THE DAY
THE MUSIC DIED

Also by Tony Garnett

The Seductions of Lucy Foster (2009)

Marine Ices (2011)

Free Love (2013)

THE DAY
THE MUSIC DIED

A MEMOIR

TONY GARNETT

Constable • London

CONSTABLE

First published in Great Britain in 2016 by Constable

1 3 5 7 9 10 8 6 4 2

Copyright © Tony Garnett, 2016

A CIP catalogue record for this book
is available from the British Library.

ISBN: 978-1-47212-273-5

Typeset in Bembo by Initial Typesetting Services, Edinburgh
Printed and bound in Great Britain by CPI Group (UK) Ltd, Croydon, CR0 4YY

Papers used by Constable are from well-managed forests
and other responsible sources.

MIX
Paper from
responsible sources
FSC® C104740

Constable
is an imprint of
Little, Brown Book Group
Carmelite House
50 Victoria Embankment
London EC4Y 0DZ

An Hachette UK Company
www.hachette.co.uk

www.littlebrown.co.uk

For the family.
The dead. The living. Those yet unborn.

Acknowledgements

A working life of many decades produces a volume of work too large for one book. It could fill many books. Included here is only a small selection with the purpose of finding connections between life and work and to discover why some productions happened at all. A full account of many others can be found on tonygarnett.com.

I mention very few of my colleagues. They all know how much I'm indebted to them and how grateful I am. The phrase 'I've only ever been as good as the quality of the people I could persuade to work with me' is literally true, not just something to say in mock modesty, picking up an award. Films are social activities, unlike novels, and each is a collective achievement.

For help on this book I thank my sister Marsha Hunt and friend Brian Winston for loving encouragement and sharp notes; my long-time comrade Jane Harris for her practical help; Tanya Seghatchian for her wise suggestions and Stephen Lacey for his academic rigour. Maggie Hanbury, my agent, assisted by Harriet Poland, has been tenacious and loyal through it all. Andreas Campomar at Constable saw the book hiding inside the material and guided me as I found it.

My sons, Will and Michael, were encouraging from the start.

Contents

Contents

Introduction

Have You Been Telling Stories?

The process . . . is not one in which the present 'I' records the events in the life of the past 'me' but one in which a dialectic takes place between present 'I' and past 'me', at the end of which both have changed and the author-subject could say equally truthfully, 'I wrote it' and 'it wrote me'.

Charles Rycroft

Our histories, whatever else they are, are coded stories about what we wanted in the past and about what we want in the future and about what we fear in the future.

Adam Phillips

To be a biographer you must tie yourself up in lies, concealments, hypocrisies, false colourings and even in hiding a lack of understanding, for biographical truth is not to be had and if it were to be had we could not use it.

Sigmund Freud

What follows is an account of my working life and some of the events which have determined its nature. It is, of course, incomplete and partial. Therefore it cannot be the whole truth. Is it truthful? That is, despite the omissions, true in the sense that it doesn't lie? It doesn't consciously lie, so the lies remaining must also be lies that I still tell myself.

I have spent my life seeking the truth. When young I was convinced it was being kept from me, that others were revealing only half-truths, keeping secrets and offering bland generalities instead of frank revelation. They either wanted to forget or they needed to escape guilt. They had the power and the secrets; they had the power bestowed by secrets. I didn't know what they didn't know.

That is rather the way many of us feel as adults about government and its 'security' apparatus. Indeed, what we feel about all opaque institutions which look over us.

Will it also apply to this book? Will I do to the reader what I complain was done to me? Will I hide as I pretend to reveal? Will what purports to be a book of revelations in fact be an exercise in public relations?

I've tried to tell the truth. But I would say that, wouldn't I? In any case it has to be *my* truth. What other truth could I possibly know?

I've tried to be true to the facts which one checks against documents and other sources, including the memories of others.

But facts are not the truth. Facts have to be contextualised in order to achieve meaning. So what I've attempted is an imaginative truth, as I try to reveal what it felt like at the time. I've tried to avoid attaching how I feel now to what happened then. Where I do, I make it clear. I have often found that what I thought was my memory was actually someone else's. I'd absorbed it and then taken ownership of it. I've tried to weigh the possibility that these memories were just a gloss and only include those I judge to be credible from other sources.

My private life is private: the clue is in the name. I'm a private man who happened to do a public job. Now, for the first time, I choose to become public but that is no reason for the lives of other private people to be made public property. I exclude, or partially exclude, many people dear to me, particularly my sons, Will and Michael, and Alex, who was my wife and remains my friend. The omissions are out of respect for them. The exceptions to this rule of exclusion are: my childhood – the child being father of the man – and my first love – for without her and what happened to her, the reader would not know why two films were even made or understand one of the main philosophies of my working life.

Why have I written it? Of course, I don't know. I think that at eighty, one has an urge to look back and make some coherent sense of what has gone before. Rebecca West said that writers write because they want to find out how they feel about something and certainly the act of setting memories down, creating that distance, gives one the opportunity to see what was once invisible. One has no time or inclination and one is too absorbed to attempt this in the middle of it all.

I do not write to seek justifications, but I am looking for connections. Many have been mined. Once I revealed them they became obvious, having entirely escaped me all my life.

I do not try to settle scores, despite the many conflicts, hurts and disappointments. I never shirk a row, but once it is over, nothing festers. Neither am I seeking to make or keep friends. I have not written thinking of other people's feelings. There is no conscious agenda except an urge to understand and to reveal what I do and do not understand.

1988

The TWA passengers from Los Angeles dribbled onto the Heathrow tarmac, sleep-deprived and shivering at the change of temperature. One of them was me, emaciated, depressed and exhausted: a washed-up failure at fifty-two.

People kept telling me I was a success. They had been telling me this for over twenty years. I knew I was a failure. What they thought of as success was actually me failing to face my past. All the frantic achievement people admired was the result of insanely focused work to the exclusion of life, a denial of who I was. A manic defence against depression.

I was running on empty and getting nowhere. There was no more road to run away on. My private life was disintegrating, my professional life no longer served its purpose and I had nowhere to go.

Except to face what I could not face.

Liberty Hall, Brum

*Uncle Jack was a painter and decorator. All the other uncles did
their own decorating or got their wives to do it. But they deferred
to Jack, who was a master tradesman. He had their respect.*

*A neighbour told him, 'Oh, Mrs Poulton. She's so good with
all the little ones, ain't she?'*

Jack looked at her. He shrugged.

'Ar. Ought to be. It's her trade.'

In the 1930s Britain was divided into two – or more – nations, as
it always has been. The north and the peripheral countries, those
centres of mining and heavy industry, suffered mass unemployment,
poverty and bitter despair. In the south there was prosperity, despite
the slums of London. There the economy, at an accelerating pace,
steamed – or rather, electrified – ahead. Houses were built, Hoovers
were bought and kitchens were plugged in to labour-saving gadgets.
Tube lines took commuters further into the country air to houses
with gardens.

In the centre of England was Birmingham, Britain's second city,
restless and insecure beneath its sangfroid; the city of a thousand
trades and the centre of the twentieth century's dominant technology, the internal combustion engine. Its centre was Victorian, laid
out by confident businessmen demonstrating civic pride, a Council
House like a provincial Parliament; a Town Hall designed for ancient
Greece; a famous repertory theatre and orchestra; electric tram cars

reaching into the far suburbs. Small workshops were everywhere, handed down from father to son, often since the late-eighteenth century. In the suburbs and the surrounding small towns were the immense factories of the twentieth century, busy with anything the world market would buy, from motor cars in Longbridge to motor-bikes in Small Heath, to chocolates in Bournville.

It was like an American provincial city – Detroit or Baltimore. Each generation restlessly smashed down what it had inherited to make way for a new architectural shape reflecting the latest fashion. It was determined to be modern. Although only one hundred miles from London it resented the capital's assumed superiority. It thought London was all show and talk. The saying was that they made the wealth in Birmingham. In London they just spent it.

Birmingham's people worked hard and spoke little. 'The less said the better' would compete with 'Don't boast' as the city's motto. The men were good at card games that demanded quick arithmetic and a poker face. Known locally as Brum, the city's abbreviation no doubt reflected the citizens' parsimony with speech. Though scarred by the slump, there was a rapid recovery on the back of world demand for engineering, especially the internal combustion engine: the motorcycle, the passenger car and the heavy, commercial vehi-cle. Vast factories produced world-famous products: BSA, Norton and AJS; Austen, Wolseley and Hillman. Thousands of workshops supplied the myriad of parts for these assembly plants.

Brum was the home of the skilled worker: the engineer, the pattern-maker, the tool-turner. The men who lived and breathed engines, who could tell you what was wrong just by listening to one; men who, in addition to a long day's shift in the workshop, would go home and spend every evening and weekend tinkering with an engine. Women worked, but it was taken for granted that after marriage their real work was in the home. Even they were judged on talents where skill met thrift – at embroidery, crocheting and reversing collars on men's shirts.

Being a city of few words, the trade in your fingers did the talk-ing, a trade only acquired through serving five-year apprenticeships. It was a city of inarticulate pride. As my uncle Harold, a deeply conservative and, I suspect, Conservative man told me: 'I've never had a gaffer who could do my job.' He would never tell me how he voted. 'It's a secret ballot!' All my uncles were top card-players: solo whist, poker, brag. They had to be. When given the small, brown envelope containing the week's wages, many would sit in a card school, playing to double it or lose it altogether. A win would mean extra pocket money. A loss meant going home with no housekeeping for the missus.

Their faces were blank, their eyes observant and their expressions unreadable. They were not easily impressed. They would sit companionably in a pub all evening, steadily necking pints of Ansells or Mitchells and Butler mild, saying little. Their humour was bone-dry and dark.

It is therefore difficult to tell how much, if at all, they cared about the attitudes they attracted. Londoners, especially, thought – and still think – that brummies are stupid and figures of fun. Brummies dismiss cockneys as 'full of themselves' or 'not backward in coming forward'. But they also say those things about mancunians and yanks. Is it defensive? As usual with the poker-faced brummies you don't know; the chances are it's an example of their impenetrable humour.

My granddad, Albert Poulton, was born in 1869, in Aston, a poor inner-city district. In 1887 he bumped into Emily Sawyer jostling in the crowds celebrating Queen Victoria's golden jubilee. He looked Emily up and down and liked what he saw.

'I'll look after you, my wench.'

That was that. They were married at St Peter's and St Paul's church, Aston, on 29 March 1891. Emily was pregnant. The baby, Annie, died soon after birth. They settled in Upper Sutton Street, Aston. Albert's father was a gun-maker and Emily's a steel toy-maker.

Aston was famous for the football stadium, Villa Park, Ansell's brewery, HP Sauce, Hercules Cycles and a warren of skills and workshops. The brewery and the sauce factories were opposite each other near Aston Cross and the heady mixture of their smells permeated the area.

Granddad loved Aston Villa, Ansell's mild and fishing. Apart from his family, they were the three pillars of his life. He was a short, bald, upright man with a moustache and a strict manner. He always wore a three-piece suit with a watch and chain in his waistcoat and a hard collar displaying a tie, even when he went to work in the packing department of a warehouse. Walking along the street – which all his life he called the horse road – he would command me to straighten my back and not slouch. He frowned upon eating so much as an ice cream in the street and women smoking anywhere were severely discouraged, although his pipe was always stuck in his own mouth.

He was a Victorian who couldn't adapt to the bold ways emerging after World War I. The twenties was the decade of gramophone records, the Charleston, short skirts and shorter hair. The abolition of the bosom. A world in which smart young women smoked through long cigarette-holders, drank cocktails and even questioned their subservience to men. He was shocked when his own daughter, Pom, appeared in a scandalously short skirt and askance at her even shorter bobbed haircut. He was unimpressed when told it was all the rage. In fact he raged, saying that, 'Your mother has never had her hair cut!'

And what on earth was this 'crystal set', with voices coming from nowhere?

He served his time to become a maker of long whips for use on a team of horses. They were made of bamboo, measured many feet and tapered along their length. A good coachman could tickle the ears of the front horses in a team of six with Granddad's precise creations. He was a skilled tradesman with good wages and pres- tige – until the internal combustion engine arrived and his trade vanished, seemingly overnight. His skills were redundant. He spent the rest of his life as a common labourer, in the language of the day. He used his skills to make fishing rods for himself and his sons. This hurt his pride, but he took it in his stride, saying '"Ought"'s count for nowt. You can only sleep in one bed and eat at one table.'

As I grew up I learned more about him. As a young man he had been wild, especially in drink. Picking up his week's wages – a sov- ereign – he would go off up the canal with his friends for the whole weekend, fishing and drinking and fighting. When Grandma heard him at the front door, she would rush upstairs with the children, only coming down in the morning to see the kitchen furniture, plates and ornaments broken up and Granddad sitting with his head in his hands, now sober and hungover, appalled at the chaos he had wrought. His love of the pub was deep and many times Grandma would march to the Hare and Hounds, slap a dish in front of him, saying 'There's your dinner.'

But he never shirked work. Like his sons after him, he never missed a shift, even if he had been carousing all night. In those days if you were even a minute late in the morning, the gates would be locked. You missed a day's money. He was never late. He was not feckless. As for the rest, age reformed him; he slowed down in his forties and when I knew him he drank little and his rage had ebbed.

He loved gardening, having an allotment in addition to the back garden. Members of the family remember him walking in to the kitchen, his arms full of vegetables and some flowers for Grandma. All his sons loved the garden, Fred becoming famous locally for his chrysanthemums.

At meal times, each of his twelve children were instructed to concentrate on the food. Any infraction – giggling or teasing – was met with severe disapproval. A really naughty child was told to go upstairs, get undressed and wait. He would finish his meal, which would take some time as he chewed each mouthful forty times, having been told this ensured longevity. He would then pick up a cane and go to thrash the child. My aunties said the waiting was worse than the caning. I understood. It was the same with my Dad. It was the same outside the head's study at grammar school, waiting to be called in.

As the children grew up they resented these beatings and started to assert themselves. One dinner time, after he had sent a teenage daughter upstairs, his way out of the room was blocked by Uncle Harry.

'Get out of my way or you'll get a taste.'

Harry stood his ground.

'Go and sit back down, Dad, all that's finished now.'

They stood head to head, like two stags, Granddad looking up at this strapping seventeen-year-old. Everyone stared, hardly daring to breathe. It promised a fight unless Harry backed off. But he didn't. He seemed to grow into manhood through this very act of defiance. Eventually Granddad turned tail and sat. No one broke the silence or dared look at each other. He never struck any of his children again. He looked physically diminished. Power had shifted in the family.

The world was changing around him. During World War I Aunty May wanted to marry the man who had been courting her, John Darby of Walsall, but Granddad at first forbade it. He said no daughter of his would marry to get the man's pension, expecting he would be killed. He called it 'blood money'. His family would not bear that shame. They should wait until the war was over. The family was lucky. The only casualty was Albert, who was wounded in the shoulder.

He could not absorb the changes that came with the war, its disruption and the aftermath. Suddenly girls were no longer subservient to their fathers. During the war his daughters had gone up the canal on a barge to Dunlops, the tyre factory, to work shifts with a soldering iron, doing the work of a man. The roads were full of the cars and lorries that had ruined his trade. He never went on an aeroplane. He just looked up at them, as though they were a mirage.

Granddad loved music. He made sure those children with an aptitude learned an instrument. Uncle Albert, the eldest, eventually became the lead violinist in the Birmingham Hippodrome pit orchestra and played summer season in Blackpool Tower. Ida, my Mom, learned the piano as a child and then gave lessons. She also played on a music stall in Birmingham market. Potential customers would ask her to play some sheet music for them so they could judge it. She spent her evenings playing the 'hurry' music in cinemas showing silent films. Granddad would sit in the front parlour, tears streaming down his face as he listened to Albert play the violin with my Mom accompanying him. He was a sentimental man.

As a small boy I was interested in a picture of a man on the wall of Granddad's kitchen. He told me, reverently, that it was Joseph Chamberlain, 'The greatest man this city ever had'. He would talk about Brum in the days before Chamberlain became mayor, when there were no sewers, of how the 'night soil men' would come round;

how the water supply was spasmodic and untrustworthy and the slums were infested with rats. How when he became mayor, he cleared slums, municipalised water and gas, laid parks One realised how important were the changes wrought by Chamberlain and why Granddad so revered him. Uncle John worked hard to persuade Granddad to vote Labour. He was a persuasive man. But Granddad never would. He was a Victorian Liberal adrift in the twentieth century.

But despite Granddad's nominal authority and severe manner, Grandma ruled. She was 4 feet 10 inches high and, by the time I knew her, bent and worn, with a severe manner that softened only when a small child appeared. Her white hair reached her waist. She wore long dark dresses, adorned with tiny flowers and, when in the house, a wraparound pinafore. She could add up but couldn't read or write. No one knew her age. As a child she had lied in order to get a job. She bore twelve children, of whom one died early: seven girls and five boys lived to maturity and themselves had children. Albert, May, Ada, Harry, Minnie, Emily (Pom), Fred, Wesley, Ida, Floss, Lottie and Dulcie. The eldest, Albert, she did not carry. He was her sister's baby, who had emigrated to Canada with her man. The idea was to better themselves, get established, and then come back for Albert. They did not come back, so Albert became a Poulton. Grandma bore a child roughly every eighteenth months until menopause.

As the years of hard work beat down on her, she became bent with a humped back. Her hands shook with a Parkinson's tremor. Her face was lined and darkened by the sun and her hair was white. But there was an observant stillness to her, a centre of gravity, a confident calm that gave her an authority which did not provoke fear. All the family felt safe with her. In her rough and ready way, she loved them and they knew it.

She always kept a good table, however little money was coming in. She believed in a family sticking together and helping each other. When Uncle Harry was sick with cancer she instructed Fred to deliver milk for his family each day without charge. There were regular whip-rounds for any one unemployed. Albert and Harry busked cinema queues, playing duets on their violins, when unemployed, but most of the others kept in work most of the time. All the daughters married skilled men. A tool turner, for instance, could take home £5 for a five-and-a-half day week in the late-thirties.

Grandma ran it all with an iron grip and her word was law even after her children were long married, living away with their own children. Everyone obeyed, such was her authority. No one seemed to question it. As they married she would say, 'When you've taken your legs from under my table, you're not to come here complaining. I'll send you straight back to sort it out. So, no tittle-tattle.' This even-handedness, this refusal to take sides, to be an interfering mother-in-law, was popular with the in-laws, who soon called her mother and truly joined the family as equals.

Wherever she went, in shops and market stalls, the sales people would be on their toes. No one tried to cheat her twice. She was aware of all their tricks. For instance, she would never buy a skinned rabbit. She would ask for it to be skinned while she watched. She knew that, during the night, men would catch cats, skin them and sell them on as rabbits. She did her shopping at the last minute, late at night, knowing that shopkeepers would be trying to get rid of perishable goods. She could drive a bargain. She only ever deferred to one man, her husband, Albert, and gradually even that became something she did in public, to save his dignity. She managed him as she managed everyone, through the sheer force of her personality.

When the family finally settled in the suburb of Erdington, 289 George Road was known as Liberty Hall and the front door of this Victorian house was always open. Anyone who walked in was welcomed, told to sit down and fed. The family would all come back to Grandma for Christmas, which was saved up for well in advance and for which preparations began in September. All through the autumn contributions were made by each wage-earner. Grandma had a jug to keep them in. By November it was filling up nicely. It was principally a food fund, with a sum set aside for booze, mainly a barrel. The amount of food was mountainous. It had to be. Christmas went on for days and days. In addition to Grandma and Granddad there would be the twelve children, their spouses and children, various other relatives and anyone else who had nowhere to go.

Olwyn from next door would drop in and stay. She was a quiet, reserved maiden lady who would not, on the face of it, be expected to approve the rough Poultons. But she did. Olwyn's father had bought 289 before the Great War, so she was our landlady. Hers was a God-fearing, low church family. They approved the way in which Grandma's children had turned out and they revered her. Olwyn behaved as though she was their eldest daughter and was loved as part of the family. The rent was low and never increased.

Everyone had a party piece at Christmas. My mom would play the piano, Uncle Albert the violin. Uncle Fred would sing songs from the music halls,

> And there's lots of girls besides,
> I should like to be beside,
> Beside the seaside,
> Beside the sea.

Even Granddad would sing:

> There ain't no sense,
> Sitting on a bench,
> All by yourself in the moonlight.

They all liked their beer, even Grandma. As a boy it was my job to go to the corner off-licence with a jug and have it filled with mild ale. I'd carefully carry it back to avoid spilling any. Grandma would set it by the hob in the kitchen and plunge in a red-hot poker; the ale would make a searing sound and give off steam. She would then drink it as she toasted bread on a fork and spread dripping from the weekend roast. I loved these cosy, intimate times with her.

My grandparents' Golden Wedding Anniversary party was a grand affair, held in the Masonic hall in Erdington in 1940. All the family were there, dressed in their best. My cousin Margaret was seven and I was four. We were sent up to them, hand in hand, me with a bouquet for Grandma and she with a flower for Granddad's buttonhole; Margaret in a gold dress and me in a golden blouse, made by Aunty Janet.

53 Neville Road

'See, what you need for this job is a left-handed screw driver. Go up the stores. They'll have one.'

'Clean out of 'em,' said the store man. 'Want summat else?'

The apprentice dithered, out of his depth.

'I tell you what, tek 'Arry a Brummagem screw driver. That should do the job.'

The store man, with a straight face, handed over a large claw hammer.

The apprentice stared at it, nervously, not wanting to show his ignorance.

Somebody was taking the piss.

But who?

My Mom, Ida, and her brother Fred had always been close. She was shy with people she didn't know. But Fred, the milkman, wasn't. One day he took her to one side.

'Come on, Ida. You're coming up Erdington with me.'

'What're you up to, Fred?'

'Dancing lessons. There's a feller there, Mick Chamberlain, teaching ballroom and you're coming with me.'

'Since when were you interested in dancing?'

'I'm not too worried either way. But you never know who you might meet.'

The fact was he already knew who 'he might meet', but he wasn't letting on to Ida. It was Janet Hughes, a flighty, nicely-built girl with a lively energy and very attractive if you could handle her. Fred thought he could. She was also a girl of very strict morals who knew how far she would go so you'd better keep your hands just there. Fred would find out. His plan now was to go with his pretty sister, palm her off and discover Janet, as if by chance. The rest, he thought, would take care of itself.

Ida had her suspicions because none of her five brothers ever did anything without a plan, usually involving Aston Villa, beer or girls. As they got older the order changed. She thought, why not? So she borrowed her sister Pom's dress. Pom was out and Ida might have it back in the wardrobe before Pom noticed it missing. The rule in the house was first up, best-dressed, anyway.

Mick Chamberlain worked at the same factory as some of the Poulton brothers. He was small and smooth and rather fancied himself with the ladies, although he remained a bachelor till middle age when he married my Aunty Minnie, then a widow.

An entrepreneurial fellow, he'd rented a room in the pub and brought his gramophone and records. A few minutes after seven he asked for the men to choose partners. Ida noticed Fred's eyes wandering and saw Janet . She looked stuck up, Ida thought. Janet had noticed Fred but wasn't letting on. Or trying not to. Then Ida saw a young man, impeccably dressed, standing a little apart, almost scowling. He was slim, wearing specs against his short-sight and his hair was severely combed back but he looked dark, polished and very handsome. Ida thought he was scary but he also seemed lonely under that hauteur. She wanted him to notice her, to choose her, to make her special.

Mick had finished describing the quick-step and as he moved to the gramophone he said, 'Everybody form yourselves as couples in a line here.' That was like a starting pistol for Fred. In an instant he was ushering Janet on to the floor. Ida was busy watching Fred and looked round with a start as she heard a voice in her ear.

'You don't seem to have a partner, so would you help me?'

He was smiling.

'I'll be useless.'

The music and the difficulties of the dance made the intense and determined young man with Ida, Tom Lewis, rigid with concentration. Ida did her best to follow. He was unarguably in charge. The problem was he'd never danced before.

'Slow-slow, quick-quick-slow,' called Vic. 'And . . . turn.' Their bodies were very close. Tom's left hand was pushing at her lower back and his right was pushing and pulling. He'd got the knack of the hands. The feet took a little longer. But after some stumbles, the embarrassments of which increased his concentration, he seemed to get the hang of it. So did she. He even relaxed enough to smile. She smiled back. She looked round. Fred was very suave, clearly now being Fred Astaire. He winked at Ida. Cheeky sod.

That's how my Mom and Dad met. I pieced it together from members of the family.

They began walking out together, in the phrase of the day, and were soon in love, making plans for their future. Tom was full of them. His motorbike soon had a sidecar and they went on day trips to the Lickey Hills and a week's holiday to Blackpool. They were married in June 1931. He was twenty-five and she was twenty-four, a late marriage at that time.

Behind the family home in George Road, speculative builders made a cul-de-sac up a steep hill and built tiny, box-like semi-detached houses, with gardens at the back. Two hundred pounds for a ninety-nine-year lease. They tempted young couples ready to take on the risk of a mortgage, couples with hopes and ambitions, imbued with a new optimism. The Great War was a memory, the 1929–31 slump was receding in Brum and newly constructed Neville Road symbolised working-class aspirations. Displayed outside most houses was a motorbike and sidecar.

So my Mom and Dad put down the deposit on one at the very top of the hill and Mom's brother Fred, with his wife – the virtuous Janet – did the same next door. I was born in the front bedroom on 3 April 1936. My cousin Margaret next door was three. I arrived surrounded by love and attention. In addition to Mom's warmth, my Dad thought I was perfect. Or, at least, he was determined to make me so.

'He thought the sun shone out of your arse, your Dad did,' said my Uncle Fred. I worshipped my Dad in return. Uncle Fred was indulgent, funny and gentle. I thought of Janet and Fred as surrogate parents and Margaret as my sister. Aunty Janet had longed for more children but had one miscarriage after another. I floated on her thwarted maternal feelings as the son she never had. There was a gap in the fence and I spent nearly as much time in their house as I did in my own. A few yards down the road was Grandma, who I revered. I grew into a confident little boy, happy to be the centre of attention.

My Dad was a garage mechanic. He then decided not only to bet his savings but also to borrow money to buy a Royal Liver insurance collection round. It was a step up from an oily overall to a suit and tie. He hadn't liked working for a gaffer. He was going to move up in the world, to be his own boss. Restless and impulsive, he was always the first to buy anything. Mom had a washing machine. It was novel in our circle in the thirties, though you still had to turn a mangle.

I can just remember the Austin 7 car that Dad bought and Fred later told me more about it. Tom had not gone to the pub with Fred. He'd saved. Working in a garage he'd kept his eye open, then drove a bargain on a second-hand car he could do up. In 1938, a 1936 Austin 7 Model Ruby 'de luxe' saloon could be bought for £70, but Dad got his cheaper. He found one in bad condition. He sold his bike and sidecar to a man from Sutton for a top price; it was a good runner. The Austin he bought in its place looked and sounded rough, if you could get it to start at all. He took it to pieces in the shed at the back of the house and tuned it up. It soon looked and ran like new, though I didn't pay much attention as he put it back together. Dad always had things he tinkered with. Sometimes bits of engines were even in the oven, which I never understood.

I'd been playing with Margaret when my Dad came to me. 'I've got something to show you.'

I followed him out the front and saw him wink at Mom, who smiled and followed.

In the street was this lovely car. I'd only seen it in bits. Other men were around it, peering under the bonnet, sitting inside behind the wheel, pushing and pulling and poking; asking questions in low voices, my Dad knowing all the answers.

'Is that ours?' I couldn't believe it. He smiled. They all smiled. Then he became serious.

'Can you drive, though? That's the question.'

'Yes. I've watched the bus driver.' I hated it when they laughed at me.

'Come on then. Show me.'

I hopped in. Dad started it up and off we went down the hill. When we got round the corner he stopped and said, 'Want to drive?'

'Yes.'

I climbed over and stood on his seat between his legs and held the steering wheel. He laughed and I gasped with pride as we went along the road. In my reality I was driving the car, not realising he was still in full control. It was the most thrilling moment of my life.

When we got back I wanted to rush in to tell Mom, but Dad stopped me. 'So, you like driving, son?'

I nodded.

He winked at me and said, 'Just between us, OK? Don't tell your mother.'

I didn't. Not only was I now a driver, my Dad and I had a secret.

Dad was admired in the district for his ability to fix anything. Not only cars and motorbikes, but all electrical gadgetry and, as Uncle Fred remarked, people would bring their stopped watches and Dad would take them to pieces, which was easy, but then put them back together with no pieces left over, which was difficult. What's more, they then started up again. He was a perfectionist and he was competitive. He disliked gardening but as he had a back garden it had to be the best, the most admired, in the neighbourhood.

He was energetic, charming and amusing. The life and soul of the party, as they said. A leader. He was also volatile and there was an anger eating at him. His father had run off with another woman, leaving a wife and three sons to fend for themselves. Dad was the eldest and at twelve had to become the father of the house, soon leaving school to earn money.

I wonder if his anger with his father for abandoning them was still burning inside him. His mother was a snob who thought her son Tom had married beneath him, Ida's family being rough working class, and she thinking she was above them. She had made him leave school to earn wages, yet her snobbishness made her despise him for his oily hands. He drew back from her and joined Mom's family. He revered Grandma, too.

My mother was petite, with large expressive eyes. She loved him but hated rows and never revealed a temper. But she would come out in red rashes round her neck, a sure sign of unexpressed feelings. The family say she loved children and cousin Margaret remembers her as kind, always ready to listen and explain. We used to stand by the piano when she played and she allowed us to play with her. That is, to indiscriminately bang the notes.

Dad's anger scared Mom, particularly after the start of World War II. Suddenly life was not going according to his plan. It was difficult to keep the insurance round going now he was seconded to a factory, on shifts. His was a reserved occupation, his skills keeping him out of the army. He must have felt that his ambitions were slipping away. He started to drink. If he found fault with his dinner he would throw it against the wall. Perfection was acceptable. Anything else was worthless. Mom was loving, meek and a peacemaker – 'Anything for a quiet life.'

But life with Dad was not quiet. It was exciting and unpredictable. He beat me regularly. For even minor infractions he would tie me to the door handle and thrash me. I remember often being woken late at night from a deep sleep to see Dad towering over me. I would draw away from him, trying to be smaller. It would be a punishment for something I must have done, but I never knew what. With the booze running in him, his face would be choleric. His leather glove would strike me as I tried to wriggle away. Those beatings didn't hurt as much as the ones from the strap, but they frightened me more. He seemed out of control. Not even my Mom, though she tried to pull him away, could restrain him.

Other nights he brought back a few mates from the pub and, bleary-eyed, I would be carried downstairs and stood on the dining-room table in my pyjamas. He would tell me to entertain them.

With Dad looking proudly on, I would sing and tap dance as though my life depended on it, their laughing faces nodding with the tune and the smell of booze in the air.

Margaret, being three years older, had vivid memories of scenes which were only a haze to me.

For instance, even with the war on, they all went to dances in town. The preparations were elaborate. Mom in her cami knickers with garter belt holding up the last of her silk stockings. They would soon become unavailable in the war shortages, until the Yanks came bearing gifts for favours. Mom and Janet would be doing each other's hair, making waves with curling tongs, which fascinated Margaret.

I have a memory of Dad's silver-plated cigarette case as he filled it from a pack, before checking his lighter. For years when I saw one of those old lighters, with its wick lit by a flick of the thumb, I thought of Dad. Most people had to flick theirs for ages, with increasing frustration, but my Dad's lit first time, every time. Of course it did. It was my Dad's. It wouldn't have dared to fail. He would then light a cigarette. As he inhaled and then blew out the smoke he would look at me and smile. That would make me happy. He was my Dad and we had secrets. I wasn't sure what they were, but we had them. Us men.

Then Mom, in her best long dress, and Dad, in a dark suit and tie, would go off in the Austin 7. I'd beg to go with them, but Aunty Janet would put me to bed, where I stood by the window, sulking. Thirties' dance band music on the radio – Bowlly, Hylton, Ambrose – still makes me think of them.

Dad's shed and garage at the end of the garden was his private domain. There was a bench with a vice and all around were drawers and shelves. Everything was swept spotless and tidy, every screw knowing its place. On the floor would be various bits of engines waiting to be assigned their role. We were not allowed into this holy tabernacle, but that tempted us to live dangerously, Margaret and me daring each other. When Dad was at work we would tiptoe around it, looking but not touching, excited and fearful, knowing that discovery would bring his wrath upon us. When he was working in there he would come out, joke and rough and tumble with us. He fixed up a swing with a rope and a piece of plank, pushing us higher and higher till we screamed with delight and fear. At these times he became young, like an older brother, rediscovering his childhood.

One day – I must have been about four – we were out the back, Margaret and me, poking about in Dad's shed. It smelled of oil and our hands got dirty if we touched anything. We were bored, just walking around this prohibited space, trying to find something to do. On the floor, under the bench, were some pots of paint, partly used. Margaret took the lid off one of them.

'That's nice,' she said. 'We could paint something.' She was always trying to be helpful.

'Like what?'

'I don't know. What would they like? What needs painting?'

She looked round to see what hadn't been painted.

'We could paint the path. That would be a good job done.'

It would, as well. Margaret was right. He'd be pleased when he got home He always had a lot of jobs on.

We found the brushes and set to work. It was hard but we kept at it. Soon the whole path from the back door right down the garden was a bright blue. It really stood out. We both thought it looked lovely and were proud. We were just standing back, admiring our work, when Mom opened the kitchen door.

'Oh, my God.'

We looked happily at her. But something was wrong. She had a look of horror and her hand was at her mouth. Had we chosen the wrong colour? It looked just right, to me.

'What have you done?'

'We've painted the path,' said Margaret.

'For Dad,' I added.

Margaret's Mom, Aunty Janet, had come out, hearing the commotion. 'Oh-my-God. Wait till your Tom sees this.' It was at this point that I knew that it was really going downhill. But it was no use now wishing we'd asked whether they wanted it done. 'It's paint, Ida. It won't wash off. You! In! Now!' Margaret went home, head down, and had it cuffed as she went past her Mom, who followed her.

My Mom looked at me. All the busy happiness had fallen away.

I was deflated. 'Come here.' I felt like a dead weight. As she put her arms around me I burst into tears. 'It's OK. You meant to help, didn't you?' I nodded. She wiped my nose. 'But I don't know what we'll say to your Dad. He'll be back soon. If I were you, I'd hide until he gets over it. Go on, make yourself scarce. I'll give him his tea and then show it to him.'

Now we had a plan. I felt better. I went back and hid behind his shed. He wouldn't find me there.

I had to come in sometime. And when he saw me, he was not pleased. But Mom had calmed him down. Maybe she had given him an extra treat for his tea. She was clever like that. He looked at me steadily, poker-face, for an agonising few seconds. Then he flicked his fingers, calling me to him. I slowly walked the few yards to my fate. His arm went up but instead of hitting me he rested it on my shoulder and he broke into a wide smile and shook his head. Then he laughed and turned to my Mom.

'What're we going to do about this little bugger, Ida? Eh?' He turned back and grinned at me. I knew I was safe, but I didn't know why. You never knew with my Dad. He stroked my face and then waved me away. 'Go on, you silly bugger.' As I turned, he said, 'Next time, think.' He tapped his head. I got out of there in case he changed his mind.

Even after the war had started, on Sundays in the summer the family would all walk the four miles to Sutton Park, Grandma and Granddad too, the little ones in the pram. Everyone would join up there from different parts of Brum. I don't know how they knew. No one had a phone. But greeting hugs were followed by the sharing of picnics and gossip and beer and laughter. As the sun lengthened the family hugged again and bantered and walked home. No one thought twice then about walking everywhere.

Some memories are stuck in aspic, vivid and unchanging, and I play them like tracks on an album. I must have been about three and my hair was long. Dad said I should have it cut, properly.

'Not poked at by you, Ida. You never cut it right. He looks like a girl. Yes, he does. His hair's nearly like Margaret's. He's not a babby now, get him down to the barber and that's the end of it.'

I didn't know what a barber was. The next morning my obedient mother took me down to Evershed's on Slade Road. Mr Evershed was a big fat man with a bald head and a big smile.

'What have we here, missus? A boy or a girl? Can't tell, can we? I say, we can't tell.'

He put a plank over the arms of a big chair and lifted me up on it. I was scared, not sure what he intended, fearing the worst. A big sheet came round me and he tucked it into my collar. I looked in the mirror and saw him coming towards me with scissors in his hand. They were getting nearer. I screamed. I fought him, trying to escape, and Mom got tangled up. She couldn't calm me. I wanted out of there.

On the way home I quietened down. 'I don't know what your father will say.' I think she did, though.

When he came home from work I made myself scarce up the garden. He found me hiding behind the water bath at the back of the greenhouse. I started to cry, seeing him towering over me, expecting punishment. He knelt down to my level, smiled and spoke softly. 'Did you think Mr Evershed was going to hurt you?'

I nodded, trying to get my breath back, heaving from my tears.

'Well, you're going to have to go back and be brave about it.'

I'd been afraid of that.

'But Mr Evershed isn't going to hurt you.'

'No?'

'No. Because I'm going to be there. Do you think anybody'd hurt you with your Dad there?'

I looked up at him. He looked amused and confident. Nobody would stand up to my Dad. He gave me his hanky. 'Come on. I want my tea.'

He lifted me up and carried me inside. I clung to him.

The next day Mr Evershed looked at me cautiously.

'Short back and sides, Mr Evershed, for this young man.' Oh, God. 'And I'll help you.' Was this a betrayal?

Mr Evershed had a little machine in his hand and it was making a racket, a loud buzzing. I shrank into myself. But then, in a way I can't put my finger on, it all turned around. Terror became excitement, anxiety became joy, fear of the immediate future became absorption in the present.

My Dad had taken the machine and with a big smile said, 'Let's play aeroplanes.' The device magically became just that and it ducked and dived over and around my head. I could see it through the mirror. I started to laugh. It was just me and my Dad. I felt safe.

'Shall we let Mr Evershed be the pilot?'

I nodded.

Hair came off and I never looked the same again. I was inspected and shown off. Everyone in the shop was consulted.

'A little girl came in here and now a young man is going out. How about that?'

There were smiles all round. I was proud of being a young man. I was three, after all. As we left, my hand in Dad's, I was proud of having him as my Dad.

Life was good. I was loved by those around me.

Especially Grandma. Always Grandma. My rock.

I was blessed.

The first black cloud was the imminent arrival of my brother, Peter, when I was three. I knew from all the activity that something was up. My Mom was in bed. Dad was home, looking distracted. Then I saw a woman arrive on a bike with a big leather bag on the back. Dad let her in. She went upstairs with the bag.

Who's that? I thought. What does she want with my Mom? I thought she must be poorly, but this woman isn't the doctor.

A little while later I heard noises. She left and I was taken upstairs to see my Mom. I went into the bedroom wanting to be cuddled. All this strange behaviour had upset me. But as I rushed in I got a shock. What was in that blanket? 'What's going on here?'

Dad took my hand and led me to Mom. They showed me what she was holding.

A baby.

At least I now knew how babies got here. I had been told that the woman had come for the delivery so it must have been in that bag.

You make an order and get home delivery, like beer at home, which Davenports' brewery did. Years later, in the playground, older boys gave their version, quite near the truth in fact, but it seemed very far-fetched to me. I thought mine was more credible and I stuck with it for years. Lots of children come to the same conclusion, I'm told. Made sense to me.

What I could not understand, or readily forgive, was the fact of it. Why order another? What was wrong with me? Wasn't I good enough? I was even more affronted when Peter got all the attention. He was not even punished for crying, shitting or anything. They just said he was wonderful. Except my Dad. I had an ally in him. He had decided that it was going to be a girl. He had one son, so now he wanted a daughter. He was so let down he wouldn't have anything to do with Peter for ages.

'Shut that bloody kid up, Ida,' he instructed her. I agreed with him. The bloody noise it made! But it took no notice. It'll learn soon enough, I thought, amazed at the risks it was taking. I wondered why he didn't just send him back and tell them to deliver what he'd ordered. That is if he really did need another.

I wouldn't go as far as Freud, who thought a new baby left the firstborn dethroned, despoiled, with a grievance against the faithless mother. But I was puzzled and hurt at the injustice of it. Eventually I made friends with him. The worst betrayal was Margaret's – my Margaret – who treated little Peter like a precious doll, suddenly ignoring me.

But I still loved her. I would follow her down to Grandma's and we'd go up to the attic of the Victorian, rambling house and explore. There were relics from another time, stuffed birds in glass cases and trunks full of old clothes. Grandma kept everything because, 'You never know, it might come in.' We would dress up in the clothes and invent adventures, being whatever character took our fancy that day.

The war began when I was three but I didn't notice it. In fact Mom took Peter and me to Blackpool in 1940. She refused to let me be evacuated. There were gradual changes, like the night-time blackouts and air-raid balloons in the sky. We had a gas mask each, carried in brown cardboard boxes with string long enough to go

over the shoulder. It had our name and address on it. Little Peter's
had a Mickey Mouse design and Mom would carry it. Mom and
Aunty Janet would make up games for us in the Anderson shelter
to practise taking them on and off. Everyone seemed to be carrying
their gas masks all the time, but the significance was lost on me –
unlike all those who remembered the Great War.

There was rationing: 2 oz of butter, 4 oz of sugar, 2 oz of tea,
2 oz of sweets, 2 oz of fats. I don't remember the rationing from
back then, but I got to know it as it didn't end till the early fifties.
Meat was a treat. A small joint on Sunday, Monday mince, Tuesday
bubble-and-squeak. Tarrans the butcher would bring our order in
the basket on the front of a bike, any day, even a few sausages.

Sweets were scarce, but Mom made us some with cocoa powder,
dried milk and a little margarine. We would roll the mixture into
balls and then roll them in cocoa powder. Lots of finger-licking.
When margarine was short, we would put some milk in a screw jar
and shake it until it had the rough consistency of butter. There was
always an abundance of vegetables in the garden. The lawns that had
looked like neat bowling greens had all gone now. Everyone was
'Digging for Victory'. I didn't even see a banana until after the war.
I didn't know how to eat it until someone peeled it for me.

Dad was sent to work in a munitions factory, a reserved occupation, because of his skills. Mom took over the insurance round, Janet
babysitting Peter and me. Uncle Fred was just too old but he joked
that delivering the milk was an essential service. He was out at nights
with the ARP (Air Raid Precautions), supposedly scanning the skies
for enemy planes but more likely passing a bottle of whisky round
with his mates. It was officially unobtainable but it's surprising what
a milkman can get in tips. We had lodgers billeted on us from time
to time.

Then the bombing started. Dad and Uncle Fred had half-buried
the Anderson air-raid shelter at the bottom of the garden and Dad
fixed up the electricity so we had lights. Every night, when the adults
heard the sirens, we were woken up and had to hurry there in pyjamas. When bombing was very bad, we went down early, treating it
as our bedroom. There were bunkbeds and two little chairs with a

table and tarpaulin on the floor. The bombing came every night for a while. Mom had a little torch to guide us down the garden. It was pointed discreetly to the ground, because of the blackout laws. We would snuggle up in the bunkbeds and drift off to sleep, listening to the murmur of the grown-ups. Margaret and I thought this was a great adventure.

Fred didn't go down because he was out with the ARP and Dad, when not working nights, stayed in the house, refusing the shelter, to Mom's distress.

'If that Hitler thinks he can get me out of my bed, in my house, he's got another think coming.' That was that. No one argued with my Dad or told him what to do. They wouldn't dare. He told everybody else what to do. It was personal, man-on-man, between my Dad and Hitler. I didn't know who this Hitler was but I would have backed my Dad against him any time. Hitler wouldn't know what had hit him.

I was sent to infant school as normal, starting in the nursery class. In those days even very young children were trusted to do things on their own. Although a good ten minutes' walk away, I was shown where Slade Road school was and that was it. I liked being with the other children, playing with plasticine and drawing with crayons.

One day in the playground I couldn't get to the lavatory in time and filled my pants. Maybe I had a bug or had eaten something upsetting. I didn't want to go back in class in that state. I wanted my Mom. So I walked home with shit oozing down my legs, crying, and miserable. Then I looked up and saw my Dad cycling towards me. Seeing my condition, he propped up his bike and came over. I was a mess. He grabbed me by the hair and thrashed me, calling me filthy, saying he was ashamed. He got back on his bike and rode off.

I hobbled home, crying. My Mom hugged me, calmed me, tugged my clothes off, washed me from head to toe and made me some toast. I felt better. I'd never been so happy to see her. She could solve every problem. She loved me whatever I did. But I knew I would have to up my game for our Dad.

The bombing went on. Coventry, just down the road, got it even worse. It was mere chance whether you 'got one from Jerry' or not. Every morning we would emerge from the air-raid shelter to see if the houses were intact. They always were. Fred continued the milk round.

I heard Aunty Janet say, 'Only takes one bomb and both our houses are up in smoke.'

'I saw a bad one this morning,' said Uncle Fred. 'Middle of a terrace. A whole house just rubble and the ones either side not looking too good. Funny thing, some of the front wall was still up by the front door. Just flattened behind.'

'One of your customers?'

'Ar.'

'What did you do, Fred?'

'I left the usual. Two past [pasteurised] and one stera [sterilised].'

'Oh, Fred.'

They laughed quietly.

Fred might have distracted the others, but not me. One bomb and our house up in smoke? My Dad'll be in there. That means he'd be gone too.

But Hitler never got him. He was brave. Nobody could push my Dad around.

So the adults just got on with life and I look back with admiration. They must have been scared in the early 1940s, worrying about the bombing and an imminent invasion. They didn't have the reassurance of hindsight. For them life hung by a thread with men briefly back on embarkation leave before going off to death, injury or prisoner-of-war camps. The fear of bombs every night. The fear of Nazi oppression. They must have shared their fears among themselves. An insouciant courage can only go so far. But these phlegmatic brummies never conveyed their fear to me. I thought it was just life and wasn't afraid. They protected me.

On Slade Road, at the bottom of her mother's garden, Madge Jenks gave dancing lessons – ballet and tap – to the little girls and some boys of the district. A wooden building, very light with an echoing floor, had an upright piano and a mirror down one wall, a bar fixed in front of it. She was a warm personality, a natural, curly blonde with lots of bounce. My cousin Margaret was a pupil and Mom played the piano there, so she took me. I was three or so and always wanted to be near her and Margaret. I joined in and still remember my tap shoes and the pleasing, rhythmic clickety-click they made, even some of the steps, although I couldn't execute them now. Learning how to tap-dance, which was fashionable in those days, was normal. Fred Astaire was a big, glamorous star.

We entertained the workers on their dinner break, often the night shift, doing our bit for the war effort. Everyone in Brum worked in the munitions factories. There would be noise from the diners as they came in and out and clattered their cutlery but we sang through it. Madge had told us to sing very loud. Aunty Janet, who was a seamstress, made the girls' frocks and made me a shirt of red satin and trousers of green satin. With Mom at the piano I would perform a duet of 'Tea for Two' with Freda Fowler from Reservoir Road, a petite brunette who was always smiling. She had a pretty dress. We would sit at a small table with dolls' house crockery, pretending to pour tea, and then sing.

> Picture you upon my knee,
> Just tea for two,
> And two for tea,
>
> Just me for you,
> And you for me alone.
> We'll raise a family,
> A boy for you,
> And a girl for me,
> Can't you see how happy we would be?

Margaret would then come on with Sheila Ferndon and Hazel MacPherson to sing:

> Three little sisters,
> And each one only in her teens,

One loved a solider,
One loved a sailor,
But I loved the man from the marines.

And I would be waiting to march on for my solo, the top of the bill! With a wooden gun on my shoulder, I launched into, 'Mr Brown of London town had a job to do . . . ' The audience roared in appreciation, partly for the combative and patriotic sentiments and partly to see an infant precociously pretending to be a soldier. Any nerves threatening to engulf me as I faced this huge, noisy audience disappeared when I looked for Mom, checking she was at the piano, guiding me. She smiled with love and pride, confident in me.

One night Peter, just a toddler, was in Aunty Janet's arms near the front and cried out for Mom, reaching to her. Without a break in the show, continuing to play with one hand, she beckoned to him. He wriggled free and went to her. He stood by the piano, his head in her lap, as the show went on. She hadn't missed a beat and neither had I. That brought the house down.

We felt safe with Mom. If we made a mistake she would know and help by cutting the music, nodding encouragement, guiding us on, so no one realised. I don't think I've ever been happier than in those moments. Staying up late with the grown-ups, on stage in front of hundreds of people, with my Mom accompanying me.

I was in the moment without a care in the world.

The Lights Go Out

The past is never dead. It's not even past.

William Faulkner, *Requiem for a Nun*, 1951

On 11 December 1941, in order to encourage an alliance with Japan, Hitler declared war on the USA. The whole world was now truly at war. Despite stiff upper lips, despite the dry, understated Brum attitude, there was a dreadful fear of the future. They could not have realised that in fact the tide had turned. The worst was over.

But for Mom and Dad life was about to become catastrophically worse. She became pregnant again. While Hitler was a nuisance, frustrating Dad's plans, another baby would ruin the family. The fate of the insurance round was the real crisis, never mind the Japanese. With Dad on mandatory shift work, they were only just managing to keep it going. They had sunk all their savings and got into debt trying to make a go of it. Mom went from door to door, keeping it alive, Janet helping with Peter and me.

They no doubt discussed their options. An abortion was one of them. Whether Aunty Janet knew, and then Uncle Fred, I don't know. They would never say. But they were family and lived next door, speaking every day.

Did Mom try to abort the pregnancy herself? There was a long working-class tradition of dubious techniques to bring on a miscarriage. She could then have said she'd 'lost the baby' and there would have been sympathy all round. Clearly, as the weeks went on, the dangers from an abortion increased.

Abortion in 1941 was a serious criminal offence, attracting long sentences, as well as being against all the conventions of respectable, God-fearing working people. Perhaps Mom did try some of the remedies of the day. Abortifacients came in the form of purgatives such as aloes or turpentine; hot baths; gin (although the economy during the war meant it was in short supply); extreme exertion and even falling down a flight of stairs. Some women risked their health by putting instruments inside themselves in an attempt to start a miscarriage, like a back-street abortionist. Every district had a woman who performed these operations. The rich could find a struck-off doctor or one taking risks with his career for a price.

Dad was told of a reliable woman in Handsworth, on the other side of Brum, who'd done lots without a problem. She had a reputation for being discreet and safe. It was two weeks before Christmas 1941. Whether Mom travelled on public transport to the other side of the city to endure an abortion and then travelled straight back or whether the abortionist came to her, I don't know. But it was done. Afterwards, trying to go on as normal, she felt increasingly unwell. The pain and fever increased. She couldn't see a doctor for fear of exposure. She decided to stick it out, hoping the illness would clear up. It did not. It's difficult to imagine Aunty Janet being oblivious. They were very close and always popping into each other's houses. By the third day Mom was pale, sweating and in agony. Not that I noticed or, if I did, I gave it little thought.

Early in the evening, really my bedtime, I remember Dad hovering, unable to decide whether to stay or report for his night shift. This is wartime and he's under military discipline. He needs a credible reason for absence. Mom says, 'I'll be OK, Tom. Don't worry.' He hesitates, undecided, then he kisses her and says to me, 'Look after your mother.'

I feel proud as he leaves. He's made me man of the house. Mom and I sit opposite each other close to the fire. She plays my favourite game. I have my sweet cigarettes and offer her one, as men did. She thanks me and I pretend to light it. But she has a real cigarette in her other hand, draws on it and then lets out the smoke as though from the sweet one. This delights me and I pretend to blow out smoke too. Then it really is time for bed.

When Dad is on nights, I sleep with her in the front bedroom, unless the siren sounds. Then we go scurrying down the garden to the air raid shelter. I hope it won't go off tonight because it's freezing outside and I love cuddling up with my Mom. She tucks me in with a hot water bottle. That will do until she comes up. She's warmer than ten hot water bottles.

I'm cosy there, very happy, having just played one of my favourite games with her. I don't have a care in the world. Why would I? Life's good. I drift off to sleep. Little Peter's in his cot at the back of the house.

The next thing I remember is being woken in the middle of the night by my mother. But the bed is empty. I look around, confused, trying to locate her, blinking the sleep away. She is on her knees, banging on the adjoining wall, trying to wake Janet and Fred. She's whimpering and giving off low roars of pain, bending double and then trying to straighten up. I go to her. I feel helpless, almost paralysed. I want this to stop. I start to panic. I'm out of my depth. I've never seen anyone, let alone my Mom, like this. I don't know what to do – I just want her to be my Mom again. At last Janet and Fred rush in and there's a burst of activity. Those final moments, with my Mom's wailing in my ears, are the end. My mind is a blank from that moment till the next morning.

Margaret, who is then eight, will tell me years later what happens next. Fred runs down Neville Road and then along George Road to wake up Dr Steen, who lives above his surgery. He's a kind man who knows the family.

Janet stays upstairs to be with Doctor Steen, while he attempts to revive Mom. Janet is the local woman, there is always one, who is called to lay dead people out, putting pennies on their eyes. In the middle of the war the undertakers are especially busy, so she would take dead babies and put them in drawers for a day or two. It is a matter of pride to say you'd put enough money away to afford a 'decent burial'. So Janet wouldn't be squeamish. The question I will spend my teenage years asking is, does she already know what is wrong and for fear of personal exposure keeps silent?

Margaret wakes up, sensing something wrong, maybe half-woken by the commotion. Seeing no one in her parents' bed she goes downstairs. The house is empty. She goes next door to my house. Her father, Fred, is in the living room with me. He says, 'Sit down and be quiet.' Then the door opens and Janet comes in.

'Ida's dead.'

They burst into tears, holding on to each other for comfort. Fred goes down the road to wake up Grandma and break the news to her. Janet carries Peter and me next door and puts us all to bed together.

Margaret tells me, 'Your Mom's dead,' but I have no memory of hearing this. It's as though it doesn't penetrate.

Mom had lost consciousness. The doctor could do nothing, so she was dead before the night was over, before Dad came home from his shift. She was suffering from what they called galloping septi-caemia. The infection as a result of the abortion was overwhelming her. Shock, multiple organ failure and death followed quickly. She was taken away and given a post-mortem. I have no idea what self-imposed remedies Mom had tried, but one relative speculated that an attempt at doing it herself contributed to her death. This would be consistent with the high reputation of the abortionist they used.

Next morning I sit with Janet and Fred next door in the living room. Nothing has been explained, but the air is thick. The heavy mood is sombre in a way I've never experienced. I feel numb but curious, in a detached way. The atmosphere is new. Something must be really wrong, because Fred's never there in the mornings. He should have been delivering the milk. Both Margaret and I sit silently by each other on the couch, our eyes going from one to the other, reading nothing. How's my Mom? I don't dare ask. No one's looking at me. Then my Dad comes in from our house. He's weeping, making the most distressing sounds, out of con-trol. Janet goes to him and puts her arms round him, whispering comforting words. He's inconsolable. I have never seen a grown man cry, let alone my Dad, yet here he is, crying louder than even our Peter ever did.

Janet walks me down the road to Grandma's. The news is out. Some live miles away, but most of the sisters are sitting round Grandma's table. She goes into the kitchen. 'What you doing, Ma?'

'Getting us a bit of dinner.'

'Dinner? Ma, none of us could eat a thing. Come back here.'

'You'll all eat some dinner. Life must go on.'

They all get some dinner down, under Grandma's gaze.

When Fred had told Grandma her Ida was dead and then the reason, she just said, 'Silly girl.' What was another baby to Grandma? She'd had twelve, in real poverty. We were a close family. She'd have looked after it. Then, I'm told, she did something which I had assumed was just a literary cliché, a phrase people unthinkingly use, not something anyone literally did. Her hair was grey and long, hanging right down below her waist. She wore it in a bun when she went out. She stood in her kitchen and tore her hair out in big, painful lumps.

I'm packed off to Aunty Pom, Mom's older sister. Her name is Emily, the same as Grandma, and that's why we use the nickname. She had loved pomegranates as a child. I still have no idea what's going on but I deduce that something catastrophic has happened to Mom – she has disappeared – so I'm already closing down, protectively refusing to feel anything, finishing the job I've clearly already started.

But knowing nothing, I do as I'm told.

I walk away from Grandma's house, hand in hand with this woman who I only vaguely remember from family gatherings, away from the streets I know, past Slade Road school, which I would never see again, to the bottom of Tyburn Road, where Spaghetti Junction is now. We get on the seventy-nine tram to another part of Birmingham, Pype Hayes. The journey is only a few miles, but to me it's another world.

Woodlands Farm Road, opposite Pype Hayes park, is a road of identical semis and we enter a house halfway down. It's like my parents', on a 1930s' greenfield estate where working people struggle to make tangible their aspirations. This house is bigger than ours, posher and polished bright. You can see your face reflected everywhere, even from the floor. It is as tidy as a barracks, no item out of place. It smells of furniture polish. Our house is untidy, the floor littered with stuff Peter and I play with. Pom is Mom's sister but very different. Unknown to me, she is recovering from losing a baby who had died hours after birth. She has been told another pregnancy will kill her. She is depressed and, in the phrase of the day, under the doctor.

What I experience is someone stern and strict, tense with a short temper, always finding fault. She had once been a slim, pretty woman. Now she is stick thin. Her face is taut and her mouth turns downwards in a grimace. She believes in 'will power' and, as she keeps reminding me, 'We're not in this world to enjoy ourselves. We're here to do our duty.' She is just hanging on. As the blows – struck by ill health, suppressed panic about the war and the grief and shame at the death of her favourite sister – rain down, she hangs by a thread.

Uncle Harold seems friendly, beneath his stern manner. But I'm wary of him. My cousin Robert is three years older. He seems nice and is very well behaved.

I do not feel 'at home'. I never feel at home there or anywhere else. My home is in Neville Road with my family. Anyway, I say to myself, whatever's going on, I'll be back home for Christmas.

But I'm not. I'm at Auntie Floss's. The atmosphere is strained and everyone is quiet. Uncle Terry's away in the air force and Floss is afraid he'll be sent abroad.

We are all sitting around buried in this subdued atmosphere when Floss goes to open the front door. My Dad walks in or, rather, he edges in tentatively, as though wary of his reception. Not at all like Dad, who usually dominates every party. He looks haunted. All his energy has vanished.

Floss says, 'Sit down, Tom. Can I get you anything?' He shakes his head. We look at each other. No one else is looking at anyone. I wonder where Mom is. Maybe she's in hospital. The last time I saw her she didn't look well. I still don't ask, maybe because I'm afraid of the answer. My mind is blank. Will he be cross with me for not looking after her? He was crying the morning after that night.

He opens his arms and I run over to him. He hugs me and I sit on his knee. He holds me tight. He's tender with me and sad. I want to say, 'I love you,' but I can't. I could with Mom but never with Dad. I don't want him to think I'm a sissy. I hug him back, though. When he puts me down, preparing to leave, I struggle to stay in his arms. I'm unwilling to let him go. There's something wrong here, something I can't think about. I want to ask him but for some reason I don't dare. Then he leaves. No one mentions him, no one comments on why he only stayed a few minutes, no one gives a clue to solve the mystery of what has happened to Mom.

I never see him again.

I've never remembered being told that Mom had died: neither the moment nor the manner. I didn't understand death. No one I knew had ever died. It was difficult to comprehend my Mom disappearing and never, ever, appearing again. But that's what it seemed like as time went on.

On the morning of 2 January 1942, three weeks after Mom disappeared from my life, Pom comes into the bedroom and closes all the curtains. I wonder what she's up to, not knowing it was the convention on news of a death. She stands by the bed and simply and quietly says, 'Your father is dead.'

I look back at her and, without expression, say, 'I know.' I don't know why I say this or what I mean. I feel nothing. She walks from the room, offering no details and no comfort. She doesn't mention it again.

No doubt she was so grief-stricken by the sudden loss of her favourite sister and so ashamed by two serious criminal acts in the family – an abortion and now a suicide – that she was barely holding herself together. In any case, in those days children were not given any information. I was often told "little boys should be seen but not heard". Usually they were just ignored.

Mom's autopsy had revealed the botched abortion. That meant her death became a police matter. A detective interviewed Dad, aggressively – according to Fred – and threatened him with arrest. He could have been charged with aiding and abetting an abortion or for withholding information from the police about a criminal act.

It might be said that the detective was just doing his job. Was there an edge to what he said? In those days abetting an abortion was a despicable crime in many people's eyes. A sin against God as well as a criminal act. This one had resulted in the death of a mother as well as an unborn baby. Any trial would have heaped more shame on both families.

A possible prison sentence was hung over Dad, though the police were really after the abortionist and the man who had recommended her. Dad didn't crack. He revealed nothing. A policeman was stationed outside the house and Dad was followed whenever he left. He spent New Year's Eve alone in the house. He wouldn't be coaxed away. He didn't want company. In fact, during the time between Mom's death and the New Year, Janet went repeatedly next door to our house, opened the back door and left some food, maybe a bit of their own dinner. He wasn't eating much.

On the morning of 2 January 1942, she went with Margaret in tow, to see if he would come round to hers for some breakfast. She opened the back door and pushed Margaret out again. She'd smelled gas. She called Fred. He turned the stove off, followed the hose and found Dad. He'd put a rubber hose into the gas outlet, a sheet under the door, checked the windows were tight shut and turned on the gas. Then he lay down with a bottle of Scotch. He didn't finish it.

I was not allowed to go to either funeral. Children didn't go to funerals. The family didn't want to upset me. I seemed to be taking it so well. I had not even cried. But I wonder if the reason was, instead, that they couldn't have borne to see her son at their beloved Ida's funeral; that they were protecting their own feelings. On the day I remember playing with some cousins outside Grandma's and saw these large cars. People came out of the house and they drove away, expressionless and dressed in black. We continued to play.

Much later I gleaned a little about my Mom's funeral. There was some nastiness directed at my Dad, I was told. The most venomous outpouring came, oddly, from his own family. Whether this was out of grief for Mom or embarrassment at the shame he had brought to their family, I would never know. Even years later my relatives refused to talk about Dad's funeral. In those days it probably was

difficult to arrange for a suicide. Bitterly ashamed, angry and grief–
stricken families on both sides no doubt wanted to move on.

Those hours and the days surrounding the funerals are the pivot
around which my life has turned. Some of the story was pieced
together later in my childhood and adolescence, the result of fierce
interrogation of reluctant relatives, upset or guilty, all still grieving
the loss and smarting in shame. But the direct memories are as vivid
as if they happened a moment ago. They play in my head, sharply
focused, the voices clear, like a film.

Who Do You Want Me to Be?

To be adopted is to be adapted, to be amputated and sewn back together again. Whether or not you regain full function, there will always be scar tissue.

A. M. Homes

Grandma called a family conference, although there was never much conferring with Grandma. Views could be expressed. Then Grandma decided. The result was my brother Peter would stay with Janet and Fred and Margaret, moving seamlessly next door, as Dad had requested. Janet wanted more children but had suffered many miscarriages. Now Margaret wouldn't be an only child, a fate to be avoided in Grandma's eyes: an only child was a spoilt child.

Apparently Aunty May wanted me but she already had three children. Aunty Floss, who only had Norah, would also have had me but Uncle Terry was away to the war and might not come back; others were similarly eliminated. In the end, as Harold was too old to be called up, Robert was an only child and Pom could not risk another pregnancy, I was sent to them. In those days to only bear one child was to have failed. It wasn't as bad as not to bear any children or, worst of all, to be an 'old maid'. But just having one child was frowned upon. Pom might have felt this.

Of course, I was not consulted. From Grandma's perspective we were one big family rather than a loosely connected group of nuclear families. So what could be the problem?

I bitterly regretted being sent away to Siberia. I'd hated that strict house during my stay before Christmas. I missed Janet and Fred and Margaret almost as much as my parents. Even my little brother Peter. Nothing was explained to me. I concluded it must be punishment, this exile to a harsh and unfamiliar world. But I didn't know what I'd done. I tried, only partially successfully, to suppress the thought that this unspoken crime was the neglect of my Mom. I only had a hazy idea of what death was. They were gone. But gone where? The last words from Dad were, 'Look after your mother.' I had not done so. She died. Then he had died. Had I killed him, too? How? I was evil, a double murderer. I felt guilty and rejected. Each time Pom shouted, 'You dirty little boy,' I felt unclean. Was this what they mean by hell? Had I died, too, and been sent there?

Pom didn't want me. She had enough to cope with. But I was told that this was my new home now. I had to learn fast, adapting to a new culture. It had unfamiliar ground rules which were never explained. It was assumed I knew how to behave. So I began a life of living on three levels.

Out of harm's way was my grief for the loss of my Mom and Dad. Possibly sensing that I might not get through it, I automatically closed down, feeling nothing. I was numb. I never cried or seemed put out. This should have caused alarm or at least suspicion but no one commented except to show relief that I was getting over it very well. I remember on a few occasions I simulated being upset, crying, saying I missed my Mom, because I thought that was expected of me. I did this feeling nothing. It was an act. That was perhaps the sickest aspect of all.

Then there was the rest of me that I kept private, out of the reach of Aunty Pom and Uncle Harold's disapproval. They were not going to be allowed to compromise or change who I really was.

On the observable surface I cultivated a self they thought was me, a self acceptable to, or at least tolerated by, my new keepers. I keenly observed the new customs and practised them, learning fast. The roles changed. My cousin, Robert, three years older, became my brother; my brother Peter, three years younger, was now my cousin. I saw him occasionally.

Perhaps all this was the beginning of me as an actor. Or rather, because we are all actors, the beginnings of me as a professional actor, in Orson Welles's sense that the difference between a professional and an amateur is that professionals do it when they don't feel like it.

One day, after I'd been at No. 40 for a few weeks, Pom must have thought I'd settled in. I looked as though I'd 'got over it'. She sat me down by the fire and quietly informed me, 'You can call me mother now.'

I stared at her, expressionless. 'I'd rather not, thank you.'

I've still no idea where that came from, the prim formality of it, odd in a five-year-old. She looked slapped. The gulf between us widened. It was never mentioned again.

They didn't change my name to theirs. I kept my father's name. It was meant well, but caused difficulties. As I left them at the end of my teens, I changed it to theirs. I'm still not sure why. Perhaps out of gratitude. Or maybe a need to belong.

The last connection with my past was severed when Pom asked me if I wanted to continue dancing and singing. It was put as an open question, as though I was free to make a choice, but the tone and her look of distaste left me in no doubt of the correct answer. I understood more years later when I read Laing's speculations on Bateson's double bind theory of conflicting messages, one contradicting the other. She gave me freedom to choose. But I could see the correct answer. I gave it. In any case, I didn't want to dance except to my Mom's tune. I doubt if I could even if I'd tried.

Then Pom put me to the piano. We were a musical family and Mom had spent her life playing the piano, so it was expected that I would. I did not respond. It was many years before I could bear even to listen to music, let alone play it. I was tone deaf and had no rhythm. I could not sing a note in tune.

The music had died.

I have no memory of any artefacts from my home, no toys or teddy bears or any little item, things of importance only to me. Have

I just forgotten? Were the others so upset and thrown by events that they didn't think to restore them to me? A decision hadn't been made about my future before Christmas. I was in limbo. Then when Dad committed suicide, our house was a crime scene and everyone was reeling from this double shock. So it is possible that they just forgot about my precious possessions of no consequence to the grown-ups. They had other things on their minds. So, my past, my life, was erased. I didn't die with my parents. I seemed very alive. But a part of me was anaesthetised and buried with them. I now had to become someone who would be tolerated in this new house, the house of Pom and Harold Garnett. The alternative seemed to be actual death; I chose to learn how to survive.

What has only now occurred to me is that at no point did anyone ask me how I felt. What I did feel was so overwhelming it was safely buried, so deep it became inaccessible. That is why it remained so powerful. My grief, if tapped, might have felt unbearable, so it needed someone empathetic and strong to see it through with me. Perhaps Aunty May could have, even Aunty Janet, because I knew her well. But no one tried. I responded to their silence with my silence. Better not to feel anything or say anything. Don't cry. Just go on as though nothing's happened.

Donald Winnicott, the great family therapist, would have simply said, 'You loved them very much, didn't you? Do you miss them?' That alone would have opened me up and the work would have started. He knew the importance of 'ordinary good mothering' and had a rapport with young children. But my family had never heard of this exceptional man. He was practising with working-class families in Paddington, but that was in London, a hundred miles and a world away. In any case my family probably wouldn't have seen the need for him. I was an adult before I'd even heard of him.

Harold never hit me, which was a welcome surprise. He didn't need to. He was stern. But he never lost his temper despite much provocation. I was grateful for that. I must have been a difficult and puzzling child. Their main concern was so worrying it was shared with the wider family.

'He does nothing. All he ever wants is reading. We can't get his head out of a book. That's not natural, is it? What's wrong with him? Wash days I get him to turn the mangle. He does it. *But all the time, he's reading a book!* Yes, I know. Turning the mangle with one hand and a book in the other, ignoring me. Now, that's not natural, is it?'

It was indeed strange behaviour in a house possessing not a single book. I read compulsively, although I don't remember learning to read. Was I mentally ill? Robert, indeed all my cousins, were normal. They did things: woodwork, played with Meccano, repaired their bikes, fiddled with radios.

'Our Tony just sits there. Reading another book. He might as well live in Erdington library. He's bone idle. We can't shake him out of it.'

But reading out loud was different. Harold would hand me the *Birmingham Mail* and tell me to read it to him. Reading the paper was an honour because I coveted his copy every evening and tried to grab it when he returned home from work with it under his arm. I enjoyed reading out loud, imagining I was the man on the wireless saying, 'Here is the news.' I read with the gravity I thought the news deserved. This tickled Harold and he smiled with pleasure, looking at Pom occasionally and nodding at the voice of this little lad who had disappeared behind the pages of the *Mail*.

Only now does it occur to me that maybe burying myself in a book was a way of absenting myself from an intolerable world; maybe it was my way of going on strike, of sulking; maybe it was an escape into a world they didn't have access to. The fantasies sparked by literature were safer than the realities facing me.

The Doctor Will See You Now

Marriages were for life, so although a mere twenty-five years was not even halfway, a celebration was planned for Pom and Harold's Silver Wedding. Our family would never pass up an excuse for a party. The hall of Gunter Road school filled up, the drink flowed and after the salad tea Uncle John called the meeting to order for the speeches.

Harold stood, looked at Pom sitting primly beside him and, with a straight face, said he was looking forward to many more years with her. She smiled and looked up approvingly at her uxorious husband.

''Cause I've been told, on good authority, the first twenty-five years are the worst.'

This brought a wave of laughter.

Pom turned her mouth down.

She was used to Harold making a fool of himself.

Harold was a practical man, an engineering toolmaker who could work to a few tenths of a thousandth of an inch. He stood at a lathe all his life, working at the Wolseley car factory and then at Hercules Cycles. Like other skilled, prudent men, he saved his money: 'Look after the pennies and the pounds will look after themselves.'

I thought this would take a long time. Why not look after the pounds and the pennies wouldn't matter? But no, penny by penny, shilling by shilling, pound by pound were saved by self-denial and thrift.

Pom was even more thrifty. 'Waste not, want not.'

Although this thrift came into its own during the days of wartime scarcity, we all continued to bathe once a week, one after the other, using the same few inches of water. I was last, by which time the water was not pristine. But it was expensive to heat. The soap, which doubled as shampoo, was a slab of green carbolic from Erdington Co-op, where Pom did the weekly shop. I can still remember our divi number – 41382 – the use of which would earn a small dividend at the end of each year. They also earned extra money from lodgers who were taken in from the factory down the road.

I was never allowed a comic, like the *Beano*, and fireworks were never allowed on Bonfire Night. 'Waste of money.' That was the judgement of anything 'unnecessary'.

But between them Pom and Harold saved and the savings bought a car. Petrol gradually became available again after the war. In Brum a vehicle was not just something you worked to make in the factory. It was romantic, a symbol of freedom. Even into the 1960s, the lure of the open road was potent. For Pom and Harold the car was not a means of keeping up with the Joneses, a snobbish symbol. It was their deepest source of pleasure. For them to be able to get into their car, and drive off anywhere that took their fancy – a day out fishing in a canal, a trip to Cannock Chase or as far as Llangollen in north Wales, with a picnic and a flask of tea - was worth any amount of thrift.

Thrift was built in, like hard work. The constant reward, from the first motorbike through a bike and sidecar, to a tiny Austen, a Ford Anglia and then the Ford Prefect, was the freedom promised by driving.

They had secured their house in the building boom of the late 1930s, just like my Mom and Dad. Three hundred pounds for a ninety-nine-year lease. Harold told me that for the first two years he was close to going under, so difficult was meeting the mortgage payments. A constant threat of unemployment hovered. If it had hit him, they would have lost the house.

But following Grandma's example, Pom tried to put on a good table and she always listened to the sound advice that cheap shoes were an extravagance. She never stopped knitting or crocheting, even when listening to the wireless or watching television. Socks were darned and collars on shirts were reversed. Neither she nor Harold ever rested. 'The devil makes work for idle hands.'

Political class-consciousness rises and falls but social class-consciousness is, like the weather, of consuming interest to the English. There were many gradations of class within the working class. Harold's family, the Garnetts, considered themselves superior to the Poultons. Harold's older sister Dorrie lived outside the Brum boundary in leafy Four Oaks and was convinced of her superiority, even though her husband Bill was employed as a plumber. When I appeared she said she would allow Robert to play with her sons but not me. I was of too low a class for her sons. The Poultons, after all, drank and partied and were rather rough.

Pom, to her credit, said it was both or neither of us. To me Dorrie was just an uptight witch and it was only later that I realised how difficult it had been for Pom to keep up with the Garnetts. She was torn between her own family and her husband's.

I was a quick learner in behaviour. But sometimes I didn't know an act was wrong. A week or so after my arrival I was outside, felt the need and promptly peed into the outside drain. Why walk all that way to the lavatory? It's what I'd always done when playing outside. Pom caught me and called me, 'You filthy little boy,' quivering with fury. I did not know she was projecting her bad feelings about the war and her own health, that she was depressed. I did know my eyes and ears must be vigilant. It felt as though my life depended on it.

She said, 'You'll be going to school on Monday.' She took me to Gunter Road primary. No problem. But I was stunned to learn that she hadn't meant just Monday, she meant every day. These were tricky people.

The school didn't know what to do with me. At eight I was put into the top class but after a few weeks I'd read all the books in the school library: not difficult because they barely filled one table in the corner. I was bored and bored children cause trouble. I played up, as they say, causing disruption. Just to pass the time. I sat at the front so that I could read the blackboard. Then the man came to test everyone's eyesight. I didn't want to be a four-eyes, the butt of jokes and bullying. So I contrived to be a monitor, assisting him. This gave me access to the document he hung on the wall with letters of the alphabet printed smaller on each line. I learned them by heart and when tested passed easily. So, no spectacles. Eventually I was sussed and made to wear NHS specs, which would look sexy years later on John Lennon but were not cool then.

One fashion item did make me stand out. I was taken into town and handed a pair of shiny new boots, a gift from the *Birmingham Mail* Christmas tree fund. As an orphan I was eligible. They were magnificent kicking boots. Not that I kicked anyone but they had metal studs on the soles so were brilliant for sliding in the frost.

Towards the end of the war, American troops were stationed near us. These glamorous exotica, bearing gifts of nylons, would court local girls, who were then dismissed by locals as 'no better than they ought to be'. But many didn't care. They would allow the Yanks to take them into the long grass in Pype Hayes park and then not try too hard to retain their virtue. We boys would stalk them, crawling through the grass, just like the Red Indians on the pictures, until we were a foot or two from them. Then we would stand up and insolently stare at them. The Yanks, their seduction interrupted, would throw gum, candy, even money, telling us to 'get outta here'. We gladly obliged. Mission accomplished.

It's difficult to convey now to a different world just what it felt like in the summer of 1945. It's even difficult to remember. I was nine. After the final victory over Germany was announced, people everywhere had a party in the middle of the road. There was no traffic. Even those who had a car had no petrol. Somehow the tables were full of food.

I was sitting on the kerb, absorbing the happy, almost hysterical noise erupting from these normally reserved neighbours, all sharing an intimacy I'd never seen, laughing and joking, arms round each other. This was unusual in our keep-yourself-to-yourself, mind-your-own-business road. When Uncle Harold appeared, I looked up at him, wondering if I'd done anything wrong. He was grinning. A wry, dry smile was the usual limit if he was in a good mood.

'Tonight,' he grandly announced, 'you can stay up. As long as you like. No bedtime. All night if you like.'

I stared back at him. What was the catch?

'All. Night.' He nodded in further confirmation and turned away. He wasn't drunk. I never saw him drunk – he would make a half last all night.

They told me later that by nearly eleven they'd found me fast asleep on the kerb and carried me to bed. All night indeed. But Harold had told me I could. This must be a special occasion.

It was.

People who were not particularly political had decided that they didn't want the 1930s again and the experience of the war had taught them that a community could work together for a common good. Why not carry on and win the peace in the same way?

For all the black marketeers and those who had done well out of the war, for all the centralised, top-down bureaucratic mistakes, that feeling prevailed for years, my formative years. The people had sacked Churchill. Amazingly, decisively, unceremoniously. Even though much of what they craved was in fact coalition policy and suggested by the Liberal Beveridge, the majority decided to trust Labour with the task.

The working class felt it was their turn now.

I was formed, not just intellectually, but deep in my bones through these years. My political stance was set. The war was over and rad-icalised men were returning. People felt closer than they had ever felt. The street that night wasn't just breathing deeply the oxygen of relief after five years of dread and deprivation. It was bound together in a community.

All but one of our family returned safely. Uncle Wilfred, Dad's younger brother, came back very ill, a skeleton who could barely walk. He had spent years in a Japanese camp. Cousin John went over on the Normandy Landings and was captured straight away. No more war for him.

My other uncles never spoke about the war and refused to answer my questions about it. Was it that they didn't want to be reminded of what horrors they had seen, to relive them? What was in their memories? What nightmares? Or was it that they were now, safely back within the family, their children around them, ashamed of what they had been ordered to do or, even worse, of what they had done on their own impulse? War is brutalising. What had they done, what had they discovered in themselves? Maybe it was all better forgotten, glossed over under the rubrics 'duty' and 'a just war'.

A few uncles had been fighting in France and Italy. Cousin Norman was a rear-gunner on a bomber flying sortie after sortie over Germany.

They must all have been glad to be home unscathed, at least in body.

But many men didn't return. My favourite cousin, Jack, was one of them. He was handsome and daring. He indulged me. I would visit my Aunty May and Uncle John in Bloxwich, Walsall, when he was on leave and looking magnificent in his Fleet Air Arm uniform. He was a pilot. We would walk side by side, like mates, even though I was seven. He would give me his cigarette and laugh, watching me smoke it like he did, stylish as a film star, and then spoil it by coughing. I adored him, worshipped him. It was like having Cary Grant as your best mate.

Just after VJ Day, the end of the war, atttempting a landing on the aircraft carrier, he overshot and went down with his plane. He'd come through the war without a scratch. I cried myself to sleep. I still often think of brave, glamorous Jack.

When the doctor deigned to visit he was treated like royalty with repeated thanks. If you were certified on a list, called the panel, you paid a little every week. Otherwise he would take what you could afford. Sometimes debt men would call to collect for him. Illness was dreaded. Grandma had no truck with doctors, although a midwife came to the house when she started labour. Once she asked

Uncle Fred to call in on his way to school and tell the midwife she was starting but the little lad forgot. By the time he came home at midday and remembered, his sister had been born, with the help of a neighbour. Once I was with Grandma on the 79 tram and passed a large red brick building on Steelhouse Lane. I asked what it was. She said, 'That's the general hospital. You don't want to go in there. People die in there.' Uncle Harry had cancer. His wife had to cope with three little children, but our family rallied round, organised by Grandma, making sure they were fed and shod. After a long spell in hospital he was allowed home and told he could eat anything he wanted. The whole family were delighted at this good news but Grandma was grim: she knew. Harry died a few weeks later.

She relied on various mysterious herbal remedies which had been handed down to her. They all tasted horrible. If you complained, she said, 'Get it down you. It wouldn't do you any good if it tasted nice.'

In 1948 the National Health Service began. It had been talked about for years. Its presence was like an enormous weight lifted from people. They were not afraid anymore. It was the single most important piece of social legislation ever, even more important than compulsory, free education. No wonder they say it's the closest we have to an established religion.

But round our way there was a bigger subject of concerned conversation, bigger even than the start of the NHS. A new doctor arrived at our surgery at the top of Tyburn Road. Dr Pilgrim chain-smoked, lighting a new cigarette with the stub of the last one, even in his own surgery. No one commented because no one knew then that tobacco was killing them. In fact, there were ads saying it was healthy. One for Craven A had a man in a white coat telling us it was 'good for the throat'. I started smoking at ten, stealing from uncles and buying packets of five Woodbines or rather getting a grown-up to buy them for me. Many children smoked. Cigarettes made me feel nauseous but I practised the mannerisms of film stars, especially Humphrey Bogart. It was cool.

Dr Pilgrim also had a crate of Mackeson stout under his desk. But no one worried about any of this. The big news spread round the district in a flash, causing consternation. It was the sole topic of conversation. He was black, from the West Indies. Black! No one had ever seen a black man, not round our way. All the women said they would never consent to being examined by a 'nigger'. All the men said they wouldn't allow it. They were revolted and scared. But what was the alternative? It was him or nobody.

Pom was seriously ill with kidney trouble, underweight and depressed. Like most housewives she starved herself to supplement the rations for her family. I remember seeing her with just a cup of tea as she put a full dinner before Harold. Robert and I were always well-fed but Harold got most of the meat and the eggs. I learned later that because of the rationing, the shortage of sugar and every-one digging for victory and growing vegetables, we were the only generation of working-class children to be well-nourished, before or since. Maybe, but I still remember looking covetously at Harold's boiled egg.

Pom went to see Dr Pilgrim with much trepidation. There were murmured, worried conversations at home. Harold went with her. The doctor put them at their ease. He was jovial and charming. He made a good impression although cautious Harold just nodded, unconvinced. The doctor secured increased rations, treated her kidneys and was such a support that Pom started to feel better. She changed her mind. So did the whole neighbourhood.

The doctor always had time. He listened politely and was not at all superior. His optimism spread through the depressed waiting room. Everyone felt better. Soon he wasn't 'that nigger'. He was a witch doctor, a man with secret powers, a healer. He was magic, black magic maybe. But ours.

All this passed over my head. I was curious about him and stared. But I liked him.

When I was about eight I cycled to Bracebridge Pool, a man-made lake in Sutton Park, with Robert. He said he was going to swim to the island in the middle. It was a sunny, hot day. Not to be left out, I said I would go with him. He advised against it, knowing that I could barely swim. Leaving me on the bank, he swam out with an easy crawl. I went in after him.

My pathetic dog paddle was soon inadequate. I was stationary in the water. Then my basic technique failed in even keeping me afloat. I began to sink, flailing around to no purpose. Robert looked back, saw my difficulty and came to save me. In my panic I fought him off. I kept sinking, emerging with a splutter, then going down again, helpless and very scared. The water seemed to be pulling me under. Then I felt strong arms, too strong to resist. A man on the bank had seen us and dived in. With his hands under my armpits he swam on his back to the shore. I remember being sick in response to his pressure on my chest, heaving heavily, but alive. The man waited a moment, checked with Robert and then disappeared.

I would certainly have died if that man had not noticed me, not been a strong swimmer, not known how to revive me and had not had the presence of mind to act. I owed my life to a stranger I could never thank. It was a simple act of humanity, valuing another's life as one's own, done without any expectation of reward, because it was right.

After a few minutes I collected myself. Robert was shaken and white-faced, probably in a worse state than I was. But now he didn't have to ride back home and explain why Tony wasn't with him. Neither of us said a word about the incident.

The World Opens Up

Our Margaret got married in Aston Parish Church, next to Villa Park, where so many of the family were also married. The Villa were playing at home that Saturday, so after the ceremony all the men went to the match. Naturally. The women went to the reception, made sandwiches and gossiped till after the final whistle and the groom returned with all the other men. The celebrations could begin. I have no idea if the Villa won. I hope so. If not, it would have put a dampener on the proceedings. When, years later, I asked Margaret why she had stood for this, she said it was what people did then.

I didn't know what the eleven-plus was. We were taken into the school hall and told to do the tests. I just did them and waited until they said we could leave. I wondered what was going on but then forgot about it. Life was full of stuff no one explained. When the result arrived, Pom had no idea what it was. She guessed this brown envelope must be from the council. It looked official, so she waited for Harold to open it.

He did so on his return from work, after the ritual of taking his shoes off, putting his slippers on, settling into his armchair by the fire and accepting a cup of tea. He did everything slowly and with considered seriousness. Life was not to be rushed. By the time he arrived back from work each evening, Pom would have the kettle on and, hearing his key in the lock, would pour the boiling water into the teapot. His cup would be offered the moment he was ready to receive it. It was elegantly orchestrated.

After he had sipped at his tea, Pom handed him the envelope and waited for him to open and read it. Finally, he looked up from it and pronounced on the contents.

'You're going to the grammar.'

That meant nothing to me. There was no clue in Harold's tone: it was neither good nor bad, just an official decision. When I discovered that my best friend down the road, Barry Westwood, was not going to the grammar but to the secondary modern, I dug my heels in. He was my best friend. We played in the playground and in the park together. We were inseparable.

'I ain't going.' This took some doing. Defying both Harold and Pom was not undertaken lightly.

They ordered me, told me not to be cheeky. I set my mouth and looked at them. Then they pleaded with me. 'You have to go. We've had the letter.' As though it was an official order, not an offer. They said it wasn't up to them. They talked ominously of officialdom. I finally relented, not knowing who exactly I was fighting. Soon I was in a uniform with a cap and tie, all of which I hated; with homework in algebra and French, which I hated even more. I still lived in the same road as Barry, but we were now in different worlds. After a few months we hardly saw each other and when we did, there was nothing to talk about.

Barry's older brother had gone to Central Grammar, which was why I chose it when asked; they were all the same to me. Pom was advised by teachers to allow me to be considered by King Edward's, in Edgbaston, because they thought I would get in. But Pom said, 'No.' It was a tram ride all the way into town and a bus ride to the opposite side of Brum. There was already enough expense with this grammar school without doubling the fares. I couldn't have cared less.

Central Grammar was a rough school with, anomalously, a baronet for a head. Sir Rodney M. S. Paisley, Bart, MA, tried – unsuccessfully – to run it on the lines of his own public school.

There was rugby and prefects and caning. I hated it. Apart from Tom Reader, my English teacher, the staff were lazy. They made boring subjects unbearable and interesting subjects boring. After a couple of years, I decided to ignore them. I would do enough to make myself invulnerable. If I made sure I came top in at least one subject each year, ensuring I received a book token at the annual prize-giving in Birmingham town hall, that would keep them quiet. I would take care of my own education.

I still had to survive in school. I was small and four-eyed. On arrival, big older boys would take you into the loos and ask if you wanted to see the goldfish. Not understanding, but apprehensive, you would nod. They then tipped you up, stuck your head down the loo and pulled the chain. Or they would ask you if you knew what the 'black hole of Calcutta' was. Not waiting for an answer, they would throw you into the corner of a wall, pushing and squeezing until you screamed. But the scariest thing they did was to hold you by your braces and hang you out of the second-floor window. On looking down, scared out of your skin, you could only reflect that two buttons stood between you and eternity. I've hated bullies ever since.

As I moved up the school I realised I needed to win my first-fifteen rugby colours. If – as I did – you ran the school library, edited the school magazine, took a leading part in debates and acted in school plays, you needed macho cover or life was unbearable. I was useless at rugby and disliked it. I decided to specialise by becoming a hooker. My reflexes were quick and with practice I knew I could win most set scrums. Whether this was enough for me to win a regular place in the first fifteen or whether I was picked because, especially on the coach to away matches, I could entertain everyone with lurid stories about lascivious Germans in the war, ravishing pretty women – all improvised on the spot – I don't know.

My friend in school plays was Nicol Williamson, a boy from the next road. He and I played all the leads. He was a brilliant mimic and his impersonations of various members of staff delighted the boys, if not the teachers when they caught him. Neither of us knew, of course, that years later I would produce a film in which he played the lead, Brecht's *The Resistible Rise of Arturo Ui*.

Harold's distant cousin, Roberta, was a rebel against working-class conservatism. She was a stroppy, short-haired 1930s socialist idealist, brave and inspiring to me. Her husband, Rowland, an architect, was posh with impeccable manners. He was quietly principled. In the war he was a Conscientious Objector, sent to work in forestry in north Wales. Neither of them had a penny. Neither knew the first thing about farming. But they rented a field, bought a cow and began their lives together.

Eventually they rented a small farm near Wiveliscombe in Somerset. With a few Guernsey cows they scratched a living, brought up their four children and were political in the Labour interest in nearby Taunton.

Harold and Roberta negotiated a deal. He paid for us to spend two weeks on the farm, enabling Roberta and Rowland to get milking cover and go to Cornwall camping. Harold had bought us a cheap holiday and enabled them to have one too.

Year after year I begged to go there. I was in heaven. Not because I had aspirations to be a farmer. It was the liberating atmosphere. There were books there about subjects I never knew existed. There I read of A. S. Neill's school, Summerhill, where children were free to discover learning, not disciplined or beaten into submission. There were even books about sex, written as though it were just another subject. Roberta and Rowland even talked about sex to me, calmly and frankly. They discussed a range of ideas around the dinner table and all the children, including me, joined in.

Rowland was a member of the Soil Association and a passionate believer in organic food. He talked me patiently through the effects of pouring nitrates into the soil and of chemical sprays on the animal world. So as far back as the early 1950s I was concerned about the environment. Rachel Carson's shattering 1962 book, *The Silent Spring*, was no surprise to me.

One day I asked Rowland what his children would do when they grew up. He raised his eyebrows and said he had no idea. 'All I've ever wanted is that they become who they are. My task is to open the way, allow them to achieve that.' I was about fifteen by then. That simple, profound wisdom resonated through me. I've never forgotten. It has been my guide with my own sons.

These sojourns each summer opened my eyes to the possibility of another world, a world of fearless intellectual inquiry, of people living lives according to principles they believed in, swimming against the current received opinion.

The Birmingham reference library was an imposing example of Victorian civic responsibility, an invitation to gorge on hidden treasures. One entered this cathedral in awe, intimidated by the scale of the central space, a huge half-sphere with long workbenches filling the floor. There was an atmosphere of silent respect for the accumulated knowledge on every wall. That is where I felt at home through my adolescence. I would look around at shelf after shelf, each book patiently waiting for me, passively ready to give up its secrets. There was no prevarication there, no lies, no refusal to reveal the truth, no one to say that a subject should be of no concern of little boys. Each book treated me as an equal, none said I was forbidden to read it. They were my friends, my teachers and my solace.

It was usually empty except for the librarians gliding and whispering; plus a sprinkling of a few drunken tramps, old, defeated men, sleeping and snoring in the warm.

There I met Freud, beginning with 1905's *Three Essays on the Theory of Sexuality*. I suppose it was inevitable that a fifteen-year-old boy should be drawn to the word 'sexuality'. But, although I did not get what I'd hoped for, it did amaze me. Could any of this be true? Who was this man? I read all the Freud I could find. I understood little of it.

I devoured the Jacobeans and the few Shakespeares still unfamiliar to me. The romantic poets took over my life for a while. For a few weeks I posed pretentiously as a suburban Byron with no one noticing. I decided I didn't wish to outlive Keats and hoped for a romantic death. My own poetry was not earth-shattering. I lost myself in the great nineteenth-century English, French and Russian novels.

I discovered serious politics and wrestled with the first volume of Marx's *Capital*: it beat me easily on points. No contest. In fact, I didn't even finish it. But I would return to it. I also read some English history, especially on the Civil War.

My addiction to reading became ingrained as I imbibed the contents of these books. Many of them I've read again since and realised that then I only understood a fraction of what they offered. Maybe that's true even now. I suppose at each stage of life we take what we can and what we need. Books were my life. They satisfied my curiosity and offered me provisional answers; fed my fantasies and absorbed my energies. They kept me out of trouble.

When I entered middle age and Uncle Harold was very old, he remarked that his biggest fear for me when I was a teenager was that I would 'get into trouble with the law, you know, one of those delinquents and end up in prison. You had that danger in you. I couldn't handle you, I know that'. The library saved me.

Examinations at sixteen were a challenge as I had done little work on the curriculum. All my time had been spent in the library or on the amateur stage. Panic rose as the dates loomed ever closer. I crammed madly for three weeks, night and day, hoping I would have enough short-term memory to get through and that my facility with words would make what little I did know look adequate. One or the other must have saved me because the results were better than I'd dared to hope. I had what Harold disparagingly called the 'gift of the gab', possessed by all those he was wary of, such as lawyers and politicians and anyone who tried to sell him a bargain. For Harold this equated to dishonesty.

His vision of true integrity was marked by slow inarticulacy and those who displayed that were people you could trust. Like my other uncles, for him 'silence was golden'. I remember watching him with awe as he slowly leaned over and picked up a red-hot coal which had fallen into the hearth. He casually threw it back into the fire, his sleeves rolled up, his huge forearms like Popeye's. His fingers were so hardened by decades working metal on a lathe that he felt nothing. I also admired his impeccable, beautiful copperplate handwriting, my own being so ugly and indecipherable. He learned his before the Great War at elementary school.

We didn't have a television till I finished my A-levels. Whether they wanted to wait until I'd completed my exams or to see if the expensive new-fangled box of tricks would really catch on and prices would come down, I don't know. But we had the wireless and as Robert and I got older we were allowed to listen to more of it. Though not the Top Twenty on Radio Luxembourg, which was 'on too late and rubbish'. So Robert fixed up a crystal set and we listened in bed every Sunday night, under the covers. You would lose face at school on Monday morning if you didn't know the charts.

The biggest treat was being allowed to listen to *Dick Barton – Special Agent*, at a quarter to seven every evening. He, with his stalwart assistants, Jock and Snowy, would extricate himself from deadly traps and fight the enemy fearlessly. Every episode, with a tantalising cliffhanger, was bliss.

So I found ways to enjoy life.

Working Class Hero

One day Uncle Fred, feeling poorly, went to the doctor. After he'd been taking the medicine for a few days he answered the front door to a panicky chemist.

'I'm sorry, Mr Poulton, but we've discovered a mix-up. At the pharmacy.'

'Oh, ar,' said Fred.

'Yes, I'm afraid you were given Mrs Tanner's prescription and, unfortunately, she got yours. I'm ever so sorry.'

'Right. Do you want it back?'

The medicines were swapped and a relieved chemist left.

'Oh, Fred,' said Aunty Janet. 'How come they did that? I say . . .'

Fred shrugged.

'. . . Mrs Tanner's! Could have been, you know, woman's trouble, you know. Anything.'

'I felt better on it, anyroad.'

Not much bothered our Fred.

In the early 1950s, in my middle teens, I worked for my Uncle Fred on Saturdays and in the school holidays. Fred indulged me. He didn't need an assistant but he wanted to help without seeming patronising. He tolerated my aggressive, argumentative company, gently deflating me.

He was a milkman for the Midlands County Dairy. As a young man, sacked in the Depression and not too bothered about it, disliking factory life, he fancied a change and started his own milk round. He bought churns of milk from a farmer and ladled it out, house by house. But bottling came in. He sold his round and became an employee: not the first family member forced to respond to technology. But he stayed an ordinary milkman till he retired, refusing offers to be a supervisor: 'I'm not coming copper on my mates.'

His round was the city centre. This was Brum before the frenzied activity of the sixties, when restless planners came back from research visits to America with big plans to remake the city. They destroyed the Victorian heritage with their car fetish to make way for concrete brutalism and motorways, people having been dismissed and human scale forgotten.

Spaghetti Junction was still just an idea (Gravelly Hill interchange wouldn't be opened until 1972), so I took the 79 tram into town. We carried crates of past (pasteurised) and stera (sterilised) across the tram lines to big insurance company offices, like the Wesleyan & General on Steelhouse Lane. Then along Colmore Row, down to the Bull Ring, serving Oswald Bailey's Army & Navy Store and the fishmongers in the market hall. From them I was given a bag of crabs' claws which, while Fred went off for a couple of pints with Uncle Albert at the musicians' club, I would smash against the side of the truck to extricate the sweet meat. It was washed down with a pint of stera milk. Tobacconists would tip Fred with Craven A cigarettes, which I would take home for Uncle Harold. Others would give me sweets, a lovely tip in those days when rationing was ending but sweets were still scarce.

At that time the Bull Ring was an open space north of the church and there, rather like a mini-Hyde Park Corner, speakers would gather, ascend their soapboxes, and harangue the multitude. That is, if they could attract one. Neglecting my duties, I would linger and began to heckle, with confidence that increased with practice. The Mormon young men asked me to speak, to argue with them, possibly because the confrontation attracted interest. I accepted. I ascended the soapbox and faced the crowd. This is where I first learned public speaking, practised conquering my nerves and learned the value of repetition, scorn and humour for contrast and humour to deflate the heckler. Without knowing it I was enrolled in a practical course of rhetoric. It was all hugely enjoyable. The practice allowed me to become the star of the school debating society. Like a barrister I would argue a case for the sheer pleasure of the contest. It was sport.

Fred was and remains my hero. He was an indulgent father-substitute. Myopic, balding, walking like a punch-drunk prize fighter, he enjoyed life. He loved everyone and everyone loved him. Maybe his sunny temperament accounted for his longevity: he died at ninety-four, having smoked a pack of twenty a day, kept Ansells Brewery in business and lived out of the frying pan. His humour was Brum-dry: on Aston Villa, the family club, 'I don't care what you say, they're the best team in Aston!' Like all my other uncles, his humour was delivered with a blank, poker face. Each girlfriend would look puzzled and ask me if laughing would offend them. The hilarious joke and the deadpan delivery were confusing.

Fred would regularly be up at five, load his truck at the dairy, deliver all morning and then get on the train to London. That evening he would go to the fights – maybe the American, Sugar Ray Robinson, against Randolph Turpin, from Leamington Spa – and then get the milk train that stopped at every station back to Brum. He and his friends, with a supply of ale, would play cards and gossip all the way home, arriving very early in the morning. Then he would go to the dairy, load his truck and do his round, never missing a beat. He confessed to having a nap in the afternoon, before a trip to the pub in the evening.

Aunty Janet got angry, but no amount of nagging changed him. He once told me that although he was a bad lad, always in the pub, 'I've never been with another woman. I've never broken my marriage vows.' On a winter evening, snug by the fire, Fred would say, 'Even if the Queen of England asked me, I wouldn't be shifted from this fire tonight, Janet.' Then he would hear Uncle Jack, the painter and decorator, whistle outside and he'd be straight up, looking for his boots to go to the pub. Aunty Janet used to hide them sometimes to stop him. But the pull of the Hare and Hounds was too strong. None of my uncles would leave a party until all the beer had been drunk. They thought that would be indecent.

When, as a young married couple, he and Janet first moved into their house, Fred said, 'I'm going to decorate the front room, Janet, so don't come in. You won't know it when I'm finished.' She was surprised and glad. What a good husband she had, she thought. She was surprised and apoplectic on Sunday afternoon when he let her see his handiwork. None of the lengths of patterned wallpaper fitted, there was paint all over the windows and some of the wallpaper had big air pockets where it didn't stick. She ordered him out, saying he was never, ever to be let near any decorating or any other job for that matter. He went to the pub, mission accomplished. Over the years Janet did all the jobs and Fred praised her extravagantly.

An old trick, elegantly executed.

Smart man, my Uncle Fred.

My teens were angry, as teens often are. But mine had an edge the origins of which I couldn't or daren't identify. It took me over and it cast itself about looking for release. No doubt some of it was turned inwards but it mainly became the engine of my questioning all authority. I would accept anything if there were convincing reasons. If not, my scorn was cold and dismissive. When very young I'd dismissed religion or at least the version of God I was offered, in the same way I'd dismissed Santa Claus. I applied the literal, patronising Christian story to my own life. If I ever meet him, I would think, he'll get a piece of my mind. 'If you're all powerful, why did you kill my parents? Oh, free will's your get-out card, is it? How cruel to then stand by and watch wars and famines and diseases. Is that fun? You're a sick bastard.'

These sentiments were not appreciated by my Church of England, baronet headmaster.

I've been a republican since I can remember, affronted by the monarchy and the House of Lords. My adolescent mind worked in black and white: nuance compromises certainty. I must have been an exhausting pain in the arse.

Getting into an argument, forcing people into combat, was difficult. How could I provoke anyone to disagree with me? So I decided
to become a Conservative and even worse, to support Birmingham
City, the Blues, the rival football club.

Uncle John, a Black Country man who lived in Walsall, was a
staunch member of the Postal Workers' Union and a Labour man.
He told me stories of going to an open-air meeting on Cannock
Chase to hear the local MP, Jenny Lee, and a brilliant young orator,
Aneurin Bevan, and how the police brutally broke it up. He was a
calm, measured, moderate Labour man and a brilliant speaker himself, always respectfully looked up to at family gatherings, chairing
them with authority. I was aching to debate with him.

He took me on in his quiet, reasoned way, never patronising me,
wiping the floor with me, of course, but always listening carefully
to my crude polemics. He would play with his pipe, filling it from
a pouch as he listened and considered, tamping it down and then
buy time endlessly trying to light it. Most men seemed always to be
playing with a pipe in those days. Smoking was an afterthought. The
pipe was a prop, a temperamental companion that had to be coaxed
and disciplined into behaving. I was fascinated by all of them, my
uncles and my granddad. There seemed to be a design fault in the
pipes which they for some unknown reason didn't want to fix. They
were like toddlers with a dummy, my aunties said.

As a relief from solving the problems of the world, which Uncle
John thought difficult and complex and I thought I could solve
overnight, he would tell me Black Country stories about Enoch and
Ali. He had a beautiful accent which he broadened as the stories
unfolded till he was barely comprehensible. They were simple, silly
and to me delightfully funny, told as they were in an affectionate,
non-patronising way. They were a lament for a world not yet obso-
lete but going by.

Supporting the Blues provided some useful conflict too. From
Granddad's time our default position as a family was the Villa. In
the late 1890s he would go to Villa Park: an alternative would be
as unthinkable as drinking in any other than an Ansell's pub, whose
brewery was yards away from the football stadium. So I now had

some good arguing in prospect. I enjoyed it for a few months. Then it palled and I reverted to the Left and to the Villa.

The loser was my younger brother Peter. I saw a little more of him now. We sought each other out, puzzled by our closeness and our separation. I didn't know him yet he was my brother. I liked him yet we knew little about each other. I had told him I supported the Blues and the Villa were crap. This was his big brother talking, so he decided to support the Blues. When I later reverted to type, I forgot to tell him, so it stuck. I only saw him occasionally and it slipped my mind. He still supports the Blues. I'm ashamed now at what I did, but it's too late to save him. Poor chap.

I still remember two speeches from my teens. One May Day I went to hear Bevan, at an open-air meeting in Calthorpe Park. It was a sharp, sunny day and he had attracted a big crowd. I knew little about him but was curious after listening to Uncle John. When he appeared he seemed ordinary, speaking in a low voice which made us all reach forward to catch it. Gradually it rose and the jabbing wit, excoriating the Tories, began. He spoke more in sorrow than in anger, as though he was sorry for these deluded politicians. He continued to lay on heavy sarcasm. There was much laughter. This was like a free seat at the Hippodrome. In fact, he was better than most comedians. Then he got serious, the scorn turned to sorrow, the sorrow to piercing anger. He finished on a call to arms, a flourish of principles which invited us all to follow our dreams of a better, more compassionate world. He had spoken for well over an hour, extempore. It captivated the crowd. The applause and the cheers were prolonged and everyone left nodding to each other. He had played a full range of notes faultlessly: humour, scorn, biting anger and then soaring high into the possibilities for humanity, sending everyone away walking on air.

The other speech was at a family party to mark Grandma and Granddad's Diamond Wedding, celebrating sixty years of marriage. I was fifteen. It was in Gunter Road school hall, my old primary school, hired for Saturday afternoon and evening. All the aunties had got together to make the meal: salad and cold meats, with Heinz salad cream. Everyone did their bit. I had been to the Bull Ring to buy some nice fresh lettuces. All the uncles had contributed a lot of booze including a barrel, the condition of which they tended like the experts they were. It had been bought days before, left to settle and then carried very carefully to its place early that morning. When I arrived, uncles were round it, conferring. This was clearly a highly technical matter. Their expressions were grave. Everyone dressed up, the hall full of the banter and laughter of around 120 people of all ages, mostly family. After the sit-down tea everyone danced, ending with the 'Hokey Cokey' and then 'Old Lang Syne'.

As the meal finished Uncle John called us to order and in the expectant hush all eyes were on our Fred. He stood up and began to speak about his Mom and Dad, who were sat next to him. Grandma's hair was up in a neat bob and on her flowered dress was a diamante broach. Granddad wore his only suit and tie, which he always seemed to wear, and his pipe was on the table in front of him. To me they looked ancient, especially Grandma, shaking a little as she looked up, smiling at Fred.

Without a note, he elaborated around the theme that his Mom and Dad were themselves diamonds, rough, unpolished diamonds, but genuine, not paste, nor imitation. That they had been formed in the only way diamonds can be formed, through the long passage of time. He continued to elaborate this image beautifully but it was only afterwards when I thought about it that I understood his artful skill. At the time, like everyone else, I was caught up in his sincerity, his simple expression of deep love and respect, echoing everyone's feelings. That day I not only learned from Fred the importance of believing what you say, but also the importance of structure to give it shape. The trick is never to let the technique show. He spoke as though what he was saying was just a few things he happened to feel at that moment. When he sat down there wasn't, as they say, a dry eye in the house. I'm choking up, remembering it as I write. Of course, he might have got the idea from a paperback giving tips on how to speak on various topics. They must have been around. But the speech was his.

Two very different speeches. Two great speakers.

I loved these parties as a child, going round with my cousins slyly finishing people's drinks, joining in the fun. Always knowing that Mom and Dad were absent but refusing to feel anything about it. I remained numb.

One day after school I was told to go to Grandma's. When I got there I was directed upstairs. Grandma was in the double bed on which she'd given birth to so many babies. Some of them, now her grown-up daughters, were gathered round. No one spoke, unusual when a group of my aunties got together. Aunty May, who seemed to be in charge, quietly told me to say 'Goodbye' to Grandma. I looked down at this wizened little woman and her lined, peaceful face, her heavy breathing rustling through the silent room, and took her hand, the large veins pushing through mottling brown age spots. It was limp. She did not return my squeeze. My love and respect for Grandma had only ever been rivalled by my devotion to and need of my parents, despite her rough justice after they had died. She was an anchor. I had always been sure of her love.

I looked at her impassively, said nothing, and indifferently left the room, feeling nothing. My protective decision not to feel was intact, guarding me and crippling me. Another grandchild was allowed into the room. Her daughters' vigil remained until she died a few hours later. When told, I shrugged. So what? Nothing could hurt me.

Apparently, she had done the Monday wash, turning the mangle. She'd tidied everything up. Then she told Dulcie, the youngest daughter, who still lived at home, 'Fetch your sisters. I'm going to bed now.' She clearly knew she was going to die and wasn't concerned. In fact she looked forward to it, to go when her time came. There was no washing-up in heaven, apparently. I refrained from asking how she was so certain. You knew how to behave in front of Grandma, if you knew what was good for you. Little boys should be seen but not heard.

Gimme Some Truth

Aynock [Enoch] *and Aylie* [Ali] *gorron the buzz and went to
the middle of Brum for a look round, loik. Getting to Victoria
Square their brains was in a spin at the size of it all and the
traffic. Aylie was looking at a great, big buildin': 'Look at that,
our kid. Is that a palace, loik? Who could afford to live there?'*
  'No,' says Aynock. 'That's the Council House.'
  'Bloody hell,' says Aylie. 'I got me name down for one of them!'

Auntie Pom and Uncle Harold had gone out for the day, he to
fish in the canal and she to crochet beside him on the bank.
'Drowning worms,' was my dismissive judgement. I couldn't think
of anything more boring, although I wouldn't be so scornful once
I'd spent a day going round the BSA (Birmingham Small Arms
Company) factory, It was an educational visit from school. It educated me. The noise in this vast Miltonian hell was ugly. It hit you in
waves, like blows to the head. Five shifts a week a man was chained
to his machine, doing its bidding. I began to understand Harold,
who had spent his life in deafening hell like this, day after day, concentrating on shaping a piece of metal on a lathe.

Sitting on the canal bank in the open air, concentrating his eyes
on a float, Harold would be in a state of meditation, calming and
healing in its silence, with just the swish of the water and the cry
of birdsong. I remembered Granddad's love of fishing and that he'd

made fishing rods. Coarse fishing was a working man's sport. I thought the idea was stupid, just to catch fish, roach and perch and then put them back. But that wasn't what it was about. Even if he'd caught nothing, not even had a bite, the day was always a success. He was refreshed.

That day Rob was also out, on his bike at a time trial.

Alone and restless, I mooched round the house. This aimless drifting gradually turned into a systematic search. I didn't know what I was searching for, but in an unfocused way I guessed there were secrets to be uncovered. This was my chance. I looked everywhere, putting everything back where I'd found it.

Eventually I entered the final forbidden place, Pom and Harold's bedroom. I searched every inch, but nothing was revealed. It was all predictably tidy and uninteresting. Then in the bottom drawer of a dressing table, underneath Pom's underwear, I discovered a pile of assorted papers and old photographs, including snaps of my parents looking casual and happy, walking along the front at Blackpool. At the very bottom I found Dad's suicide note, in his own careful handwriting.

To whom it may concern

It is now 3 long weeks since my sweetheart was taken from me and I feel I cannot carry on without her, the house is just an empty shell now. I have missed her and the kiddies. I know the step I am taking will shock a lot of people but time will heal as it will never with me. I am going to try to find her. When my affairs are settled I think they will realise about £600 taking into account our house and contents my insurance and interests in the Royal London book together with accrued pension and wages still at Lucas's etc. I wish my estate to be equally divided between Peter and Tony Lewis to be used for their education. Mrs Janet Poulton to bring Peter up as one of her own. Tony I will leave to the families discretion but in any case to be brought up in the true Poulton way and not the Lewis way, who never did anything for my darling with the exception of Wilfred. I should like Mr Kendall and John Darby to settle everything for me.

*I am taking this step because from a certain conversation I had today
(Thurs). I understand that all my relatives still think I was the cause for my
darling's death.*

Goodbye and thanks a lot for a happy 10 years amongst you all.

Thomas E. Lewis

I read it three times, very carefully, willing it to reveal more
secrets. What was this 'certain conversation'? That phrase hung in
the air, tempting me to speculate but giving no satisfaction. I then
carefully returned the note, still carrying its tantalising secrets and
covered up my tracks. I felt nothing, as though it was nothing to do
with me. I was detached. I didn't mention it to anyone.

Did the family in effect kill him? Which family? He wrote, 'all my
relatives'. But what was this 'certain conversation' and who had it
been with?

Many years later, a story came to me that the youngest sister,
Dulcie, who was still living at home in 1941, had heard Grandma
giving my Dad a piece of her mind. A telling-off from her must have
been like napalm. At that moment, considering his deep respect for
Grandma and the fact that she was the head of the family, it must
have seemed to him like a total rejection, a death sentence. Was it
the incident that finally broke his will to go on living? Did it feel
like the completion of his isolation? He was now without Ida. The
detectives were threatening imprisonment. He must have felt guilty
about his own part in Ida's painful death. Was Grandma's excoriation
the final push that made him end it all?

What did she say? Did she accuse him of making her go to the
abortionist? In which case he was a murderer. Or did she accuse him
of not stopping her? In which case, in the conventions of the day,
he was a bad husband. But Grandma, overcome by her own grief,
would not be sensitively attuned to his feelings.

If your world has judged you and rejected you, maybe the answer is
to leave the world? No wonder, in his grief, he felt he couldn't carry
on. Would he be allowed to keep Peter and me in the circumstances?

I can only imagine his guilt at having gone along with the abortion, even possibly having pressed for it. By all accounts he was deeply in love with Mom. Contemplating life without her would have been difficult. Like so many assertive men he needed the love and support of a woman. Life in these new circumstances could just have seemed impossible.

I would never blame him for committing suicide.

Odd, though, that it might have been my own revered Grandma, one of the steady rocks of my childhood, who could have killed my Dad.

The discovery of my Dad's suicide note renewed my determination to dig out the truth. Aunty Janet and Uncle Fred bore the brunt of my restless, forensic cross-examination about my parents' death. I had been told virtually nothing. In those days grown-ups believed the less said the better. It was, also, no doubt painful to go over it. I had forced fact after fact from reluctant family members but sensed there was more. During my childhood and, increasingly in my adolescence, anyone who I suspected knew anything, even among my older cousins, was interrogated. They might have overheard some detail. By my early teens, after relentless, obsessive effort, I'd exposed the bare facts, revealing the abortion and forced confirmation of the suicide. I suspected a cover-up. What else was there to find out? What other dark secrets were buried out of my reach?

If anyone knew these secrets it would be Janet or Fred. They had been there, or at least next door. I confronted them, suddenly turning up at their house, subjecting them to an inquisition. They had always welcomed me, Janet making a fuss, hugging me and feeding me. They were patient, refusing to be baited by my anger and after a while gave me more harrowing details than they wanted to remember or they thought I should know. They confirmed my own memories of Mom's last night.

To this day I suspect some facts went to the grave with them. Had my Mom told Janet she was pregnant? Probably. They were like sisters and saw each other every day. Before the abortion was considered, it would be natural for Mom to tell her she was pregnant and how worrying that was. Did Janet know about the abortion? Mom would be well aware it was a serious criminal offence. She may have hoped to claim a miscarriage. She would not have wished to implicate Janet. But it was possible. So underpinning this cover-up might have been guilt. To know and not tell was itself a criminal offence. Maybe Janet and Fred thought they should have prevented it, if they were in on the plan. This would have meant Mom confiding in Janet without telling Dad that she had. Everyone was afraid of him. She might have been in conflict, not wanting to go through with it but unable to stand up to Dad. Would Janet have told Fred even after she had been sworn to secrecy?

I writhed and wrestled, unable to sleep, trying every permutation. But I had few facts and no one who had been involved would tell me the truth. Or at least, that's what I sensed.

There was a press report which tantalisingly seemed to raise more questions than it answered.

Buried among the ads for Vic Cold Relief and exhortations to 'Turn the gas fire down. Save fuel for the factories', the news of MORE WITHDRAWALS IN MALAYA and Jack Payne's Orchestra on the wireless, I found in the *Birmingham Mail* archive:

HUSBAND'S SUICIDE

Coroner's comments on tragic story

An inquest was held in Birmingham today on a 38-year-old man – the father of two children – whose wife died on 12 December as a result of a septic abortion and on whom an inquest was held in Birmingham, an open verdict being recorded.

The husband was Thomas Lewis, of 53 Neville Road, Erdington, who was found gassed lying in bed in his own home on the second day of the new year.

Mrs Janet Reid Poulton, a sister-in-law of Lewis and a neighbour, recounted how she gave evidence at the inquest on the wife. In reply to the coroner she admitted that women had called at the house from time-to-time during the blackout and that there were certain suspicions. Witness said the cause of Mrs Lewis' death had not been established.

A note from Lewis had been found and, commenting on its contents which mentioned £600 left for the care of the children, the city coroner said it was a very sad affair. From the note it seemed that Lewis was a very steady man and was very concerned about his wife's death. In fact, it appeared that he was a good father and a good husband.

Detective Inspector Hawthorn said in view of suspicions arising out of the inquest on the wife he interviewed Lewis. Witness wished to know if Lewis knew anything about a woman called Ivy.

The coroner – 'Were you suspicious of Lewis himself?' – 'I had no grounds but I thought Lewis could help to trace the woman.'

Addressing the police officer the coroner said: 'I hope you will be able to find the criminal abortionist and there ought to be the severest punishment considering the tragedy which has been caused here.'

A verdict of suicide while the balance of mind was disturbed, was returned.

Whose kitchen table was it? Dad had an Austin 7 but no petrol. Even if Dad had accompanied Mom, the return journey on public transport would have been trying just after an abortion. If at our house, which was suggested at Dad's inquest, was Janet looking after Peter and me? In that case, was it possible that she didn't know what was happening? Some months later the woman was arrested and tried. Apparently she was a stalwart of her local church and her vicar appeared as a character witness. She was sent to jail.

I didn't blame Janet or Fred, however they were caught up in it all. I didn't even blame the abortionist. It's difficult today to imagine

just what shame and fear the word 'abortion' provoked in a respectable Christian family in 1941.

I just wanted the truth.

At sixteen I knew I wanted to be an actor but I had no idea why. I
also didn't know how to go about it. I needed to buy time so I said
I wanted to be a teacher. In those days teachers were looked up to. I
was allowed to stay on into the sixth form. Another two years with
me eating and not earning was a big decision. In our world then it
was unheard of. All my male cousins left school at fifteen to start
their apprenticeships. The girls got work, preferably in an office,
until they were married: that was the real start of their careers. To be
still at school at eighteen did not seem natural. Pom said, 'Well, you
can stay. But thank God your Grandma's dead.' Grandma wouldn't
have tolerated such nonsense.

I loved my time on Fred's milk round because the wages took
me to every first night at Stratford for two seasons. Booking the
cheapest seats early, I saw the Oliviers in *Titus Andronicus* and many
other legendary productions. Once, the school took a group of us
to a matinee. I was almost expelled. The performance of Laurence
Harvey in the lead role in *Romeo and Juliet*, in an unoriginal production, was so laughably bad that at the curtain call I stood up,
shouting, 'Author, author' in an ironic attempt to shame the actors.
The school authorities were not amused. I concluded they did not
care about the theatre.

In those days the National Anthem was played in all cinemas and
theatres. As a republican I stolidly refused to stand despite the foul
looks, the sanctimonious hisses and even physical threats around me.
At any formal dinner there would be a toast to whichever Windsor
had the job at the time. I would remain stubbornly seated, ignoring
the hostile stares. This angry flaunting of authority could easily have
been dangerous. The 1950s were intolerant of dissent.

Each year our school made us perform a cross-country run. Bad
enough. But the supervising gym and games teachers went round
the run on their bikes. I made a banner, protesting the hypocrisy
connected to this compulsory athletic nonsense, and marched around

the course, refusing to break into even a jog. Some lads marched with me until they were threatened by the teachers.

The next day I was called in front of the head. He asserted his authority, telling me in icy tones that I was an inch away from permanent expulsion. This was a poker game. We had a small sixth form. I was one of the rare pupils expected to sail into university. He didn't want to lose me. But expulsion would have dented me severely.

I just made it through.

I started an exclusive club with a few fellow pupils. It was by invitation and male only as it had to be, being a boys' school. Amusingly, rather like the London clubs I've since refused to join.

We convened each lunchtime in a caff over the road, which was cosy and warm, filled with cigarette smoke and served drinks and snacks. The tea was strong and we sat around one of the tables in our school uniforms, ordering bacon butties and pouring large mugs of the tea as we loudly solved the problems of the world. The other customers were local workers, including a couple of coal delivery men who left black fingerprints on their white bread sandwiches. In those days the coal man was a familiar sight. It was hard work, carrying sacks of coal on your back all day, delivering from house to house. They tolerated our exotic presence. I think they were amused. We were loud and no doubt full of ourselves, knowing how to improve the world and practising long words. I would engage them in debate. One day they threw us by turning the tables to discuss us. We became the objects of their scrutiny.

'I wouldn't stand it for any kids of mine, keeping 'em on like this.' They continued and, despite the ribbing, we rather enjoyed being the centre of attention. It meant we had been accepted into their world. One of the coal men nodded at the woman who ran the caff. 'Ar, that's what I think. Get the buggers out to work, paying some rent. Look at this lot, grown men, really, none of 'em working.'

'No,' said the woman. 'I mean, I'd lose them. I don't want that.' What she said puzzled me until I realised she hadn't meant that her children would leave town but that they would pass into a different culture and be alienated from her.

This remark has had an effect on my whole life.

We early products of the 1944 Education Act were the first generation of working people to be educated in the universities of the professional middle class. Only a small group of us, but we were offered skills and social mobility hitherto unavailable to people like us. Would we use them to help and be loyal to our own people or would we join the middle class, becoming technicians serving the ruling elite and forgetting the people we left behind? Would we climb the ladder without a backward glance or fight to get rid of it, fight for a more equitable society? Sentiments like these seem odd now. They are politically unfashionable. But I never forgot what the caff owner said.

The sixties' social revolution reversed the drive to appear posh. It became fashionable to claim working-class origins. Actors who couldn't convincingly talk posh, like Michael Caine, Albert Finney and Tom Courtenay became stars, partly due to their talent and partly because they were from working-class roots. I began to benefit from these changes, too. Such is the power of fashion. Just as a game of 'lefter than thou' was played among political activists so some exaggerated the poverty of their childhoods, out-bidding each other in hardship stories. I thought this was ridiculous: my family was Labour aristocracy and proud of it.

But beneath all this lay a feeling of displacement, of being declassed: guilt and anger as I left one class behind, no longer feeling truly accepted, and was offered membership of another class which I didn't want to join. I valued all the cultural and professional opportunities the acceptance into the new world would provide but I respected my people, their culture and values.

On the last day at school a few of us got drunk and I led them in a final act of rebellion. We systematically let down the tyres of all the teachers we hated.

They were probably relieved to get rid of me.

I look back now, grateful to Pom and Harold who kept me out of a sense of duty and their love for Mom, steady people who gave me a predictable environment which I could kick against.

When I was a boy and was despondent, fearing I'd failed at something or other, Harold would say, 'Did you do your best?'

'Oh, yes, I always do my best.'

'Well, that's all you can do.'

That's what I feel about them now. They had enough on their
plates without me. They were out of their depth trying to understand, let alone cope with me.

But they did their best.

When I was an adult we became closer as I began to understand
them and myself. Harold retired and gradually they became more
vulnerable. I tried to help but they were steadfastly independent.
Harold accepted a colour TV too large for the room. It gave them
great pleasure. But when I suggested putting in central heating he
would have none of it. In truth, I wanted it for the visits I made
during the winter. By then it was the mid-1960s and I was aged
thirty before I experienced central heating but after that first cosy
winter I went soft and I've never been without it since.

As a child during a cold spell, the ice would form even on the
inside of the bedroom windows, and getting out of bed to get
dressed in that freezing temperature required all the willpower that
Pom could invoke. I could see my own breath. The only warm bit
of the house was a space in the living room just in front of the fire.
Sitting there the front of my legs would go red from the heat but the
backs would still be cold. But no, Harold dismissed the suggestion
of central heating all those years later. 'Dries the air!' That was that.

The idea of putting in a phone, if only for emergencies now
they were getting older, was similarly dismissed. 'Don't need that.
Wouldn't use it. Waste of money.'

I visited regularly and they always made me welcome in their
understated way. The moment I turned up, Harold would be out
front to see what silly car I'd rolled up in. From Jaguars to Mini
Cooper S's to Triumphs, either the cars had been assembled or parts
had been designed and manufactured nearby. Harold would be there
on the little front drive, shaking his head, a look of patient amusement on his face.

Each Sunday morning it was a ritual for all the cars in the street to be displayed on their drives and men would adjust their internal workings or wash the outsides or hoover the insides. They would all crowd round my car, which would inevitably be one at least part of which they had worked on in the factory and a car not one of them could afford or be barmy enough to buy. We lived near the body plant at Castle Bromwich and round our way the minis were called 'cocoa tins'. They stamped them out but wouldn't buy them.

I stood to one side and let them get on with it. I neither understood what they were saying nor was I interested in it. But it entertained Harold no end, shocked though he always was at my extravagance.

Our Robert bought a cheap, clapped-out MG. As my Dad had done, he took it to pieces, got the engine and transmission to work smoothly again and then spent months patiently spraying, rubbing down and spraying again until the bodywork looked new.

You started with a second-hand motorbike, which you took to pieces and re-engineered until it flew like a bird. Holidays were spent at the Isle of Man TT motorcycle races. When you started courting, a sidecar would be added. The summit of achievement was an Austin 7 or a Ford – that was really making it in life. It would never see a repair shop. Each car was polished, burnished, prepared, adored and talked about in competing panegyrics by owners who knew every idiosyncrasy of every vehicle. I thought it unwise to ask their wives what they thought of this devotion.

Men earnestly talked in their arcane jargon of carbs and camshafts and exhaust manifolds and male and female joints, pieces of metal that slotted neatly into each other, a phrase used by them neutrally without the slightest frisson of innuendo. They were practical men who spoke utilitarian prose. But the sounds and rhythms were poetic to me.

True Love

I love you the more in that I believe you have liked me for my own sake and for nothing else.

John Keats, letter to Fanny Brawne

In my mid-teens I would go to St Mary's youth club on Varley Road at the edge of a council estate. There were dances, where I was clumsy, the music having died and debates, where I could show off. The vicar, a kind man, would engage in theological dispute with me, probably amused by this precocious atheist in the middle of stolid Brum indifference.

One year he invited three of us to share the sermon on Empire Youth Sunday. I wanted to give freedom to the Empire, not glorify it, but the occasion was an opportunity to speak out. The church was unusually full that Sunday evening, some proud relatives, others no doubt just curious. Even Pom and Harold came dressed in their best to hear me. This was an honour. Harold only went to church for hatches (births), matches (weddings) and dispatches (funerals) – and VJ Day. He would maintain, defensively, that not all the best people go to church, although he sent Robert and me to Sunday school. I doubt if it was an occasion for uninterrupted sex. Pom didn't trust contraceptives. Or that was her excuse. I bet she didn't like sex. She thought it was a dirty business only acceptable for procreation. Probably that was why poor Harold was always in his shed, playing with his tools. On Sundays, instead, he chose a peaceful hour with the *News of the World*.

Robert liked Sunday school no more than I did. He collected train numbers so that's what we did. It was tricky when we went home and Harold asked about that day's lesson in church. Robert was struck dumb. I would guess that Harold remembered little of his childhood Bible education so I said things like, 'Oh, Moses in the bulrushes today.'

I stood in the pulpit that Sunday evening before a full house and tore into everyone. My theme was hypocrisy. The Church, the clergy, everyone in the congregation. No one escaped. What about the poor, here and overseas? The evils of empire? Was God English? What a convenient miracle! I accused the congregation of being Sunday Christians; most of them not even that. And so on. For an increasingly embarrassing twenty minutes I flayed them. When I finished there was a buzz of hostile conversation, unusual in a church.

For a long time my family did not mention the evening. I must have shamed them in front of the whole neighbourhood. Eventually Pom said, 'Are you satisfied now? I suppose you think you're clever.' I wisely didn't answer her.

The incident was reported in the *Erdington News* and the poor vicar was severely hauled in front of his bishop to give an account of himself.

I hated the 1950s, the years of my growing up, for its automatic respect for authority, its philistinism, its narrowness and its repression, especially of sexual feelings. I was contemptuous of the social snobbery and the rigid class system. It was authoritarian, illiberal and timid. I rebelled. Pom wasn't sympathetic: she respected tradition. When I grew my hair long a decade too early, Pom gave me an ultimatum to get it cut, short back and sides, or go without dinner. But I just grew it again.

Radio Luxembourg was a must, but I despised most popular music: Eddie Fisher, Doris Day, Frankie Lane and songs like '(How Much is) That Doggie in the Window?' Only the theatrical excess of 'Unchained Melody' appealed. It was a bleak time culturally. My friends loved Elvis but to me his songs were trite. Brum watch committee banned Bill Haley's film *Rock Around the Clock*, which sums up the times. The film would corrupt the youth, apparently. We had to go outside the city boundary to see it. The film didn't cause the end of civilisation as we know it, unfortunately.

The sixties didn't get any momentum until 1964. I was twenty-eight. I was indifferent to the Beatles. 'I Wanna Hold your Hand' was for twelve-year-olds. Only when John Lennon found his real voice did I sit up. At last here was someone who mattered. I admired him especially for embracing a belief, and then having the moral courage and intellectual honesty to reject it when he found it wanting. He was restlessly inquisitive and brave. All the rest were also-rans. But in the fifties I suppose he, like me, was chafing anonymously against a smug, mean world and showing it no respect.

In hindsight I can understand my anger, my contempt for this stifling, deferential world of racism and sexism, a world where joy was confined and the traditional unthinkingly revered. My reaction was inevitable.

Some of my family were musical but none had ever shown an interest in the theatre, even as audience members. But I loved it and was soon looking for roles with the Varley Players, whose theatre was St Mary's church hall. One girl there I really liked was Merry Legge and we soon became friends. She was warm and sympathetic without any mean spirit, believing in people's goodness. One of life's innocents. She was passionate about the theatre, later going to drama school and becoming a pro and a drama teacher. I loved her.

But it was her younger sister, Topsy, who I fell in love with. I was still in the sixth form and she was barely fifteen. My first girlfriend. Our love was intense, as first adolescent love can be, but it was deep and it lasted. She was very pretty, with a womanly body and a girlish innocence. Her hair was almost to her waist and she wore it in the fashionable ponytail. She liked tight jumpers and full, knee-length skirts, replicas of the clothes worn in Hollywood movies. Her parents thought clothes like these were too revealing and inappropriate for a teenage girl. This was the middle fifties and conventions were on the move again in an echo of Granddad's disapproval of short dresses and even shorter hair in the twenties.

Of course she would have turned any boy's head, but why did she take my heart? Since I was five I'd followed the rule 'once bitten, twice shy'. I'd closed down emotionally and refused to feel anything for anyone for fear of it all being snatched away from me. I didn't want to be left bereft again. But with Tops I was defenceless. What really drew me to her and cemented my attachment was her inner beauty. It was innocent and guileless. Her love for me was unconditional and pure. She made no demands. She gave me a love I drank from thirstily, hardly believing it could exist, let alone be offered to me. I had returned it, made a commitment, even before I could marshal my defences to resist it. I was hers.

I never looked at another girl. I had no need to.

We stayed true to each other. This first love just hit me, as it does. One has no say in it, one is not consulted. In a moment your life is turned wonderfully, disconcertingly upside down. You know it will never be the same again. Adolescent love seems permanent but usually isn't. This one was. I was lost to her, although with my customary swagger I didn't admit it. Except to her.

She had no pretensions. I had plenty. Her emotions were an open book. Mine had been locked away. But when she said she loved me I simply believed her. She changed my life. I was a better person for her presence in it.

I was introduced to her family and they made me feel at home. They were exotic and eccentric. The first names of the children were a hint. I'd never met people like these. They rented a tiny semi a short tram ride away from me. There was no one like them our way. They were all different and didn't seem to care about conforming. Harry Legge, the father, was a member of the Communist Party, an electrician who'd been blacklisted by all the employers for his militant work and political beliefs. His victimisation was relentless. He ended up as a labourer at Hams Hall power station, undaunted to the last. His final years were spent teaching the children of bargees on the canals to read and write. A man of unmovable principles, an autodidact, stubborn, rigid and argumentative, he had been radicalised as a young man. Serving on one of the first submarines, he was one of the few to escape the slaughter at Gallipoli in World War I and hated Churchill from then on. I agreed with him on so much and it was a revelation to find someone with his beliefs and his fearless embrace of them. We also had wonderful rows.

Through him I first started to think about Stalinism. He motivated me to read Marx and Engels and other socialist writers. I respected him but thought he was slightly barmy. In 1956, after Khrushchev's incendiary speech to the twentieth party congress denouncing Stalinism and the 1930s show trials, Harry was unmoved. Many members left the Party, but Harry claimed it was all CIA propaganda. He actually looked like Khrushchev and could be just as aggressive. I was learning early on in my political life the difference between the brave principles of individual members and the treacherous betrayals of the Party apparatus.

Ann Legge, the mother, was from Surrey and had a middle-class background. She was a creative cook, was very welcoming and always made lovely sandwiches whatever time we came back. I loved this atmosphere of culture and politics, relaxed and warm, where I felt I could discuss anything. There were two sons, one away at university and one little one, who would stand at his bedroom window cheekily watching Tops and me kiss and cuddle in the street when he should have been asleep.

This was a world of culture and I was accepted into it.

Tops and I were inseparable.

A high point was Merry's decision to direct a dramatised version of *A Tale of Two Cities* and to cast me as Sydney Carton. This was madly ambitious for a group of inexperienced amateurs to perform convincingly on a shelf at one end of a church hall, made more difficult by a teenage brummie lad trying to convince as a suave aristocratic hero. I must have been dreadful. At least there is no public record of my excesses. My friend Ken Loach started as an actor too but I never saw him work; he saw me on television many times and has never stopped sending me up about it. His glee would have been unbearable if he'd seen me at the Varley Players, especially as I also played Petruchio in *The Taming of the Shrew* and Ernest in *The*

Importance of Being Earnest. But the local audience was generous and we all had a wonderful time. I was glad of Merry's confidence in me even though I think it was probably misplaced.

I had truly caught the bug. I remember those people with affection, tolerating me, an awkward adolescent. It was warm and homely, everyone joining in and having a good time. After each show, from the stage someone would say, 'Thank you, vicar, for the use of the hall and thank you, Hilda, for making the tea.'

Topsy and I graduated to Highbury Little Theatre in Sutton Coldfield, a big step up. Here was a proper theatre run by professional amateurs to high standards. We thrived there, playing leads in a William Saroyan play, *Beautiful People*. This was the first moment I truly witnessed Topsy's magical hold over an audience. All eyes were on her. She was oblivious, just becoming the character, seemingly not acting at all; no one could see the wheels going round. For her it was easy and enjoyable; fun, but nothing to make a fuss about. I was outclassed but I didn't mind. We were in love, doing what we loved, together. It was a happy time.

I had no idea that what was revealed to me as I watched this unconscious magic would years later become a focus of my life. It would be central to every aspect of how I approached casting and how I set up a film. Here, watching the effect her guileless work had upon an audience I found the key to my professional future.

Through her I discovered why animals and children are so effective on screen. They live in the moment. For them there is only the moment. Some adults have it and, when combined with a little technique and professional discipline, it marks out the difference between magical and journeyman work. It is a lack of self-consciousness and inhibition without any intermediate split-second of filtering, of intellect. There is no audience, just the predicament. The spectators are observers, almost illicit observers, and can hardly breathe in case they are discovered. It is like watching birds land in the garden and forage around oblivious to your presence. Actors like this are in touch with the child inside, able to indulge in make-believe.

It was gradually and reluctantly dawning on me that I didn't have this magic. It took years for the penny to finally drop. But this insight wormed its way inside me and grew into an epiphany which would not be gainsaid. Eventually I decided to seek out those with this magic gift and create working conditions where it would be loved into existence and treasured.

But all this was in the far future.

By the time I came scarily close to A-levels I was still not doing any work. I was too busy with acting and too much in love to care. Tops and I spent every moment we could together. As I did with O-levels, I left it late, panicked and did a crash revision before the exam period and during it. Maybe I got lucky with the questions or maybe my bullshit covered up my ignorance but they went well.

I didn't much care. Acting was my life although I didn't have a clue how to make it my life. The Apollo was a cinema on the Tyburn Road, just down the road from Topsy's house. She and I would stand outside looking at the photos advertising the film of that week. They were shots of the stars in scenes from the film 'playing now, continuous performance'. Two teenagers from an amateur drama group finding their photos outside the Apollo was as unlikely a fantasy as Uncle Harold ever winning the football pools. But just as his disappointment every Saturday didn't puncture his dreams of riches we continued to dream each time we went to the Apollo to cuddle and kiss in the back row, out of the cold. We dreamed of watching ourselves in our own films and having our photos outside the Apollo. But by the time *The Loneliness of the Long Distance Runner* and *The Boys* opened in Brum, the Apollo had closed, for ever.

We never saw ourselves there.

I expected to be called up for national service like everyone else so I walked into the medical accepting my fate as a done deal. The examination over, I was sent to stand before a desk. Behind it was a bored man, who looked up. 'You have a very weak right eye.' Why tell me something I've known since primary school? I wisely did not say this aloud. 'Mmm. It's your shooting eye.' What fantasy is this idiot living in? The Russians haven't invaded, have they? After basic training, I'll probably be in an office somewhere. He offered a lackadaisical wave of dismissal and I went home.

The Poulton family home known as Liberty Hall, the front door always open to anyone.
(Author's Personal Collection)

A formal photograph of Grandma and Granddad with their twelve children.
(Author's Personal Collection)

(above) Grandma and Granddad with his fishing rods around the time of their Diamond Wedding Anniversary. *(Author's Personal Collection)*

(left) An invitation to Grandma and Granddad's Diamond Wedding celebration. *(Author's Personal Collection)*

(*above left*) Me with my brother Robert, aged six. *(Author's Personal Collection)*

(*above right*) My cousin, Jack, a Fleet Air Line pilot, who died in 1945. *(Author's Personal Collection)*

(*left*) Uncle Albert. *(Author's Personal Collection)*

(*above left*) Harold's two sisters. On the left is maiden lady, Elsie; on the right is the snobbish Dorrie. *(Author's Personal Collection)*

(*above right*) Auntie Janet and Uncle Fred, the milkman, happy on their wedding day. *(Author's Personal Collection)*

Some of the family paddling at Blackpool beach. *(Author's Personal Collection)*

(*From left*) Uncle Harold, Auntie Pom and my Mom and Dad, on holiday together. *(Author's Personal Collection)*

Mom and Dad on his motorbike. *(Author's Personal Collection)*

Pom and Harold with their wedding cake. *(Author's Personal Collection)*

Pom and Harold on their bikes. *(Author's Personal Collection)*

Mom on holiday. *(Author's Personal Collection)*

Mom and Dad's wedding in Birmingham, June 1931. Granddad *(back row, second from right)*, with pipe and hat as always, looking stern. *(Author's Personal Collection)*

Topsy as a young actress. *(© Irving Teitelbaum)*

A week or so later a letter came: grade four. Not wanted.

What a piece of luck. The army and I would not have got on. It would have been a fight to the death, no doubt mine. From what I'd heard, submitting to arbitrary authority was the essence of basic training. I doubt I would have survived a week. I'd even been sacked from the cubs for insubordination, refusing to obey an order, so I had no chance against the army. Aunty Pom used to say, 'If you tell our Tony to do anything, wild horses couldn't make him do it; but if you ask him nicely, he'll do anything for you.' I was reliably informed 'asking nicely' was not custom and practice in the British army.

Highbury had been founded by John English, who also ran a professional theatre company, the Arena. He offered me my first job, seven pounds and ten shillings a week as an assistant stage manager, which sounded rather grand to me, until an old pro told me it was the 'lowest form of animal life'. I was also cast in small parts. I accepted. I was in my late teens and I ran away to be an actor, to Harold's bemusement. They'd sacrificed to keep me at school so I could go to university. Why was I turning it all down for this insecure life?

But off to Cardiff I went for a summer season, playing in a large marquee twice a day, afternoon matinees for the children and evenings for the adults. We did *The Owl and the Pussy Cat*, in which I played the magpie in act one, the sea-green porpoise in act two and the piggy-wig with the ring on the end of his nose in act three. It wasn't the silly costumes that bothered me or having to shout above the din of hundreds of excited children. It was the fact that the mid-summer temperature was stiflingly hot and I was stuck for ages in a pink eiderdown. Welcome to show business. With inexpert slabs of make-up I opened *The Rivals* as an old, bent coachman. This was after I'd opened the curtain, which was very heavy. My face must have looked grotesque but after wrestling with the curtain the bent stance was genuine.

Thus began a number of professional engagements, including another for Arena, this time a winter one in Newcastle. Topsy got a job in the wardrobe department, so we were together in theatrical digs away from home, which was bliss.

From this I went from gig to gig, fetching up in St Anne's being interviewed for a repertory company which was fortnightly, one week there and one week in Blackpool. Weekly repertory was too much of a scramble and if I got it this would be a leg up; though old actors told me about twice-weekly repertory when the play was changed each Thursday to compete with cinemas that had started showing two films a week. The idea of pressure like that made me wince, although television soaps do the equivalent assembly line work now.

The interview took place in a large office where I was faced by one man behind a desk and another in an armchair at an oblique angle. They talked about me in broad Lancashire, as though I wasn't present. 'What d'yer think, Arthur? Likely looking lad?'

'Aye, not bad.'

'Character juve, I reckon.'

He looked at me. 'Wardrobe?'

'Oh, yes.' In those days an actor in repertory was expected to bring with him a suit, evening dress, a sports jacket and so on. He needed to be equipped for all except uniformed parts. I had few clothes and couldn't have cared less. One old hand told me I would never make it in the business. Another said contemptuously that I must be the worst-dressed actor in rep.

But these men took my word on trust. If I got the gig, I'd worry about wardrobe later. 'Right. How much?'

'Er . . . thirteen?' I thought thirteen pounds a week would be fair.

'Thirteen? Thirteen? How about that, Arthur? Repertory's dying, lad. I'm offering eleven.'

'Thank you very much.' This is an example of my ruthless negotiating skill. It never improved. As I left I saw both men get into a luxury late model Armstrong Siddeley.

Repertory seemed very much alive.

I went round the country doing a range of work in different reps. But like all actors after a while the temptations of London beckoned. Going to 'Town' and trying one's luck was the next step. But luck is the word: who knows how it will turn out? I remembered my state scholarship. It doesn't exist now, but the Ministry of Education awarded them on the basis of A- and S-level results. They were more generous than most local authority grants. One was waiting for me.

I'd nearly missed out on any grant. They were means tested, so a form had to be filled in and signed by a JP. Harold flatly refused to divulge his income. He regarded it as private. I pleaded with him.

'My wages are of no concern to anybody else. I'm not sharing my private business. And that's the end of it.' But at the last minute he relented. I raced off to ask a local JP for his signature. Harold's condition was a sealed envelope, only opened for the JP's signature. I was puzzled by all this nonsense. Only years later did I realise that he didn't want anyone to know just how little he earned. I remember him commenting on a man down the road who had complained about having to pay £20 a week in tax. 'I'd like to have to pay £20 a week in tax, I'll tell you that.'

It was 1957 and the grant was over £300 a year. I could live in London on that even if I had no acting work. My house nut, as they say in the theatre, would be secure. All I needed was a university. I applied to the psychology department of University College – I didn't want to study English. I thought I could do that by myself. I was curious about the scientific method and experimental psychology was my only hope of approaching it, having taken no science subject at A-level. For the interview I stayed with an actor friend and his wife in Bloomsbury. On learning it was my first visit to London, he said, 'Yes. And determined not to be impressed.' He knew me too well.

It turned out to be not only an interview, but hours of intelligence testing. Its great advocate, Cyril Burt, appeared to be still alive in Bloomsbury. I got in and was under the illusion that I would learn how people ticked, including myself. I soon learned differently. The fashion was learning theory, all rats through mazes and pigeons pecking away in little boxes. Behaviourism might have excited B. F. Skinner, but it held nothing of interest for me. I couldn't have cared less about rats. In any case, I was busy elsewhere. Jobs as an extra gave way to small parts on television and films. I spent the long vacs doing summer seasons in the provinces. I started to run the university drama society which at that time performed on a shelf at one end of the gym but our ambitions were not dampened. I got more and more involved, neglecting everything else. My tutor, Dr Kelvin, stopped me in the corridor one day, during a rare visit to the department. 'Ah, I saw you on television last night. It would be so nice to see you in a seminar occasionally.'

I could have been thrown out. They were very tolerant.

When I first left for London Harold had taken me to one side with a request. He made me promise to write to Pom every week. I found this a chore, I'm ashamed to say, and my brief letters were perfunctory compared with her replies, full of the latest gossip about the family. But I managed to keep the promise. Years later Harold confessed to me that he feared they would never see me again. 'You'd be off to a life in London and not give us a second thought. I was afraid we'd just lose you.'

This puzzled me. I felt an obligation to them and had no intention of cutting myself off from the family. At the time of my parents' death they could have sent me to an orphanage. Grandma and all the other aunties had tried to spoil me, remembering my Mom. I spent years rejecting each of them, literally going on strike, even down to refusing to appear on family photographs. In those days there was an advertisement for something or other which said, 'Accept no substitutes'. My Mom was dead. If I couldn't have her, why would I want a substitute? Go away. But they didn't. They were always there for me, not accepting my sullen rejection. I was family. They loved me. I was in my fifties before I truly felt their love, in retrospect.

I was by now twenty-one, the age then when you reached formal manhood, so as I was packing for London, Pom gave me Dad's suicide note, just saying, 'It was a wartime tragedy. A terrible time.' She refused to discuss it further or to blame him, saying, 'It takes two.' She was scrupulously fair to my father's memory. I doubt she felt what she said but she didn't want to poison my feelings about him. He was, after all, my Dad.

She and Uncle Harold then gave me a few hundred pounds, which was a lot of money for them, for most people, in 1957. It was the product of Mom and Dad's effects, divided equally with Peter and dedicated to be spent on our upbringing. They had not spent a penny of it. Harold earned a skilled craftsman's wage but they had to watch every penny. They hadn't touched what she said was my money.

I was struck by their resolute integrity. It was ingrained.

The deeper surprise was they actually cared for me. They wanted to see me again!

A Foreign Land

Pom and Harold came to London to see my Hamlet. *That was a big occasion for me, as well as for them. A trip to London was not undertaken lightly.*

'It's a bit overrated. Full of themselves down there.'

But here they were.

This would be a Shakespeare first for them, although they had dutifully attended the earlier amateur shows. The Christmas panto at the Birmingham Alexandra theatre was more to their taste.

I saw them afterwards. Harold was blunt. 'I think you overdo it, myself.'

That was his sole comment.

He was probably right.

I remained unimpressed by London. My Brum uncles had trained me well. It was big. Strangers on the street would walk all over you and the cockneys thought they were a superior race.

But Soho was fascinating. Italian grocers full of stuff I'd never heard of. Nothing like that in Brum. I'd never even tried pasta. I'd heard of spaghetti in tins but not this stuff coming in all shapes and sizes, that they ate instead of potatoes. Just like the restaurants in Chinatown, where they had rice with their dinners. I couldn't get my mind round that one. Rice was for rice puddings! And as for the Indian places, the smells were enough to make me want to choke. I hated garlic.

Reeling from these culture shocks, I changed only slowly. One evening a nice young student from the Slade invited me for dinner at her parents' house in Hampstead. Her father was in publishing somewhere. I think they wished to meet 'interesting undergraduates'. I turned up. They were friendly and informal. It was a large, rambling Victorian house with a family dining table in the basement, where the kitchen was. There were a few other guests. We all sat down. I'd accepted a glass of wine because I didn't see any beer and didn't want to cause a fuss. The hostess brought in a leg of lamb and started to carve it. As she put slices on plates, I could see she had really messed up.

Poor woman, I thought. It's really underdone. She should have left it in a lot longer. Even my inexpert eye could tell. It was all bloody. I felt really sorry for her. But instead of being embarrassed and apologising, taking it back to the oven, she continued to dish it out as thought there was nothing wrong with it.

She's got balls, I thought. She's just going to carry it off.

Pom would cook a shoulder of lamb until it was a crisp brown on the outside and dark grey all the way through.

So I thought I'd better say nothing and follow the others. I tasted something nasty in addition to it being nearly raw. Ages later I found out it was probably bits of garlic all over.

They were certainly different down here, I thought.

The pea soup fogs were chokingly bad. You could hardly see a yard in front of you. But it added to the excitement, especially in Soho, which looked especially sinister and sinful. Late at night as you strolled around, the lights from the sex shows and clubs would emerge from the fog and entice people in. Prostitutes would openly solicit in doorways. Good thing Aunty Pom wasn't here, I thought.

In Soho I began occasionally to eat in restaurants. I'd never been in one except when at the seaside on holiday for fish and chips and ice cream, but there I did try pasta and even rice in a Chinese. They were OK, but I decided I preferred potatoes.

It was all exotic, like going abroad but staying at home.

It certainly made going into Brum on the 79 tram or to the dance at the YWCA in Stechford seem a bit ordinary. But I preserved the correct stance. When home and interrogated about London, I would proclaim to general satisfaction, 'bit overrated'.

What I didn't tell them was that London for me was freedom. Neither London, nor anyone in London, cared. Everyone was anonymous. I could live my life just how I wanted to live it. I realised that this freedom – having my own flat and life with Tops – allowed me to feel more relaxed at Pom and Harold's house, with them.

At first I shared a flat with an old friend from Brum, Philip Dudley, who was a call boy at BBC Television Centre. His job was to call the actors to the set. The job title amused us but the BBC seemed oblivious to its other meaning.

One evening he was doing *Hancock's Half Hour* at Riverside Studios and I joined him afterwards in the pub opposite. Everyone from the show was there. I was a big admirer of Tony Hancock, so it was a thrill. He was the nation's favourite comedian and his show was very popular.

Then I made a big mistake. I told Tony Hancock a joke.

It came out of a combination of innocence, a wish to impress and youthful arrogance. Plus I thought it was a very good joke – although it can't have been that good because I've now forgotten it. I haven't forgotten my feelings of that night, though. They still come back in embarrassing waves. The pub was crowded and Tony had his jaws around a large drink. He endured the joke, looking at me with a steely, narrow-eyed glare. I should have sensed danger but it had gone too far. I had to finish. I delivered the punchline. Silence. Everyone was looking at Tony for a signal. He held the silence. It seemed like two years but was probably only fifteen seconds. Finally, he broke it. Speaking softly with a murderous smile, he said, 'Oh, yes. My word. Very funny. Yes! Hilarious, that one! Just one to open the show with . . .'

A perfectly timed pause.

'. . . and leave the country.'

He then returned to his drink. I was dismissed. Conversation returned. I was alone. I wanted to die.

I have never, ever since told a comedian a joke.

That's what they do.

Topsy, who had trained as a children's nurse, had come to work in London so that we could be together. It was bliss getting away from Brum, where there was nowhere to make love. We used to look at lit-up bedrooms as we walked past, longing for somewhere like that. In the summer we would walk to Penns Hall hotel, which was very posh, drink in the bar, although she was years too young, and then make love in a field behind the hotel. But the winters were difficult. In London we felt free to live our own lives. She started to go up for acting roles and, after some time as an extra, moved up to small parts.

We decided to do the natural thing and live together. Insensitively and self-righteously, I decided to tell everyone. We were not ashamed. I'd read Friedrich Engels and Bertrand Russell. I thought marriage was a heinous bourgeois prison. I could rehearse all the arguments but I wasn't able to put myself in the shoes of traditional, respectable people in Brum in the 1950s. It's difficult to explain it now. Every girl was supposed to be – or at least pretend to be – a virgin when she married. Living in sin was living in actual sin. It wasn't just a form of words. It was shameful. The female would be a fallen woman and the man was clearly a rotter. One aunty had married hurriedly years before and in my lifetime a female cousin had walked up the aisle pregnant. Events like these were scandalous.

When I casually announced it they were dumbstruck. They couldn't digest it. After nearly a week, Uncle Harold took me to one side. 'Are you trying to tell me you two are actually going to live together as *man and wife*?'

'Oh, as far as that goes, we've been doing that for years.'

He was stunned. After he had collected himself he told me not to tell Pom. It would kill her. Harry Legge, Topsy's father, was disgusted. His politics might have been modern but his morals were distinctly traditional. He advised me, with distaste, that if I felt I had to do such things, I should use prostitutes.

That shocked me.

It would have been easy just not to mention it. But that would have been hypocritical and unacceptable. When I realised what I had done and understood the painful fallout, it was too late. I'd caused reckless, avoidable hurt. I began to see that rigid principles might make one feel pure, but sometimes sympathetic flexibility is more human.

I almost sabotaged my acting career before it had kicked into gear. I went to the BBC to audition for Gilchrist Calder. The part was tiny, but I would have taken a walk-on for Gil. He was one of the realist producer/directors who paved the way for our work in the sixties. His manner was clipped, business-like and courteous. He told me I could have the part of Driver Brown on one condition: 'Get your hair cut.' It was more than fashionably long. As I left he asked me, almost as an afterthought, if I could drive. I nodded nonchalantly, as though to say, Can't everyone these days?

I could not drive. The rule with actors is never lose a role because you lack a skill. Always say, 'Yes'. Then, if you are cast, deal with the problem. I decided it probably wasn't important. I would improvise around it. Anything complicated would be done by a stuntman.

A day's filming was scheduled at the parachute regiment's base in Aldershot, so I went to Lime Grove film studios to change into uniform before being driven down there. The writer, Troy Kennedy Martin, shared the ride. We hit it off. A friendship began which lasted till his death in 2009. He was the sweetest man. I later acted in an episode of *Z Cars* which he wrote and John McGrath directed. I punched Joe Brady on the nose and made it bleed. Another delinquent role.

I loved Troy and his talent; he became arguably our greatest screenwriter. *Incident At Echo Six* was based on his experience in Cyprus during his national service. I think I only had one line, but my part was crucial to the plot. Driver Brown was shot during this day's filming and then had to lie dead, back in the studio. That sounds easy but I was not dead. I could lie absolutely still but had to breathe, at least occasionally. This was not good enough for Gil, whose voice thundered down from the gallery, 'The bloody corpse is breathing. Stop it breathing.' Unknown to me at the time I had an arthritic spine which affected the ribcage, making my breathing shallow. Consequently I needed to breathe more often and couldn't hold off for long. I thought my lungs would burst. Eventually he was satisfied and I was free to breathe again.

The filming was a bigger problem. On arrival in Aldershot, Gil came over to me and pointed to a mammoth army truck, the kind you have to climb up steps to get into, and said, 'Get in.' I did so, as nonchalantly as I could, but leaving my heart and all my professional aspirations ignominiously on the floor. He would tell me to drive it. I could not drive a Ford Anglia let alone a huge army truck. Yet the character I had signed up to play was called Driver Brown. I would be sued by the BBC, word would get out I was not to be trusted and I would never work again.

I just sat there stewing in remorse, desperately trying to think of a way out. Perhaps I could feign illness? But what would be believable? Gil and others were by the camera on a rise thirty yards ahead, playing with a gun on a stand. After fifteen minutes of stewing in agony, I saw Gil walk towards me. He was clearly about to tell me to start the engine and drive towards the gun, which would then shoot me dead. I wanted it to shoot me dead, for real.

As I was madly looking at the dashboard and the pedals trying to figure out the damned thing he leant into the cab and said, 'I'm most awfully sorry but we can't make this work. We just can't get the shot if this truck is moving, so I know this is a difficult bore, but I want you to cheat it. Some chaps out of shot at the back will rock it so we give the impression it's moving. You'll have to pretend you're driving it. Do you think you could manage that?'

'No problem, Gil.'

'Good man.'

My career was not in ruins.

The climax of my faux student life was a production by Roy Battersby. He completed his PhD, but scorned an academic life in favour of directing. I played Hamlet and, as the old gag has it, Hamlet won. But we enjoyed it. We played the first quarto and gave it a psychoanalytic interpretation, consulting the lone analyst in the psychology department with the glorious name of Dr Cecily de Monchaux. That's just what an analyst ought to be called, I thought.

In those days national drama critics would attend university productions and I was generously reviewed but probably because they were making allowances for youthful enthusiasm.

One good thing came out of it: Philip Dudley invited Peter Dews. This was scary. Peter was a big producer at the BBC. I'm told he sat in the front row and sent it up, which I'm glad I was unaware of. He was preparing TV productions of all Shakespeare's history plays, from *Richard II* straight through to *Richard III*, the early ones live transmission, all in the studio. Some wag inevitably named it 'An everyday story of county folk', after *The Archers*. Peter asked me to join the permanent company, which would be supplemented by star guests. I said, 'Yes,' to this big chance, planning to leave UCL before finals. I didn't need a degree. Then I was told that the ministry could ask for my grant back if I had no excuse, like a medical certificate, for cutting finals. I didn't know if this was fact, but decided not to risk it. Peter said I could join late.

It was a glittering cast, although none were stars at the time. Sean Connery before *James Bond*, Judi Dench, Eileen Atkins, Robert Hardy and Violet Carson, imminently to become Ena Sharples in *Coronation Street*.

A separate 'green room' had been allocated to the actors during rehearsals and there I listened to the jokes, no doubt old, and honed, but new to me. I loved to hear talk about the mysterious characters in *Hamlet* who never appear. What is the dramatic purpose of Else, for instance? We hear the question – What matter Else? – but she is not there to answer. What about the Chinese character, What Ho? Actors in mock serious, academic tones pursued these conceits to my delight.

Each week we waited to discover if we had a speaking part or would just be a 'spear', stuck in the ranks. One fellow company member, on hearing that he had been cast as the Constable of France in *Henry V*, phoned his mother with the good news. Her response – 'Oh no, not another policeman' – deflated him and amused everyone else.

One rehearsal day, in the crowded green room, above the usual moans about agents and gossip about who was doing what to whose wife, I heard a voice which threw me. It was, unmistakably, that of Dick Barton – special agent, the hero whose brave escapades had inspired my childhood at 6.45 every weeknight on BBC radio. I was awestruck. This was my boyhood hero, here in this room. For a moment it was like finding I was sitting on the tram next to the captain of Aston Villa. I looked round and saw the voice belonged to a ripe, overweight, charming actor, Noel Johnson. Now I could put the voice to the face, he didn't look as though he could fight his way through Harrods' sales. He played aristocrats. They sometimes unkindly say someone has a good face for radio. Well, Noel certainly had a good voice.

I was a just a spear one week and a small speaking role the next. Frank Windsor, a fine actor with a wonderful voice, who later became famous as Sergeant Watt in *Z Cars*, befriended me and showed me the ropes. He came from Walsall and we got on famously.

Peter Dews ran it all like the schoolmaster he had been. One moment he was the benign, warm, very funny older brother; the next he was in a rage, telling you to get an atlas down your pants, you were in trouble. He and I became good friends and he was very fond of Tops. Years later she and I went up to Yorkshire to see him play King Lear in an amateur production. A week or so before, he'd married a nice girl, who he referred to as 'the hairdresser from Bradford'. I didn't ask her what she thought of spending her honeymoon watching Peter on stage. It was certainly an experience: the only Lear I ever saw who had an irrepressible sense of humour. He really was like an elder brother to me and I was sad when he died young of a heart attack.

Topsy and I took a flat just off the Finchley Road in north London with mice that seemed to be permanent squatters, defying all our attempts to discourage them. They had been residents before we moved in, so probably had a case. We moved to nearby Swiss Cottage, close to Roy and Audrey Battersby.

My back had been aching for a long time and seemed to be getting worse. Eventually I went to see Dr Nick Mallinson, the medic for UCL's student health, apologising for wasting his time, saying I was probably imagining it.

He was kind and calm. 'If your back aches, then you have back ache. That is something you're experiencing. So we must find the source and do something about it.' This was a new experience. A wave of relief lifted me. Where I came from you had to be at death's door before a day off work or school was sanctioned.

At University College hospital they X-rayed and examined my back. The consultant quietly listened to his juniors and looked at me from all angles. I was called in again for a meeting with a young medic. He was Welsh. I imagined him to be a hard-drinking scrum half, tough as old boots. All the UCH medical students I knew were boozers. When I was a boy the GP was revered and held in awe. Now I knew some of the next generation I realised they were people learning a trade and, like garage mechanics, some would be better at it than others. Once you've seen them hungover and heard their black jokes about patients you see their ordinary humanity.

This scrum half was brutal. I later guessed this was a ploy to make me take it seriously. 'You have ankylosing spondylitis,' he said. 'It's an arthritic disease affecting the spine. Vertebrae fuse, ossify. You've seen people on the street walking bent double? Also called bamboo spine. That's what could happen to you. We don't know what causes it. There is no cure. Severity varies from person to person. So does the pain, which will be intermittent. Take Disprin. Only stuff tackles it. Lasts twenty, twenty-five years or so, then burns out. The calcification between the vertebrae, the fusion, will be permanent. What you're left with is what you live with. So keep moving. Swimming is good. But don't do anything silly, like shifting pianos or riding horses. Good luck.' He muttered something about radioactive treatment but didn't sound too optimistic. I was dismissed.

I walked out into Gower Street knowing I had some decisions to make. I would have to face occasionally crippling pain, maybe become a cripple, or whatever the correct word happened to be at the time. I wasn't good at physical pain, being a bit of a wimp, but this was a test. Sobering. It was another reminder that anything can happen, arbitrarily, and you just have to take it on the chin. It was a fact and I had to adapt to it. I decided to fight. It certainly wasn't going to be used as a prop or an excuse for failure. Anyway, I briskly said to myself, whistling in the dark, there's plenty worse off than you, repeating one of Aunty Pom's dismissive judgements.

Topsy was wonderful, taking it all in her stride. She was brave and optimistic, wanting to help me with everything. As I saw her longing to nurse me, I loved her more and more. Why does she bother with me, I thought. I'm such an irritable sod. I decided not to be an invalid. I wouldn't tell anyone except family and very close friends. I didn't want to be defined by it or reduce myself inside it and I didn't want my career to be compromised or insurance jeopardised.

I immediately signed up for horse-riding lessons. I had never been near a horse. The posh rode horses. My family rode bikes. I knew it was stupid even at the time but I needed to fight back. It was my way of saying 'fuck 'em' – whoever 'they' were. The God I didn't believe in, perhaps? I rode every week for years. My horses were supposedly staid and sensible creatures, more Morris Minor than Ferrari, but riding was still scary. I persevered doggedly, even taking jumping lessons, usually going over before the horse or even leaving it behind. After painfully picking myself up I would see it staring insolently at me.

The pain came and went. When it was bad, first thing in the morning – having been in one position all night – I found it difficult to get started. It would take me forty minutes of struggle to get my socks on. I would weep with frustration, but couldn't allow Topsy to help me. Soon I was on sixteen Disprin a day to keep the pain bearable. Then there were remissions. It was unpredictable. Gradually my ribcage lost expansion and some vertebrae did ossify.

At Easter, with Topsy away on a long provincial theatre tour with Peggy Mount, a UCL friend named Jeremy Hornsby invited me to stay at his family home in Chorleywood. I noticed that my eyes were sore but ignored it. Within a few days I couldn't bear it, so after Easter I saw a medic. I had iritis, an inflammation of the iris that was common among those with ankylosing spondylitis. It would recur over the years but I got to know the symptoms and would catch it early. This time I'd left it very late and by now it was serious. I might have become blind. I had it in both eyes. In the late 1950s treatment was prolonged.

I went home and Pom took me every few days to the Birmingham eye hospital for heat treatment, which we also did at home using hot poultices. My eyes were bandaged. I could not read. That was purgatory. Just the radio. *Mrs Dale's Diary* for company.

I experienced a side of Pom I'd never known. She was tender and attentive, welcoming me back, looking after me as though I was a little boy in a way I hadn't experienced when I had been one. I had regressed, feeling so helpless, and was glad of her care. Her health had improved. The worries of the war were long over. The family tragedy was now a scar rather than a raw wound. She even put on a little weight. I saw her smile. We became closer during these weeks. We talked. She was lonely and I filled her days. She felt useful and I warmed to her affection.

In those days my default position was denial. Ignore illness, defy pain. It was magical thinking. 'Don't encourage it,' I would say, as though it was a conscious enemy. Once I even went on stage in a leading role after a diagnosis of pneumonia, having that very afternoon been told to go straight to bed and stay there. I necked a large Scotch and got through the performance. It wasn't anything to do with theatrical tradition. Later I put up a large slogan in my office. '"The show must go on": was a con invented by the management'. It was macho foolishness and clearly showed I was not connected to myself.

The pain in my spine lasted, as they had said it would, for about twenty-five years, gradually disappearing during my forties in the Californian sun. Its lasting effects are what they are.

In the end, even this illness was just an inconvenience – not life-threatening.

Crest of the Wave

When Uncle Harold worked at Hercules Cycles he was told that a doll's house was to be presented to the young princesses, Elizabeth and Margaret. Hercules was to make a tiny bicycle, just a few inches high, and it had to be in working order. He was told to make the wheels.

Years later I found one of these in our shed. It was tiny, but a real bike wheel, with spokes and it went round the tiny hub. When I admired it, Harold was dismissive, saying it was a reject. He pointed out the defects with distaste. I couldn't see any of them.

His perfectionism almost rivalled my Dad's.

I was a jobbing actor on TV and in minor films. I worked consistently. Some of it was embarrassing, like an episode of *Compact*, a silly soap about a magazine, but all of it was experience. I made a rule only to do a very few episodes of any serial. I did six of *Emergency – Ward 10*, an easy gig lying in bed playing a patient: no moves to learn and a pretty nurse, played by Jill Browne, bringing me drinks and comfort. I also played a couple of episodes of *Probation Officer*. I was up for any show needing a Teddy Boy, preferably a violent one.

This work led to a big agent. I must have been recommended as a bit of fashionable rough, because it seemed odd finding myself in the company of the Grade Organisation. Its office was in Regent Street, near Oxford Circus, and it was run by Leslie Grade, Lew's brother. This was the most famous family in show business.

I was to meet Robin Fox. He was not so much flash East End as smooth Mayfair. Urbane, chain-smoking cigarettes with an elegance I'd always failed to accomplish, he welcomed me with easy old Harrovian charm. I sat in his elegant office trying not to feel intimidated and guardedly observed him. Awarded a Military Cross in the war, he looked like a movie star. Tall and slim, he wore his elegant, navy suit as though it were an obedient detail. I only had one suit, bought years before from Weaver To Wearer in Birmingham, and I felt it didn't really like me and longed to be worn by someone better able to appreciate it.

Robin always seemed relaxed, even slightly bored by business. Work was evidently just a detail in an otherwise fascinating life of which I knew little. Forget being an agent, I thought, who represents you? This is what Cary Grant must be like. His list was full of equally posh actors like Vanessa Redgrave and Sarah Miles. What on earth was he doing, bothering with a ruffian like me?

But he offered to represent me. I liked him. He and his formidable colleague Ros Chatto were friendly as well as intimidating. We got on well. Maybe, just as I rarely came into close contact with people like them, they rarely met anyone like me. Seeing the way the industry was changing, they might have been interested in me as a specimen. Their assistant was Meg Poole. Her father was Lord Poole, the chairman of the Conservative Party. I was duly invited to Ros's house to meet him. He was charming. They were all charming. We argued politics. Of course, they were amused by me. It was not the only time I have been used as entertainment by people too secure to feel threatened. I duly did what was expected of me but declined future engagements. I was not going to be the performing socialist seal for their after-dinner diversion. But Robin's wife Angela was not just charming, she was kind and thoughtful too. I became very fond of her, although I saw little of her. She was a homebody in their country place.

The quality of the work stepped up a notch. I was put up for film leads with little hope of being cast unless Albert Finney and

Alan Bates and Tom Courtenay were not free, but things became qualitatively better. Robin later represented Topsy. They all adored her, of course.

None of this work cut any ice in Brum.

'Our Tony? I don't know, really. He's been on the telly a bit.'

Harold, especially, was unimpressed. His view all along had been that I was wasting my life or at least treading water, just messing about, when I should be doing a serious job. Had they kept me at school those extra years for this? 'You've had all this education. And you're just play-acting. When're you getting a proper job? With prospects?'

As one relative told me, 'Actors are the sort of fly-by-nights who live in furnished flats.'

He was right about me. I lived in a furnished flat.

Then I accepted a part in a laughably bad but very popular cop show, *Dixon of Dock Green*. Everything changed.

I'd nearly turned it down. I was glad I hadn't when I went home the weekend after its live transmission. The star was Jack Warner. Harold was an admirer, more so because people had remarked on a physical resemblance with Dixon. He was a fan of Warner and his sisters Elsie and Doris Walters, who had been great comic favourites during the Blitz as Gert and Daisy.

'Saw *Dixon*. So. What's he like?'

'I didn't have much to do with him. But he seemed a nice enough chap. Very pleasant with everybody. Quiet. He was OK.' I was running out of things to say.

'Jack Warner. He's been around a long time, hasn't he, Pom? I say he's been right at the top a long time. They won't make any more like him. Broke the mould when they made him. Remember *The Blue Lamp*?' With awed respect he added, 'He was a comedian as well, you know. Do everything, that man.' He looked at me and nodded. I'd just worked with Jack Warner on *Dixon*. Actually met him, in the flesh. I was evidently going places after all.

Don Taylor created both David Turner and David Mercer's careers. No one has heard of any of them now, such is the fickleness of fame.

Don was another working-class scholarship kid, in his early twenties, just down from Oxford, picking and directing important single plays on the BBC. He was a star. He was also arrogant.

Once in rehearsal, to make conversation, I showed him an interesting book I was reading and said, 'Have you read this, Don?'

He looked at me imperiously and said, 'I don't need to read books. I've had an Oxford education.' Was he serious or was he sending himself up? Either way, I was stunned into silence. But we got on. He was picking interesting plays and we could talk.

I had been called in to read for him. Sitting in his Television Centre office was David Turner and at that point I knew why I had been asked along. I'd met David years earlier, as a schoolboy when he'd coached me for a speaking competition. He was from a poor part of Brum, Nechells, and had become a teacher. He was kind and gentle, with a Parkinson tremble. But he had courage. When, in 1964, Mary Whitehouse launched her media clean-up campaign in Birmingham town hall, David was there and got up to heckle. It couldn't have been easy speaking against the tide of hostility in a packed town hall. My last memory of him, in the late seventies, was visiting his home in Leamington, he and his wife near death with terminal cancer. He gave me a last embrace and pressed on me the gift of an Allen Jones print.

I acted in two of David's plays. *The Train Set* starred Robert Shaw, a man so macho and competitive that he would give you a fifteen start at table tennis, beat you and then give you twenty start and still beat you. No wonder he later became a James Bond villain. He looked like the sort of bruiser you'd avoid in a pub. A heavy, muscular build and a fierce face didn't seem to go with being a gifted novelist. But he was. He taught me to appreciate Hemingway for the way he had reinvented prose style. He hit on Tops, which amused her; seeing her sweetly reject him amused me.

Tops and I were in *Trevor*, about a working man's difficulty with his sexual performance. Mary Whitehouse objected, presumably on the grounds that working-class sex shouldn't be encouraged by the BBC. I didn't know it then, but she and I would become deadly enemies.

Don Taylor called me in again. A tubby man with glasses and a small beard sat in the corner of his office, looking mysterious. He said nothing. We then went to the bar at the BBC club and I learned he was David Mercer, a train driver's son from Wakefield who, like so many bright people I knew, had failed the eleven-plus. He finally became a writer after an aimless drift, battling with depression and booze.

Don cast me as Colin Waring, who appeared in two of David's trilogy about nuclear weapons, *The Generations*. It culminated in *The Birth of a Private Man*, when Colin is shot to death on the Berlin Wall. At last I was given the role of a complex, intelligent man, written by someone who thought about politics.

I got on with Don and David. We talked the same language.

Colin's death was actually shot in a disused brewery, Watford way. Such is the glamour of filming. Bitterly cold, I stood on the wall and grabbed the barbed wire as I fell. A man dying from rifle fire is unlikely to look carefully down to protect his hands so I grabbed as I fell and on each take the spikes in the wire penetrated my palm. I was bloody by the end of the night but I'd have bled for ever to achieve that shot. A still was used on the *Radio Times* cover.

Later, Don and I would become estranged. He was moving further into a literary, poetic tradition of drama and I was obsessed with pursuing a distilled naturalism. Don lost out when the BBC's head of drama, Sydney Newman, took away the choice of material from directors and gave it to producers. I sympathised with Don. It was a layer of management added purely to better organise a growing and varied production base. Had Sydney kept the old system where directors chose and worked with the writers, I would have become a director rather than mainly a producer. One wants power over the material and the freedom to make decisions.

Another big break around that time was to be cast by director Sidney J. Furie in *The Boys*. I had been in a couple of short cinema films, shot at Merton Park Studios, just junk stuff, but working with good actors like Warren Mitchell and enjoying the precision of the film camera.

Sidney was unthreatening and all of the actors got on: Dudley Sutton, Jess Conrad, Ronald Lacey and me. We were playing

London lads on a night out, arrested and brought up at the Old Bailey on a murder charge. Richard Todd prosecuted and Robert Morley defended. We shot the courtroom scenes at Elstree Studios.

We met during filming in the commissary, where we would drink tea, chat and lark about. Films are made mostly spent waiting. I was always up for a lively discussion, partly to relieve the boredom. One day as I loudly proclaimed my republican and socialist beliefs, I saw Richard Todd. He didn't often deign to visit the commissary. He was getting hot under the collar, so I made my remarks more incendiary. He stood up, quivering. 'How dare you? Your infantile remarks are insulting and you must withdraw them this instant.'

I looked at him, naively thinking this was just the opening salvo of a stimulating argument. Good, I thought. A real reactionary.

But no, he had no intention of engaging with me. He was a star and he meant it when he demanded an apology followed by a respectful silence. Despite wise, muttered advice all round me to cool it, I responded, matching his attempt to put me down with blistering sarcasm. This was a mistake. I was in danger. Those were the days of strict hierarchy. Even the chief cameraman was deferentially called Mr or Sir. A star was high in the hierarchy and Richard Todd was especially sensitive because his star status was in decline. He was going out of fashion. He rounded on me with a spirited defence of the monarchy and the usual, tired instruction that I should go back to Russia.

I would not back down.

Robert Morley saved me. 'I agree with you, old boy,' he said. 'My advice is never lend the banks any money. It only encourages them. Always invite them to lend to you. Have you noticed they always have the best sites in any high street? And the largest buildings. What on earth do they do? Make money out of money. What magicians they are.' He continued like this, his chins wobbling and his eyes sparkling while all around were chuckling as this establishment figure mocked the establishment, taking the heat out of the moment. He continued to hold the floor, turning it all into a harmless comedic moment.

Richard Todd retreated in a foul temper. I later heard that he had demanded I should be sacked.

Robert was a joy. I became very fond of him. He loved young people. He certainly was good company. Fat and jovial, he just enjoyed life. Rumour had it that he and fellow toff actor Wilfrid Hyde-White would not 'accept any offer of an engagement during the flat racing season'.

Now I had the chance to see close up how they made films. During the cross-examination scenes the camera would be set and the location lit for shots of each barrister. The boys would play all those scenes out of shot throughout the morning. After lunch the camera would be moved round and the same scenes would be played on one boy after another. It had nothing to do with the passage of events or the emotional quality of the moment and everything to do with the schedule and the convenience of the camera crew, handling those inflexible 35-mm cameras. It was static and dead. This puzzled me. Surely the emotional truth was what mattered. Why not facilitate this?

During the morning, when the camera was on Richard Todd, we boys were in the witness box responding to his questions. During the afternoon when the camera was on us, he had already gone home and the first assistant director woodenly recited his lines.

This wasn't the first time or the last when I longed to revolutionise the way films were made, to overturn the hierarchy. A sign, although I didn't know it, of things to come.

The film ended with a verdict. Three of the boys were convicted of murder. My character was acquitted and, as the film ended, I walked free.

As soon as the film was released Pom and Harold made a special trip into Birmingham to see it at the Odeon, New Street, a cinema which charged more than our local. That in itself was a compliment. As they walked out at the end after my character's release, Pom said, 'I knew our Tony wouldn't get mixed up in anything like that.'

Life was suddenly good. I was being offered plenty of work and the quality was improving. Topsy was doing even better. Michael Elliott cast her opposite Edith Evans in an Anouilh play for the BBC, *Time Remembered*. Most young actors would have been overawed at the prospect of meeting this great lady. She was quite old, by then, with a formidable reputation. She had been a star for decades. But Tops just thought it was a nice role and went happily to the read through. They hit it off from the start and the Dame adopted her. It may have been because Tops wasn't overawed. She treated the old lady respectfully and politely, as she would any old person, but was naturally herself. She would not have been awkward or trying to impress, just ready to go to work. There was a picture of them side by side on the front cover of the *Radio Times*.

The offers continued to pour in. Sure, we knew so much of it must be luck. I reckoned it wouldn't last, with the typical Brum pessimism that promised every cloud had a black lining. Tops didn't seem to give it a thought. We were happily living together. We began to talk about buying a house, somewhere of our own, before starting a family, which Tops longed to do.

Don Taylor offered me a BBC play which was ordinary TV fodder but it was the lead and I enjoyed working with him. After the usual couple of weeks outside rehearsal we went into Studio One at the TV Centre for two days in preparation for recording on the evening of the second day. I was given the number one dressing room. A short time before, I'd worked in this studio as a non-speaking extra. After the first day I drove home to Swiss Cottage in my little open sports car through the back streets, looking forward to seeing Topsy and exchanging the gossip of our day.

In Kensal Green I took a shortcut, driving over a crossroad – my right of way – and was smashed in the side by another vehicle at speed. Its driver clearly hadn't looked. I should have, right of way or not. It disappeared. My car spun sharply round on the impact, throwing me clean out. I landed in the street. Dazed, I gradually picked myself up, noticing that my head was inches from the kerb. If it had hit its edge, I would have been dead or brain dead. After a few minutes I gingerly drove home, both the car and me bruised but still serviceable. Nothing broken. Topsy tended to me and I slept. The following day, I stiffly got through the show, not mentioning the accident to Don. It had come arbitrarily, out of a clear sky, when everything was going well. I shouldn't have been surprised. I've lived most of my life half expecting the roof to fall in: the only thing I knew was that I couldn't predict just when or what form it would take. Life really does hang by a thread.

I was doing well, but Topsy was now being recognised as exceptional. I looked at her work with pride and awe, although she thought little or at least less about it. For her it was just natural. She was play-acting, being childlike. She still had that capacity to quietly and unselfconsciously be in the moment. Many actors are formally well educated and some are highly intelligent. It is always humbling to admit but neither is of much use. Technique, especially in the theatre, is important, but if you hide behind it you are an empty shell. At this time I was reading the psychoanalyst Erich Fromm. He made a distinction between being and doing. Actors like me were doing, Topsy was just being.

I thrived on my intelligence, intensity, technique and determination. I was also fashionable. So was Albert Finney. But he had something more. When I saw *Saturday Night and Sunday Morning* it reminded me I was outclassed. He just 'was'. He seemed to possess an effortless authority and credibility. He knew when to leave off trying. One had to look at him. He was always in the moment.

What Topsy and Albert had revealed I saw later in Carol White, who played the lead in *Cathy Come Home*. Ken Loach, another ex-actor, had seen the light, too. We both got it. This more than anything made me want to work with him. I have continued to pursue that quality with other directors since, trying to open the eyes of those who did not yet see.

Topsy was cast by Tony Richardson in *The Loneliness of the Long Distance Runner* with Tom Courtenay. He then invited her to go to Stratford for a season to play Hermia in *A Midsummer Night's Dream* and other roles. But that was to clash with another film. John Schlesinger was to direct *Billy Liar*, again with Tom Courtenay, and he wanted Topsy to play opposite Tom. Her career was taking off at this time in ways you could only dream about. All her friends were delighted for her.

Topsy carried this magic so lightly it drove the rest of us crazy. She just shrugged. What was the fuss about? She enjoyed it but would just as soon go to the launderette as she would rush the decision on whether to do Stratford or *Billy Liar*. She was a homebody. 'I'm off now.'

'Hold on. What if John Schlesinger calls? Tom said he would.'

'Oh, tell him I'm up the tumble. I've got the washing to do. Can't sit here all day.'

Sure, I'll tell John Schlesinger, 'Sorry, she's up the tumble, can't speak.' No problem.

How cool was that? But it was all done innocently.

She never quite understood the fuss she provoked. Wherever she went, people, especially men, stared at her. She seemed oblivious. I would take her into the bar at UCL and order her a pint. In those days 'girls', as they were called, drank Babycham or port and lemon, maybe a shandy. But she could drink a bunch of rugby players under the table.

Leaving school at fifteen, Topsy was not academic, although she read voraciously, loving Tolstoy and almost any nineteenth-century English or French novel she could lose herself in. We shared a love of poetry. She loved Keats and I liked Shelley. She would listen as I held forth, no doubt pretentiously, on some matter, using ill-digested political jargon. Then she would ask a penetrating, naive question, using simple Anglo-Saxon words, leaving me spluttering. It was done with no edge. Her love was so guileless, so complete, I never doubted it. No one had loved me so totally since I was five. She became everything to me, emotionally, although I still kept the tough exterior. Our emotional intimacy was without barriers. We trusted each other.

Topsy's role in *The Loneliness of the Long Distance Runner* had been bittersweet for me. I was delighted for her but pissed off that Tom was doing better than me. We had been contemporaries at UCL. He was frail, not very active in the drama society and failed his degree. When he said he wanted to be an actor all his friends warned him that it was a rough and tough world and wondered if he would survive.

He survived.

He was accepted at RADA. His first job was as Konstantin in the Old Vic's *The Seagull*. His second was to take over from Albert

Finney in the West End's *Billy Liar*. Then a film career. I don't know about the other friends that Tom and I shared but I for one learned never, ever, to give another actor career advice. What did I know? He remained a nice man and I wished him well. I just envied him his success.

Everyone hustled Topsy for answers on whether she was going to take *Billy Liar*. She was in no hurry and didn't seem impressed. Eventually, after much lobbying by Tom and John, she turned down Stratford and agreed to the film. We knew we would be apart for some weeks. She was off to the north of England and I had the third part of David Mercer's CND trilogy coming up, a big, difficult role. We wished each other luck, kissed and parted.

That was the last moment I saw her.

Whatever Gets You Through the Night

Creative people who can't help but explore other mental territories are at greater risk, just as someone who climbs a mountain is more at risk than someone who just walks along a village lane.

R. D. Laing

Two weeks or so after departing for filming *Billy Liar*, Topsy unexpectedly walked in the door. She was unrecognisable. Fat, dishevelled, her hair lank, she walked and talked in slow motion. She only vaguely reminded me of my Topsy.

I called Robin Fox, our agent, who said that John Schlesinger had sacked her and recast with Julie Christie because the camera could read nothing in Topsy. Her eyes were dead. What had happened? No one seemed to know anything. We were all perplexed as well as concerned. It was beyond my experience. My anxiety turned to panic. I tended to her, thinking it had all been too much and that some love and rest would make her better. This was complicated by her indifference, her assurance that there was nothing wrong. She seemed to be only half with us, having drifted off into another space. None of this was the Topsy I knew. What was I to do? My filming dates loomed. She said she might go home for a while. I approved. Her Mom would look after her.

Her Mom took one look at her and understandably took her to the family GP, who immediately sent her up to Highcroft Hall, the local bin. They just plugged her into the mains, giving her a course of electro-convulsive shock therapy (ECT) supplemented with psycho-pharmaceuticals. On this news, my concern turned into panic and that into anger. I called the hospital. Eventually I got through to a nursing sister.

'Who are you? she asked.

I told her my name.

'No, I mean what is your relationship with the patient?'

'I'm . . .' What was I to say? Lover? Friend? 'Er . . .we live together and I'm concerned. I need to talk to someone about the treatment.'

'I'm afraid we are not at liberty to discuss our patient with some-one who has no status.'

'Status? What do you mean, no status?' I was now beside myself.

'You are neither a relative nor are you married to the patient. We cannot discuss her with you, except to say she is comfortable.' This nurse, of course, was correct. I did not have any status in the matter.

Shock therapy was routine. It seemed to my inexpert mind to be nothing more than cruel physical abuse. The patient is strapped down and given an injection to relax them. Electrodes are put to their heads and a powerful electric shock is administered. After a while the convulsions stop. They say this barbaric practice shakes them out of depression or whatever they're suffering from. It's still used in some hospitals today.

Leaving aside whether Tops was depressed or suffering from some-thing else, what did they think they would achieve with ECT? They also prescribed the crude drugs which were then becoming fash-ionable but achieving nothing except what R. D. Laing graphically called a 'functional lobotomy'. It was an ignorant, pseudo-scientific assault. Beneath their defensive jargon, the doctors at that hospi-tal knew as little as any of us. They had no convincing ideas as to the cause of Topsy's condition, no cure and nothing useful to say on prognosis. They just threw everything at her, hoping for the best, possibly doing more harm than good. Maybe they were just experimenting.

But my opinions were of little use. I wasn't a psychiatrist and when you're in anguish your judgement is skewed. I'm sure the medics were doing what they thought was best for her. They always want to do something or they have to face up to defeat in the face of an intractable problem. But the woman I was in love with and planned to spend the rest of my life with had gone away to work and come back seemingly the same woman but was actually someone I didn't know. She was a person who now only vaguely reminded me of the woman I loved, the woman I'd shared almost every moment with for over ten years. I was seeking an answer.

Why is she like this? What happened?

They had no answer. Physically assaulting her and filling her with pharmaceuticals did not change her. If anything they made her even more unreachable.

If she had suffered brain injury in a car crash I would have known the cause. Maybe the medics could have described the damage and made a stab at a prognosis. It would be just as devastating, perhaps, but concrete, definitive, easier to come to terms with.

She had been sent back someone else, not just in physical form but in her personality: the opposite of the woman I knew. Getting fat and lacking all interest in personal hygiene, even to the extent of not combing her hair, I could cope with. But her lack of affect, the zombie slowness, the disinterest, plunged me into a panicky despair.

Who was she now?

She had no interest in anything except filling her mouth: suddenly chain smoking, drinking heavily and raiding the fridge in the middle of the night. She was not my Tops any more. She was reduced to a slow-motion oral fixation. She was alone in her madness but denying it. When she talked she made little sense. I still loved her, cherished her – or at least my memory of her – but I could not help her. Nor could her desperately upset, loving family.

I blamed myself. Had I not loved her enough? Had I and my friends pushed her into taking her chances which were impossible to turn down, at least in our eyes? Had she for some reason not wanted this success? Had it all been too much? Or was the cause something in me, an evil I carried, which meant anyone I loved was doomed?

She never regained herself. She remained who she had become, a broken person barely able to look after herself, with an impoverished horizon.

When my filming finished she returned from Brum. She was worse. Listless and indifferent, with no energy: the opposite of her previous personality. They had diagnosed schizophrenia simplex. It seemed to me to be a dustbin diagnosis of no use to her or them. Behind the medics' obscure jargon they were as puzzled and as useless as the rest of us. She was a psychiatric mystery and so she remained.

I kept a belief that if I loved and cared for her enough it would turn out to be just an episode. She was ill and ill people can recover. I had no basis for this belief. It was irrational. It was for my benefit, I now realise. The busy hope that I could make her better kept me from total despair.

This went on year after interminable year. Harold's cousin Roberta and her husband Rowland generously allowed us to stay with them on their farm. They were now arable farming in Gloucestershire. Dairy had proved too demanding as Rowland got older.

Topsy and I got married there, something I felt in principle against, but I relented to please her father. Harry was in hospital and very poorly, terminally ill from prostate cancer as I later learned. The fact of the marriage repaired the rift with both families, just at the time the world was becoming indifferent to such niceties.

We had always planned a family, even indulging in fantasies about it. Somehow she knew not only that we would first have a boy but also what his name would be. She had only been in her mid-twenties and her career had been rocketing, so although she was longing to start, I had said we should wait a year or two until she was really established. Now, there was no reason to wait. Clutching at straws, I hoped a baby would shake her back to us. She gave birth to a healthy boy, who we called William. But she was unable to cope. She was like a little girl with a doll. Eventually, to save him from neglect, her Mom looked after the boy. Luckily she was warm and competent and loved him.

I had given up work, turning everything down. Topsy was erratic and I often had to rescue her, drunk, aimlessly wandering around town. Sometimes the police would bring her home to me. After a year or so we were short of money. She was incapable of earning and I was a full-time carer. I could not leave her alone for long, so going away on location was not an option. In any case, I was too upset, too raw, to want to expose myself as an actor at that time.

Dilys, who lived with David Mercer, offered me a temporary way out. She was a lovely person, a no-nonsense geordie whose common sense brought David down to earth. She was a high-powered civil servant at the Ministry of Housing and would return from work quite tired. Asking David about his day would produce long moans about the terrible burden of being a writer. She would counter, 'Well, it's all in your head, isn't it? Just write it down!'

But she was very kind. She suggested I work for a while at the Ministry, helping to conduct a survey for their architects. The progressive idea was to interview people before they were rehoused and ask them, for instance, whether they wanted a front room or whether they would prefer a bigger kitchen or just one downstairs space. Because of my psychology degree and familiarity with statistics she thought I would be useful. So I did that for a while. It earned enough to keep Topsy and me above water and it wasn't too onerous. In fact, I enjoyed it, talking at length with lots of East End families. It was the start of my interest in the housing question. I had no idea where it would lead.

My despair deepened. I felt a useless failure. Tops tried my patience. She just wasn't a person any more in any way I could relate to. I first became depressed and then physically ill. In the end, I reached a full stop. I was physically and emotionally exhausted. She had drained me. My despair was engulfing. It was a relief when she said she might go home for a visit. I had nothing more left to give this stranger. I was ashamed of that. But it was a fact. She went back home. Her Mom took the strain. She was a competent, caring woman but Topsy was a trial even for her. All her family were as upset as I was and just as helpless.

The builder I'd hired to do up the old house in Islington we'd bought had run out of my money with little to show for it. I hid myself away in the basement of this potentially lovely home, surrounded by bare walls and half-finished work. It seemed to mockingly symbolise the wonderful life which had beckoned and was now in ruins. I became immovable, masochistically enjoying the discomfort. It was in tune with how I felt inside. My life was over.

I fell into an almost catatonic, deep depression, staring at the wall with tears streaming down my face, feeling I had failed her. I knew I had lost her. For months I could barely move, barely look after myself. I rarely answered the phone. The pain was numbing, dull, heavy and impenetrable. This was the closest I've ever got to suicide. I contemplated it, in a detached way, as though I was someone else. Living was too painful. What was the point, anyway? I had lost everything that mattered. Underneath was an insistent voice telling me that I'd killed her, not realising that this was an echo of a repressed belief about my mother.

OK, the decision is one thing, I thought. What about the means? Do you have the balls to actually do it? Thinking about it is one thing. Throwing yourself in front of a tube train? Would you crack and draw back at the last second? Cutting your wrists? Long and slow. Better do it in the bath. Less mess. You don't have a gun. That'd be dramatic. Get some booze down you and gas yourself? Do you really want to repeat the gag? If you're going to end it, at least try something original.

I beat myself up with scorn. Then I got serious and decided to try the wrist slashing.

So what about Will? You haven't thought about him. Is he to grow up without a Dad as well as virtually without a Mom? Can you do that to him? Really want history to repeat itself, don't you? Just because you won't accept reality as it is now and the responsibility that goes with it.

No one actually knew what happened after my Mom became pregnant. No one in the family blamed Dad. But what if he'd persuaded Mom and put pressure on her? I'm sure she would have accepted the argument that a third baby in the middle of the bombing was unwise and that the insurance round would have to be relinquished, crushing all their dreams, leaving them broke. I couldn't believe the abortion was her idea. It didn't ring true.

I could believe that Dad, a strong character, dominant and persuasive, pushed Mom into it. Mom was obedient, as wives tended to be then. 'Anything for a quiet life,' she used to say. So, in effect, Dad killed Mom. He didn't mean to, and paid the price, but he killed her.

So did I have his curse? Was I, as they say, a chip off the old block? I certainly had some of his characteristics. Why not this one?

Did it follow that anyone I love would be in imminent danger, then? I should keep away, to protect people. Or get out of the way altogether if I was so toxic. These morbid thoughts took me over. I felt the way my Dad must have felt. Maybe they had decided together to take the risk. The reputation of the abortionist was so good. It was the criminality that probably worried them. If caught, their lives would have been unbearable. But thinking about how he must have felt in the few days after her death and haunted by his ghostly presence when he sat me on his knee on Christmas Day, I knew he must have believed he'd killed her.

I had no idea how but I was sure I'd caused Topsy's existential death. Even though I loved her, even though she was like life itself to me, even though she had loved me as only my Mom had loved me, I had killed her. Never mind how, let alone why. So wasn't my Dad's way out the only honourable one?

Freud committed suicide. He requested that his physician administer a lethal dose of morphine. The pain from his jaw cancer must have been unbearable. It was the rational act of a stoic, a man of the enlightenment who had looked at the comforting delusions of religion and not blinked.

But I pulled back from the brink. Some inextinguishable spark, some stubborn refusal to give in saved me. Maybe I was actually deterred by my Dad. I later joked that I'd wanted to end it but decided not to repeat the gag. The joke fell flat. There was something about suicide's irrevocability perhaps. I had no conventional religious feelings. Popular ideas of an afterlife were just silly. It might have been my curiosity to see how it all turned out. A detachment.

Was it the knowledge of little Will's existence that saved me? I knew that Tops was lost to me. Lost as surely as if she were physically dead. But he was alive, the baby we had talked about. I was his father. Was I to deprive him of a father as mine had been wrenched from me? He didn't deserve that.

I write this still not knowing why I stepped back from the final act. It's draining to feel guilty of many crimes, not knowing why you've done them or even how. Just with the weight of the evil secretly eating you away.

Topsy never recovered. Her family kept an eye on her. I remained close to them. She limped along, another person, unreachable, unknowable; infuriating and distressing.

Starting Over

Uncle Harold was born in 1901 and survived the Depression in the thirties. I was a child of the post-war boom. We were formed in different economic climates. Years later, when I said I'd taken a job at the BBC, his eyes lit up.

'Oh, that's good.'

'Yes, it's a nine-month contract.'

His face fell.

'Couldn't you get on the staff?'

'Staff? Hell, no! Last thing I want, to get on the staff.'

That was the most unhip fate I could think of. He looked at me very seriously. 'They're a good firm.'

I was persuaded to take one gig. It was only a few days' work and I sensed I must try to stir myself out of the hole I was in or I would for ever be in this no man's land. On automatic pilot I went up to Manchester to record a half-hour play, *Catherine*, written by Roger Smith, directed by Ken Loach and produced by Jim MacTaggart. I had no idea at the time of the importance of this meeting.

I played opposite Kika Markham. I was very drawn to her warmth and humanity. She was drawn to me, too, and we spent some time together. She was unhappy, trying to extricate herself from a difficult relationship. But I was still paralysed. It would be many years before I would be able to have anything but a platonic friendship with any woman. My heart was still with Tops. Kika and I remained friends.

It was an old-fashioned studio show with TV cameras. Ken, just off the directors' course, was too busy avoiding knitting the camera cables together to offer any direction. I formed no opinion of him. He made no impression. I liked Jim from the start and quickly made friends with Roger. He was energetic, immersed in life and full of ideas about TV drama. We talked for hours. He even brought me out of my depression for a while, provoking me to debate him. My heart hadn't been involved in the gig. I felt dead inside. I went back to my basement and descended again, sitting, lacking energy. It hadn't worked.

Roger began to call and invite himself round. I tried to deter him but in the end hadn't the energy. He said that Sydney Newman at the BBC had asked Jim MacTaggart to produce a season of contemporary, single dramas and Roger was to be the story editor, tasked with finding them. It was too big a job for him to do alone. He wanted me to give up acting and join them in the venture. I wondered why I was being offered a job I had no experience in. I had written a reply to a piece in the drama magazine *Encore* by Troy Kennedy Martin called 'Nats Go Home', which foreshadowed my later idea about a distilled naturalism. But that in addition to a few conversations with Roger seemed to make a flimsy case. I turned him down. He would not take 'No' for an answer. I thought he would give up and look elsewhere, eventually leaving me to stew. But he clearly wasn't going to. In the end, with many misgivings, I agreed. Maybe it was Roger's relentless determination; maybe something in me clutched at it as a means to get me engaged with life again.

I was told to go to the Television Centre in Shepherd's Bush to meet the legendary Sydney Newman. I walked down Wood Lane from the tube and presented myself at the gate guarding the large doughnut of the Centre, by now a fully functioning programme factory. I was checked and allowed to go to reception, where I was checked again before being told to go to the fifth floor. I knew the rituals well, having turned up many times as an actor.

Sydney's office was bigger than some flats I'd lived in, with his desk by the door and beyond a sitting area with a sofa and easy chairs, what he casually called 'the living room'. Short, stocky, moustached and swarthy, he looked like a Hollywood Mexican bandit. He had a natty bow tie and a relaxed, informal Canadian manner. He gave me an amused look. The meeting was actually a formality. Sydney was hands off, and trusted Jim, who in turn trusted Roger. But I didn't know that. I didn't much care either way.

'Oh, hell, I don't know what to ask you. What did you think of the show last night?'

The 'show' was *Hamlet*, shot on location with outside broadcast TV cameras by Philip Saville. Luckily, knowing about this meeting, I'd watched it. I launched into a detailed and pretentious critique, demonstrating my knowledge of Shakespeare and *Hamlet*. He let my lecture run its course, a benign smile playing on his face. At long last I paused.

'Uh–huh. Well, Philip wanted to do it. And I didn't know the play . . .'

Had I heard right? This is the head of BBC TV drama telling me he didn't know *Hamlet*? Was he being faux naive or was he really pig ignorant? As I got to know him I discovered he played this trick with everyone. No one knew the truth. I doubt he cared. I later thought it was part of his plan to shake it all up, to force everyone to deal with the real world and the popular audience. He had done this with spectacular success on ITV in Armchair Theatre. Time and again he repeated it, throwing people, sometimes into a rage. I remember one rather pretentious director tried to persuade him to allow a production of a play by a new writer. 'It's wonderfully avant garde. So evocative of Ionesco.'

'Ian who?'

He shook my hand again in a fatherly way and the three of us began work on *The Wednesday Play*.

So the Television Centre was my new home. I'd known it before it was finished and had worked in its studios but now I had an office. Television Centre was circular with a hole at its centre, like the BBC itself. One was in danger of going round in circles. We walked around the fifth floor to the area where all the other single-play producers gathered. My tiny office was next to Roger's and opposite Jim's.

I threw myself into the work in a manic defence against my depression or at least a flight from its incapacitating power. I put in ridiculous hours – including weekends – reading screenplays and making notes. I would be at the Centre so early the only ones there would be the all-night staff striking sets in the studios. They had a canteen where I would go for breakfast. Jim didn't read, except with a pistol to his head. In his office were piles of screenplays, all unread. I went to his flat and found more. I systematically read them all, picking out ones I thought Roger should also see. Jim wasn't a producer. He was a director, a loyal BBC career man doing Sydney a favour but longing to go back to his real job.

As I looked around I saw a few people with similar backgrounds to Roger and me. This was 1963, BBC Two was being planned and it was a moment of opportunity, just as the start of ITV had been a few years before and Channel 4 would be in the 1980s. Hugh Carleton Greene, the Director General, with the help of Stuart Hood and others, had clearly noticed social trends and was busy trying to persuade Aunty to get rid of the corset and try a mini-skirt. He was opening up recruitment to a wider background.

There was some suspicion, indeed, resentment of working-class ruffians, especially of ones like Roger and me, coming in on raiding parties. If it weren't for the need to expand I doubt we would have been thought the right sort of chaps. Up till then recruits, whatever their background, tried very hard to fit in with the BBC style as well as its ethic, a style rather like the senior civil service or academia. Huw Wheldon, the voluble Welsh presenter who rose to be the boss of BBC TV, actually told me that he thought his senior producers should earn roughly the same as 'someone with a chair at a good university'.

Most of the people I met, mainly from middle- or upper middle-class backgrounds, alongside a few newcomers with scholarships, were traditionalists keen to absorb the BBC ethic. This embraced modest, socially liberal attitudes but didn't rock the boat. Their

attitude towards the uneducated masses was to assume the responsibility of conveying the best of received culture with a patronising
attitude towards the masses themselves. The appointment of Sydney
was a dramatic signal that Greene wanted change. He was clearly
afraid that the BBC would miss the tide.

As I got to know people, I realised there were some, even in
senior management, who had been infected by socialist ideas in the
1930s, who had had a good war and carried with them an idealism, remembering both fascism and mass unemployment. This was
the aftermath of the war, when a reformist Labour Party had been
returned with a huge majority (though people forget that while
they achieved twelve million votes, the Tories achieved nearly ten
million). But as now, it was only possible to survive if one's politics
were within the prevailing cultural norms; the difference being that
these have today shifted markedly to the Right.

These people at the BBC counterbalanced the Corporation's
traditional Tory view of the world by favouring a mildly reforming
Labour Party, although none would ever openly commit to a political position on anything.

Not all had been successfully inoculated by their skirmish with
left-wing ideas. For instance, I was astounded that Stuart Hood, who
rose to senior status, was a Marxist. He was difficult to read, subtle
and sophisticated, giving little away. He had a background in intelligence and one sometimes wondered if he was still an agent; and if
so, for whom. I asked him what the BBC was really like. 'It's like
the Kremlin,' was his tantalising answer.

But most were natural establishment characters who didn't want to
tarnish their reputations as they proceeded up the ladder. As the saying went, 'They knew how to behave' and it became second nature.
Nothing has changed since then, except now almost everyone with
any management power has absorbed the free market ideology and
combined it with a Victorian sense of hierarchy.

I noticed that, psychologically, BBC people divided into two
groups: the parents and the adolescents. The parents were usually
in management, some strict, some relaxed; the adolescents thought
of themselves as privileged creators and demanded freedom without

responsibility. They were like teenagers chafing against a home they daren't leave, incapable of surviving in the wider world but always complaining about their parents not 'understanding' them. They tended to be full of disdain. The parents at that time were understanding and rather too indulgent of their children's irrespon- sibility with pocket money but they did give these tiresome adult refuseniks room to create. They were slow to weed out those who were uncreative moaners. Different from the BBC parents now who impose a tight discipline, improving the teenagers' behaviour but crushing their creativity.

I realised how complex, flexible and sophisticated the BBC was: a reliable part of government that not only managed to pretend it was independent and separate from the power of Whitehall but also believed it. This was either a necessary delusion or it illustrated the old truism that the English invented hypocrisy. Commerce was for others, the monarchy was sacred and the government of the day must be treated with deference or at least with care. It contained all that was good and bad in the inheritance of the BBC's first Director General, John Reith.

In fact, although I wouldn't have lasted five minutes in Reith's day I admired much about him. He was principled, honest and had a noble vision of the BBC. He wanted to carry 'the best of everything into the greatest number of homes' and saw it as an equalising, democratic force. Good, I thought, I will pursue Reith's ideals, but perhaps not in the way he would have tolerated.

I had a secret life. Three times a week I contrived to slip away, making sure I had scheduled no meetings. I would quickly drive over to Hampstead to spend an hour with a kind, elderly gentleman. Few ever knew where I went or why. Dr MacDonald was a psycho- analyst. I thought I needed help to lift me out of depression, to give me a reason to go on living. I knew I couldn't do it on my own. I thought my problem was getting over the consequences of Topsy's illness. Nothing, I now realised, was going to save her now. She was lost to me and lost to herself. My love was irrelevant. I could not find her and bring her back to life, back to me, again.

Of course, the source of my unhappiness was even deeper, but I was not about to face what I had defended myself against since I was five. Shedding even more tears about Topsy became yet another retreat from engagement with events so deeply buried. We talked about Topsy, of course, and I held forth on Freudian theory, running rings round Dr MacDonald, enjoying the intellectual exercise. It was as though I wanted a painless experience, conducted on a cerebral level where I felt safe. But paying the fees and turning up on time doesn't get you a certificate awarding you happiness. As usual, I was too clever by half. I remained in denial, in torment and depressed, continuing with my frantic workload as a way of avoiding what I needed to face. For years I continued to visit Dr MacDonald, becoming fond of him for his warmth and kindness.

Roger was brilliant. I watched and learned. He was looking for fresh ideas and experiences. He encouraged and commissioned new writers. One of them was Dennis Potter. They had been friends at university though I sensed their relationship was fraught. We visited him one evening. Roger had a hunch he might write a screenplay for us. We were made at home in their suburban semi by his wife, Margaret, who I instantly liked. She, too, was working class and from the Forest of Dean.

When Dennis's book *The Glittering Coffin*, a precocious 'state of the nation' book, was published, he was lionised for a while and invited everywhere. One day at a drinks in Hampstead a Labour toff, making conversation, said to Margaret, 'And do you write?'

'Ar,' she said, 'I can read too.' She was unaffectedly warm, had no side and reminded me of my girl cousins.

Dennis, showing early signs of psoriatic arthropathy, an arthritic disease, was then a television critic for the *Daily Herald*. Roger persuaded him to try his hand at writing a screenplay. This started with *The Confidence Course* in *The Wednesday Play* slot and then Roger asked him to write a play based on the experience of fighting a parliamentary election, which Dennis had recently attempted.

Vote, Vote, Vote For Nigel Barton was a sharp, critical piece about a young man fighting a safe Tory seat. It was made without incident but just before transmission Sydney told us there were problems. Executives from BBC Current Affairs objected to the negative portrayal of the Labour constituency agent. He had been written and been played as a cynical and jaded pro rather than an honest believer in the Labour cause. Roger and I exploded and immediately put our resignation letters on Sydney's desk. Jim MacTaggart was not so precipitate but was concerned, not least at the prospect of his team falling apart with most of the series yet to be made.

Sydney was clearly in a quandary. Senior management on the sixth floor had been persuaded that the BBC's relationship with one of the major parties was in jeopardy for a mere play, basically a piece of entertainment. His task was to take the heat out of it, avoid the resignations and buy himself time to fight a rear-guard action. I knew he was a sophisticated political animal with his rough-hewn manner a disguise but at the time I was in no mood to appreciate his subtlety.

We marched into his office and a row began. He needed to keep us there until we had withdrawn our resignations. I didn't want to leave without satisfaction. It continued for hours. Looking back, some of it was hilarious but at the time I was too full of self-righteous fury to notice. I was affronted at this censorship. Who the hell were the Current Affairs people to stand in the way of a drama? It was none of their business.

He and I faced each other, yards apart, and screamed appalling abuse. Sydney was a street fighter. But there came a point when he stopped shouting and made a huge effort to reclaim self-control. His voice became a whisper. 'Tony, I want you to understand their position is that the BBC cannot abuse one of the great political parties of this country. It's a national institution. It's not the BBC way. How can I explain this? Look. In this country. For instance. You understand this. You *cannot piss on the Queen*. But if you do . . . you have to do it *very carefully*.'

What I didn't appreciate at the time was that this was partly Sydney's own attempt to understand the BBC and his adopted country.

In the end we agreed a compromise. The show would not be banned. It would be delayed so that we could make some changes which would address the problem. I made it clear that my resignation letter was still on his desk.

Sydney had won.

But, of course, although we did make some changes, we actually were careful to make it even more cynical, doing the opposite of what had been demanded. Sydney didn't care. He could go back and announce a good old British compromise. We guessed – correctly – that the Current Affairs censors would not even bother to watch this time round; they would have something else on their minds.

We went down to a cafe on Shepherd's Bush Green where Dennis was waiting to tell him the good news. He was as grudging and as churlish as ever. No thanks from him, no sense we were working together. It didn't surprise me. The more I got to know him the less I liked him. As the years went by I felt more and more estranged from him. He was laughably arrogant, literally asserting he could walk on water. He would deliver a slipshod first draft and then defend every word as though he was a barrister for the defence, protecting his client. He was bright and polemical and abrasive, contemptuous of any comment which fell short of awed praise. We are all defensive and don't enjoy being criticised, but part of a pro's job is to achieve a little distance and work with notes, sift them and try to ratchet up the quality of the writing.

It's not necessary to like someone you work with. It's the talent you need to love, not them. But if you actively dislike them that is a problem.

I saw signs that Dennis was moving rapidly to the Right politically. He was also moving towards a style involving fantasy and away from distilled naturalism. We wanted to plough different furrows. I was happy never to work with him again and rarely saw him. I certainly disliked the work I did see.

We met decades later at a colleague's funeral in Kensal Green. The weather was bleak and cold, a fitting background to a sad day. After the burial I looked round and as usual there were people I hadn't seen for a while. I saw Dennis. We looked at each other and nodded. As we walked off together I noticed he looked strained and even thinner than I remembered. I expected we would drift off and go our separate ways but although nothing was said we didn't. We walked side by side.

We ended up in the Portobello Road, finding a corner of a pub. It was as though an unspoken decision had been made to meet. We sat there, me with a Guinness and Dennis with his familiar Scotch clutched in a fist twisted over the years with arthritis. I asked after Margaret, really to make conversation. After a long pause, he began talking in his high, slightly whining voice, very quietly. He was blunt. Plain. Matter of fact. There were no preliminaries. 'She has cancer. We don't know how long. Soon. Weeks. Maybe days.' He drank a slug of whisky. I took his hand and squeezed it. There was another long pause. 'The funny thing is, so have I.' He looked up at me and smiled that sardonic smile I had once associated with his sarcasm but that now broke me up. 'Not long. Imminent is the word. Nothing to be done.'

His manner was detached, but it was easy to see through the pose. I held his gaze. What was there to say? It was as though he was making his peace with me. I liked him more during that hour than I'd ever been able to. He was vulnerable, drily witty, stoic and even warm. We held each other's hands for a while longer, squeezing them, saying nothing.

Margaret died a few days later and Dennis died soon after: June '94.

Almost on the eve of his death he gave a high-profile television interview demanding two rival channels co-operate to produce his last two screenplays. How does one refuse the wishes of a dying man? Particularly when they are broadcast, making the public your witness?

He was a controlling, manipulative, egotistical self-publicist to the last.

Had there been something extra contributing to my feelings about Dennis? I was sympathetic because I knew first-hand what his arthritis was doing to him, although his suffering was much worse than mine. Daily life must have been intensely difficult to sustain.

I tried to discuss it with him once, making the obvious connection between his angry skin, which had erupted in an itch that was exquisitely painful, and the twists and distortions of his arthritis, with his internal life. I suspected that he was tortured inside and that his physical symptoms were a somatic expression of his inner torture. Certainly the conflict between his Old Testament, sexually repressed upbringing and his compulsive interest in prostitutes suggested one unresolved tension. His response was instant, vehement scorn. He would not discuss the idea. I had overstepped the mark. Instead of trying to tease out his inner torments, he preferred to wallow in his physical misery. He was hostile to the idea that we are an interconnected organism of integrity. He preferred the Cartesian view, or at least was more comfortable denying the existence of the flesh.

What was lost on me at the time was my own denial of the body, the retreat into intellectual detachment and the refusal to truly face the past. I might have been perceptive about Dennis, but I used that to bolster my own refusal to look inside myself.

I was shocked that he used his illness as a weapon to buy sympathy. To him it was a currency. This seemed to me shameless and opportunistic. He told everyone. The details were all over the media. The result was, 'Poor, brave Dennis'. He not only used it as dramatic subject matter but played journalists and various media celebrities.

So his final manipulative interview was to be expected.

All this behaviour was not the Brum way, or at least not my family's way.

For years one name was associated with everything Dennis wrote: the man who became his producer, Ken Trodd. Ken had been at Oxford with Roger and Dennis. He had been teaching in Africa and on his way back to Oxford had popped into the TV Centre to see Roger. We had a drink at the bar and Roger asked him why on earth he wanted to be a don when he could be working in television, telling him to look around him at all the beautiful young women. Ken did. He changed his mind. Roger engineered a job offer and Ken became an assistant script editor, giving up academia. This was towards the end of our year doing *The Wednesday Play* and restless Roger was about to go off to write a novel in Greece with a girl he'd met at the Royal College of Art. The result was that he willed Ken to me.

We rubbed along well enough, working together or alongside each other for some time, but we got on better when we didn't work together. Ken is intellectually bright and I enjoyed that but he is also eccentric and difficult or, rather, he and I found each other difficult. His mind is complex, political and conspiratorial. He schemes and whispers in ears. If casting a Medici cardinal he would be my first choice. But his achievements are substantial and they've never been fully acknowledged.

Year after year, through one drama series after another, Ken nurtured Dennis, coaxed material and rewrites from him, prevented him from committing professional suicide and also made a material contribution himself. He knew more about thirties and forties dance band music than even Dennis did, for instance. One cannot know how Dennis's career would have developed without Ken but he owed the career he had first of all to Roger, who had persuaded him to write drama in the first place, then to Ken. They would bicker like an old married couple joined at the hip. It had a 'can't live with him, can't live without him' quality. But Ken would go down to Dennis's home and come back with material only he could extract from his irascible friend.

Roger also found Jimmy O'Connor and they became close friends as he listened and encouraged material from him. Jimmy had served life – around ten years – in Dartmoor prison for a murder he spent the rest of his life denying. He was a rough ex-villain from Paddington, whose mother had been a part-time prostitute.

He married Nemone Lethbridge, a barrister. Physically, it was beauty and the beast, Jimmy's leonine, lined face and short, powerful body ducking and diving, him smoking a cigarette furtively, looking around as he took a drag and then hiding it behind his back as though he was still on the wing at Her Majesty's pleasure; she, strikingly pretty in an imperious way, charming and impeccably mannered, revealing her origins in her every gesture, as we all do. She was from the West Country, the daughter of a general, with all the social self-confidence that conveys.

Jimmy was one of the stars of that *Wednesday Play* season. The legislation to end capital punishment was making its way through

Parliament when we transmitted Jimmy's play, *Three Clear Sundays*, an autobiographical piece about a man condemned to death. Jimmy's character really was hanged, a ritual we showed in detail. We drew loud protest, particularly and oddly from those who believed in hanging. The lead was played by Tony Selby, who had been in Roger's own play, where we first met. It was a model piece for us: taken from the headlines, realistic and overtly making a case. I had always been horrified by capital punishment, which is just state murder.

Roger also commissioned original work from established writers, like John Hopkins, Simon Raven and David Mercer, encouraging them to be daring. Some writers were inexperienced and had never been produced. Neville Smith, the actor, was one. Did they have something to say? If so, Roger helped them say it. He was also lazy and volatile, working intensely for a few hours then disappearing, rolling in just before lunch the next day, if at all. But led by him we began to assemble fresh, lively, original material.

It was during this frantic year of reading and discussing hundreds of screenplays that the obvious thought hit me: the important question, the one dominating all others is the simple basic one. What are we saying with our material? What aspect of experience are we exploring? What is our stance towards our fellow man? Making screen drama is so complex, involves so much varied expertise, that this simple truth gets lost.

Of course, I never had a 'eureka' moment when the clouds lifted and I saw the future suddenly open up for me. Insights accumulated, mostly just beyond consciousness, until I was able to say, 'Of course, how obvious.' It began when I observed the truth in Topsy's acting at the very beginning, and continued with the frustrations I felt when acting in a conventionally shot movie at Elstree. Then I saw the simple fact that it is the 'What?' question that is primary. At this point everything coalesced and gradually came into focus. I not so much decided my life's work. It presented itself to me.

Of course, when I became the one to answer the What? question, the links between those answers and my early life were exposed.

But I remained unconscious of most of them. It's possible that I'm unconscious of some of them still.

It was a relief to be so busy. Everything else could be buried. A small voice told me this was no answer, that I really had to face up to my depression at some point. But not yet. At six Roger would take me to the BBC club bar. Jim would join us. He taught me to drink Scotch. We would drink with a writer or two and then leave for the evening's adventure.

We would call on the painter, Pauline Boty, and the literary agent, Clive Goodwin, or at Troy Kennedy Martin's flat, dine at the Tratt, a fashionable Italian (my tastes having become more catholic) and then we'd go on to a club such as the fashionable Scotch, the noise and triviality of which I found boring. Or a party somewhere with theatre producer Michael White, the painter Derek Boshier or Jimmy O'Connor and Nemone Lethbridge, where there would be tough villains and actors, politicians and lawyers all chatting, exchanging gossip; and John Bindon, the criminal-turned-actor, waving his impressive cock at everyone – his party piece.

Roger and I had each bought Triumph Spitfire sports cars. He would whizz off with me trying to follow and keep him in my sights. I was never an F1 driver.

Roger was not only gregarious and socially confident, which I had never been. He was generous, including me in his life and intro-ducing me to everyone he knew. I reciprocated. It further filled my time and prodded me alive again. He not only changed the course of my life by insisting I work on *The Wednesday Play*, he brought me back from the brink and helped me to start afresh.

We were scheduled to go on the air in October 1964. One evening during the summer, our plans well advanced, Sydney Newman took us out on to the terrace of the BBC club for a drink. He told us our show would not begin as originally planned but he promised it would start three months later. We thought he was stringing us along and should just tell us straight that Donald Baverstock, then the Channel Controller, had won. We knew he didn't want single dramas. None of them do. They're expensive – no economies of scale, each a one-off – and renewable one-hour series and soaps guarantee larger audiences. Of course, we now know that battle is long over. But those who mourn the loss of single dramas do not know how long the battle raged. Sydney insisted it was just a delay. We were to carry on and not to worry.

'Oh, Baverstock,' he said almost as an aside, 'He's dead. He doesn't know it.'

A few months later Baverstock resigned and we hit the air. I thought, don't mess with Sydney.

Later Sydney told me more of his past and I began to understand him. At first he was a puzzle, an exotic creature, one new to me. I'd known him for over a year when someone remarked on his Jewishness. I looked puzzled. Everyone laughed, not believing my puzzlement. They said one look at him was enough; and the name Newman was an Anglicisation of Neumann. Was I joking with them, having them on? I then realised I'd never consciously met a Jew. Neither the religion nor the people were ever mentioned at home. I had met some in literature. I read Fagin as a nasty criminal and thought Shylock had a case: it was a class issue and his spoilt, privileged opponents were the villains. But the Jewish people and their sensibilities were new to me.

Sydney was working-class Canadian, from immigrant stock, who had been influenced by John Grierson, the great documentary figure. He admired craftsmen, his hobby being woodwork. Learning in a hard school and surviving working on the TV series of dramas, General Motors Theatre, with the sponsors at his elbow, demanding changes, as the dramas were being transmitted, he could handle the politics of the BBC. He was tough, volatile and his anger made men quail. He was like my Dad. His reputation was on the line and the need for us to get an audience was imperative. It was not enough to make some nice drama.

We were committed to trying to square the circle: do serious, uncompromising work, and make it popular. That is, to achieve the biggest audience we could, but do it the hard way. I used to say anyone can get a huge audience if that is the sole ambition. Put on a public hanging every Saturday evening. Huge ratings. Anyone can put out the accepted version of received culture if the audience size is unimportant and claim to be able to run BBC Radio 3 before breakfast. We were guided by Huw Wheldon's famous aspiration – to make the serious popular and the popular serious.

The National Theatre of the Air. I began to use this phrase as a mantra. It summarised my idealism and ambition. Ken Tynan and others had for years been agitating for a National Theatre, but here we were with the means to create one for people of all classes. In the middle-1960s television was watched avidly by almost everyone. Millions like my family wouldn't ever think of going to the theatre. That was for other people. But week after week we had the opportunity to speak to millions. I saw it as an almost sacred responsibility.

My childhood had been enriched by access to the BBC, as it had been by access to the Birmingham reference library. As the penny dropped, I began to see that we were also linking with the Workers' Educational Association (WEA) and those earnest socialists from the educated middle class, right back into the nineteenth century. I became hooked on the possibilities of television, work which would touch the audience directly and reflect their experiences. We refused to lazily rest on the usual rehash of received culture.

Cultural snobbery still assumed that truly serious people worked in the theatre or in small audience art films, or at least worked uncontaminated by the compromises needed to be popular. I was contemptuous of these snobs. I didn't want to beg a few short ends and show a film to a handful of like-minded people in a Soho basement. I thought the challenge of this opportunity couldn't be ducked. I've never lost my belief in it. Even though I've mostly failed to square the circle of artistic ambition and popular appeal, it remains the only worthwhile ambition.

Having spent a year off the screen preparing the material, we launched into a busy production schedule. In 1965 we transmitted over thirty original feature-length dramas. We would hammock a difficult play, say a David Mercer, between two genre pieces, a comedy and a thriller. The pace was relentless, which suited my need to bury my problems in work. Towards the end of 1965 the exhaustion began to show. We had coped with and survived big controversies and could never relax into a predictable professional rhythm. Each show was a one-off challenge and each transmission was a test of our resolve not to compromise, whatever the press or enemies inside the TV Centre threw at us.

We dealt with capital punishment, racism and crime; we shocked right-wing Christian Mary Whitehouse by showing working-class people swearing and drinking and enjoying sex – even outside marriage; we showed the effects of criminalising abortion. It was all exhilarating and educational: I was learning fast and my own ideas were rapidly gelling.

The Penny Drops

The BBC spreads 'the propaganda of disbelief, doubt and dirt . . . promiscuity, infidelity and drinking.'

Mary Whitehouse

Ken Loach became the workhorse of the series. He had gradu-ated to big singles, despite getting microphone booms in shot and knitting the cables in episodes of *Z Cars*. He always hated live TV drama, with the ponderous equipment and technical problems getting in the way of the actors. But in those days fledgling directors survived small blips. Jim MacTaggart could see his potential and he grew in that arduous year on *The Wednesday Play*.

He and I gradually gravitated towards each other. Our back-grounds were similar: respectable, skilled, working-class Midlands families, he from Nuneaton, me from Brum and part of that cohort in the fifties allowed into the better universities. He was not political then: he has since blamed me for his politics. Roger Smith, who was his contemporary, said he was a theatrical aesthete at Oxford.

I noticed his quiet tenacity and his capacity for relentless hard work despite looking as though a gust of wind would blow him over. But what clinched it for me was his original casting and the truthfulness of the performances under his encouraging eye. It was not something he reached for and gradually perfected. It was there from the start. The penny had dropped. He got it. His work also had a lightness and an energy. It was alive. We were both admirers of Joan Littlewood, of Theatre Workshop.

Our conversations were brief, considering the radical sweep of our intentions, mainly over at his place in Barnes. It all seemed inevitable. We had little need to argue it out. I got on well with his wife Lesley who, like me, came from Erdington and had worked at Highbury when Topsy and me were there. The kids were arriving at regular intervals and I got to know them too.

We rejected TV drama made with electronic cameras in studios. We loved TV as a way of reaching millions on the same occasion, creating an event. We wanted to make films, on location, with a 16-mm, handheld, blimped camera. We both hated writing writing, acting acting and directing directing. We had a vision of a completely different approach. It was all settled between us with no fuss or disagreement.

These were the principles which have governed both our professional lives ever since.

My task was to find and work with the writers, develop the material, deciding what we were going to make and then to organise it all and guide it through the BBC on to the screen without compromise, protecting everyone and giving them room to work; to deliver each day to the camera what was needed to accomplish this vision.

Those were the days of such revolutionary optimism that I thought we could make a film and change the world. Events rather dashed this youthful arrogance. There was no revolution, either in form or content. The status quo prevailed. But in the nineties, with low-budget series like *This Life* and *The Cops*, I was able to introduce a new generation to the basic principles and techniques we believed in.

A clear fact about drama on television is that it exists as part of a flow of material, unlike a cinema film, which is a separate event that creates its own world. *The Wednesday Play* succeeded the *Nine O'Clock News*. We wanted a style which would be seamless with the news, so that the audience would take what we were offering seriously. We didn't want it to seem like a conventional drama. We wanted an audience to think our drama was actually happening.

This would lead me into endless difficulties and an attempt to get us off the screen.

At that time it was just possible to record and do limited editing with the electronic equipment but for budgetary reasons most TV drama was recorded as though it was live. In order to justify this management had invented a phoney aesthetic which argued that continuous performance allowed more authentic work from actors.

I still remember being in a live production of Ben Jonson's *The Alchemist*, ninety minutes of the cast running from set to set, no chance to retake any of it, hoping for the best. In another play I had to seduce a number of women. There were different cafe sets, with tables for two. The writer had carefully arranged which character spoke first or last. He had given the last speech to the woman opposite me. She spoke into thin air, because I'd disappeared. I was running across the studio, changing my costume as I went, just managing to ease into a seat at another table as another woman finished her speech into thin air, giving me my cue to start.

For years I'd thought all this was ridiculous. TV drama was a bastard child of the cinema and the theatre, lacking the attributes of both but carrying all the disadvantages. In the theatre people gather in the same space to create, as player and audience, an unrepeatable event. The audience is an essential part of the ritual. In film you can, on real locations, gradually build your reality, knitting it all together, thoughtfully, later. A film is the accretion of private moments. It lends itself particularly to the realistic or naturalistic conventions that attract me and to special effects visual spectaculars – that don't.

I longed for us to make films. So did Ken. The cinema in the UK was mainly commercial and not sympathetic to my interests, even though directors such as Karel Reisz and Tony Richardson were pushing for change. It was always a long hassle to put one together. The BBC – and Granada – were more daring. At that time, the audience was at home watching TV.

We wanted to show people's lives back to them, their recognisable experience; working people's lives, in their dignity, without the condescension and the caricature they were used to.

There was just one problem. BBC management was committed

to studio electronic drama, which we thought constricting. The only location filming allowed was confined to a shot of the taxi drawing up to the door. The TV Centre had not that long been built and it was constructed around big studios for dramas and shiny floor, light entertainment. As Michael Peacock, then Controller of BBC One, put it, 'I want A-list dramas not B-movies.'

Disappointingly, the biggest potential beneficiary, Jack Mewatt, Head of Film at Ealing, was formidably opposed. It would have enlarged his empire at the expense of the electronic studios. But traditional ideas of 'quality' blinded him. He insisted that 35-mm Mitchell cameras were needed for drama, on grounds of technical capability. That was unacceptable to Ken and me. Mitchell cameras were heavy and clumsy, with short reels and would make our style of film-making impossible. Jack certainly felt vindicated when he saw the results of our work. The shoot was usually in low light, the stock pushed beyond its tolerance. The transmission engineers were also appalled. I sometimes had to go to the TX rehearsal (transmission) on the afternoon before transmission to sweet-talk them when they were on the verge of refusing what they sniffily described as 'virtually untransmittable material'. Ken – and Tony Imi, our cameraman – were each known as the Prince of Darkness.

We were talking a different language to that of management. For years I had seen and, as an actor suffered, the life and spontaneity being leached out of films in order to get a set beautifully lit and had been made to contort myself and dance for the lights. We wanted to shoot on real locations which the actors could feed off; do everything to allow the actor to be in the moment, not in a film: to free them to just be their characters. There is a hierarchy of priorities and we were inverting it. Part of my zeal was never to repeat those procedures which ensured creative death, when the actor is thought of as just another technical element to be used. That had been my own experience.

As an example, one small change marked the break with the past. Ken end-boarded each shot. A slight inconvenience for the cutting room and a liberation for the actor. He would silently indicate to camera and sound, then quietly say to the actor, 'In your own time.'

A big improvement on a camera assistant pushing a board in the actor's face at the start of shooting, shouting out the shot and making a loud noise with the clapper, before even the most intimate, emotional scene. That had been my own experience for years as an actor.

The camera had to find the actor. As for the actor, the camera shouldn't exist; one of the reasons for long lenses. They not only gave a feeling of eavesdropping on private events but helped get the camera away from the action and prevent the film crew turning it all into a circus. It was not the actor's job to entertain the crew. There was no audience. There was no camera. There was only the character in an environment. There was only the circumstance.

Roger was exhausted, fractious, thinking of other things. He was restless when in the office. He felt his job was done and he wanted out. He left. Jim MacTaggart went on holiday. I saw my chance.

Ken had drawn my attention to *Up the Junction*, a thinly fictionalised account of the lives of a group of adolescents in Clapham. It rang true. Author Nell Dunn wrote episodes, accounts of incidents and adventures, which were loosely connected through the friendships. There was no conventional narrative. It glancingly moved from one life to another. I admired it. I knew it played to Ken's strengths. He ached to direct it. He was like a boy salivating over a train set in Hamley's window.

The theme of *Up the Junction* has drawn both of us over the decades. The sheer life force of working-class young people, their energy, optimism, fearlessness and naive hopes for their future contrasting with the objective bleakness of actual experience, their ambitions extinguished by their status, their options closing off. It moved and angered us. Ken and I had been allowed to escape.

I immediately put it into the machinery. Pre-production began. We had a start date. By that point in the run of the series, transmission was close to the lock-off dates of productions. There were few finished shows waiting in line.

I scheduled just a few days of filming and booked TV studio time, making sure no alarm bells were triggered. I knew that Ken, with Tony Imi on camera, could shoot quickly. TV studio material was backed up by telecine film, which was poor quality, but usable. So it could all be on film, with Roy Watts editing.

When Jim returned from holiday I told him. He read the book and exploded. This was unusual for him. He was a calm, tolerant man. We had a stand-up row, but it was what I had predicted and the reason why I had not consulted him. Even though he had been in the forefront of experimentation, this was going too far. He rejected the material on the grounds that it was not a coherent screenplay, just a list of scenes with no plot, no beginning or end, a jumble. His incandescence increased when he realised there was no chance of cancelling it. He would have had to tell Sydney to expect a black screen or a repeat.

He accepted the inevitable and told me to take the producer credit. He didn't want his name on it, hadn't earned it. I refused, telling him he was the series producer. I didn't want anyone to say I had tricked him and gone behind his back to steal a screen credit.

Jim was by then a friend as well as a protector. I was fond of him. But none of that made any difference to my determination to make the film happen. Nothing would deflect me. It was cold ruthlessness. I didn't think this through at the time. I was just focused on my goal. Fortunately, our relationship survived and lasted.

Ken found Carol White, who had also been in *The Boys*, Cleo Sylvestre, Vickery Turner, Tony Selby, who had been in *Catherine*, on which Ken and I had first met; plus many from Joan Littlewood's repertory of actors. It was a fine, credible cast.

Tony Imi was a staff BBC cameraman. Over six feet tall, and built like a lock forward; he had a sunny disposition and a long fuse. He could shoot rock-solid hand-held all day long and he had a good eye. Between them they shot some brilliant material in just a few days.

In one section the character Ruby discovers she is pregnant. A backstreet, kitchen-table abortion is arranged. This action is played through. As the abortion is being performed, we hear a voice calmly giving the facts, listing the numbers and the avoidable deaths caused as a result of criminalisation. This was my GP's voice, Dr Don Grant, who specialised in pre- and postnatal care and had delivered countless babies. His voice was kind and authoritative. He later became the Loach family GP.

I told no one, not even Ken, that this scene alone would have persuaded me the film must be made. Ruby survives, but Don's voiceover makes the dangers clear. I wanted no more unnecessary deaths or orphaned children. I hated that law and wanted it abolished. Those shocked by my ruthless deception at the BBC had no idea of its roots. I would have cut off my arm to get that scene in front of the public.

A bill to legalise abortion was actually making its way controversially through Parliament as *Up the Junction* went out in November 1965. So, of course, that scene was the focus for complaints. My nemesis, Mary Whitehouse, used the film as a weapon to bait the BBC. I thought she had a future as a copywriter. Her prose was pithy and arresting. I was surprised she didn't ever invoice us. Partly thanks to her, the audience was large, the publicity enormous and the controversy enjoyable. We'd even delivered a film before I had formally been made a producer.

Ken and I were joined at the hip.

But that was a mere battle. I needed to win the war. It was the biggest challenge of my professional life.

It seems odd now, when shooting TV drama on location is normal and unquestioned, but it felt like a fight to the death then. I argued and pleaded and shouted. It went on for many months. Sydney was not a film man, so he didn't understand my increasingly furious arguments. He was on my side personally and didn't want to lose me. He disagreed with me but believed in me. I think he liked my spunk. So his neutrality gradually moved to support. In the end, Michael Peacock, to his lasting credit, put aside his own misgivings and said I could do a 'couple or so'. Maybe it was just to get rid of me. I'd become a nuisance and a distraction. But it was also an example of BBC management style then. In the end, if a creative person really believed in something, there was a listening ear. It was the capacity to allow. The opposite of the top down management which later damaged the BBC's creativity. Now they would probably just sack such a troublemaker.

So, Ken and I were ready to go. Sydney made me a producer. I told him I would be my own story editor but wouldn't be in charge of a big volume of films. I wanted to develop my own bespoke productions and really produce.

I was on my own now. I had to deliver.

Topsy's impenetrable illness had been so absorbing I'd lost myself in it. For years fundamental changes had been gestating within me and I hadn't assessed their significance. But now I realised that I'd accepted Roger's invitation not just as a way of igniting my life again but because I'd been moving towards something like it for a long time. I'd been a lucky actor, playing leading parts, but I was down the pecking order, behind Albert Finney and Alan Bates among others. For someone in their middle twenties it was going well. But 'well' was not enough.

Was it conceivable I could be the best? The cold answer was 'No'. And I only ever wanted to be the best or right up there. Plus, there are very few actors in any generation who can influence events, who have enough clout to make something happen. I was never going to have that clout.

The brutal truth was that I'd recognised it years before. The moment I first saw Topsy work her magic at the amateur Highbury Little Theatre I knew I didn't have it. But it took more than ten years before I accepted the truth. It hurt but at last I was honest with myself. I loved acting. To be in a good piece with good people is an indescribable buzz, difficult to explain to those who haven't experienced it. But I didn't like the life of an actor. The passivity. Having to sit by the phone waiting for an invitation. Knowing that all the important decisions have been made before I played my part. It was frustrating.

After a few months on *The Wednesday Play* I was able to put these thoughts into words.

To make a drama you have to answer three questions: What? Who? How? At the BBC and Granada (the only other realistic option), the person controlling all three questions at that time was the producer. There were institutional constraints, of course, but inside them there was opportunity. The producer decided the most important questions of all: what are we going to make? What is the piece saying about the world? To the world? If the producer also picks the team, answering the 'What?' and the 'Who?' that means the 'How?' is already largely answered. That prize was worth giving up the joy of acting for. It was time to grow up, to use the screen in the way I believed it should be used.

Of course, each art form exists within a system of conventions. It is artificial, a confection. Accepting this artificiality is the condition for entering the world of the artist.

If form is content, what form did I want? To say what exactly? Now my disparate thoughts were connecting and coming into sharp focus. They emerged through struggle, sometimes in spite of an unwillingness to give up previous assumptions but gradually became a conviction, a certainty. One consequence was that I didn't even want to go to the theatre, let alone act in one. In the transition I thought the theatre was rather like cricket, more fun to play than to watch. I would go to even small spaces and wonder why these actors were shouting at me. I was not convinced, just seeing acting acting, watching the wheels going round. Some highly technical actors were Rolls-Royce performers. I admired them. But I didn't believe a word. And to play basically naturalistic pieces on a large shelf at one end of a space, putting actors on a three-sided set and telling them to project, was absurd. Why did they pretend the audience wasn't present?

The only theatre I admired was Joan Littlewood's Theatre Workshop at the other Stratford, in east London. Through the 1960s her company's work was so exuberant, so consciously theatrical, so passionately political it swept me up in its life-embracing enthusiasm: and she discouraged stage make-up! I saw everything they did. She was a big influence on me. The film she directed, *Sparrows Can't Sing*, was beautiful. She believed in ordinary people, saying to me, 'Everyone's a genius.' I loved her. Over the years we planned to do a film together but it never happened. She was mercurial. Though always busy, she would never plan far ahead. I would take a call from her, say on a Thursday, telling me she'd start the following Monday. I tried to explain that the BBC didn't work like that.

I hardly ever go to the theatre now. Not because, as my friends say, they tend to do it at dinner time. I became tired of being bored and walking out in the interval. I realise this is my loss. I once tried opera. I went to Covent Garden and spent the evening suppressing the giggles. I'm blinkered. Once my ideas came into focus and I knew I'd found my future it was to the exclusion of anything else. I concentrated on the furrow I intended to plough. It's been a single-minded life's work learning how. I failed even in that. But my focus closed off any appreciation of other conventions. My loss.

Of course, art should be a great circus with lots of acts, a range of styles and experiments. Let everyone be free to plough their furrow. I just wanted to be left alone to gather like-minded people around me to pursue my vision.

From the day I arrived in Siberia aged five, I studied each human face around me, striving to read the expression and interpret the mood. It felt as though my life depended on my accuracy. I constantly expected rejection. Your parents can't throw you out, it's your home too. But after they died and I'd been taken in by my relatives I could just as easily be banished. Where would I go? I had to anticipate what would be tolerated. When, over the years, I've been asked about various screen drama traditions, I've truthfully said that special effects and fantasy are equally boring. The only interesting landscape is the human face. I'm fascinated by three sets of connections: conflicts within an individual; face-to-face negotiations, that is the personal politics of small groups and the major forces in society which affect everyone. Complex stories are made from the relationship between all three. At least the ones that interest me.

The connections between my response to my childhood predicament and the obsessions of my film life are obvious. I wonder how it could have escaped me.

Thanks to Sydney and others, I not only had the chance to express myself, but I now knew how I wanted to express myself.

Cathy Come Home

*C*athy *was shown on a Wednesday. The following weekend I went home
to Brum to escape the fuss. I was greeted, as usual. No one mentioned
either the film or its impact, which I knew had reached Brum because we'd
shot some scenes there and the local bigwigs were up in arms. It had been on
the front pages for days. I said nothing, staying cool. By Sunday afternoon,
preparing to go back to London, I could stand it no longer so, adopting a
casual manner, I said, 'Suppose you didn't happen to look in on Wednesday,
did you? By any chance?'*

There was a pause. Harold nodded. 'Yes.'

*I waited, deciding in the pause that he would say no more about it. He'd
actually answered my question, after all.*

'We watched it all the way through. Didn't we, Pom?'

She nodded, not taking her eyes off her crocheting.

It was all that was ever said.

In our house that was real recognition.

Jeremy Sandford was married to Nell Dunn. He was a dishevelled
man, his hair untamed by a comb, his scruffy indifference to smart
fashion making him seem lost in the world, unable to cope. In fact,
he was in a long tradition of minor aristocratic eccentrics, oozing
old Etonian charm and good manners, socially confident, seemingly
oblivious to the impression he gave. He was a tenacious investigative
journalist more than a screenwriter, working usually for popular

Sunday newspapers. He and Nell had left Chelsea, crossing the river to settle in Clapham, which they found more congenial. I liked both of them. Nell had shown me a screenplay by him. The BBC had turned it down twice, saying it 'was not a political platform'. I think he must have been reading Jack London, because it had a hopelessly uncommercial title, *The Abyss*. It was a jumbled mess but the subject matter and the story embedded in it was one I couldn't ignore.

A neighbour of Jeremy's had disappeared with her children and Jeremy, his investigative instincts aroused, began to ask questions. No one seemed to know much, but he dug away, revealing a story which eventually turned into *Cathy Come Home*. She had been sent to Newington Lodge, 'a place that God had forgotten', basically a dumping place for homeless women. They waited there in overcrowded squalor, with their children but without their husbands.

At that time there was some discussion of a housing problem and it had been an issue in the General Election but few were aware there were many homeless families. The public knew about tramps, as they were called, but not that homelessness was wider. Ken and I were as ignorant as everyone else. Talking to Jeremy made me determined we should make this film even though it seemed like a hopeless proposition. I could hardly believe it was true and was ashamed.

I insisted on a new title, although it was only finalised later, on the assumption the BBC would not remember the project. The voice-overs and the end captions, which were to cause much of the trouble, were put on towards the end of the editing. Some of the voiceovers were recorded by Jeremy after the shoot. I prevaricated with the management, saying vaguely that Ken would improvise most of the drama; it was just a little piece about a working-class couple starting a family and so on. A 'love story'. In fact, Ken did improvise some of it. For instance, he would get Carol White, playing Cathy, to knock on a door and ask for accommodation. Tony Imi would be filming on a long lens. Then Penny Eyles, who did continuity, would approach the real landlady with a permission form.

Ken was involved with Jeremy in working on the material. They went round the locations, talking through the story. The research was cast iron and needed to be. That was Jeremy's strong suit. He didn't let us down. Many tried to puncture the eventual film, saying that this or that was not so, and all of them failed.

The budget was very tight and it all had to be shot in three weeks. It was a big cast of over a hundred, with locations all over the place, but I knew Ken, with Tony Imi, would cope. It was to be shot handheld, very flexibly. There was no time for formal lighting set-ups. This scramble worked in our favour. It looked like a grabbed documentary. We learned an important lesson: leave things a little rough round the edges. Honing and polishing reduce a screenplay and a film. It's too easy to inadvertently iron the life out of material. The only perfection is in death: everything alive is imperfect and feels unfinished.

We didn't want the audience to dismiss it as 'just a play'. Because of an outdated Equity union agreement, some of the production had to be shot in a studio but that was edited with the location material, as we had done in *Up the Junction*. John Mackenzie was the first assistant director. He pulled it together so brilliantly, with such relentless energy, that I later gave him his first directing gig as a reward.

Ken had wanted Carol White again. She was the only serious candidate for Cathy. Her emotional availability and her quality of entering believably into an imaginary world were central to its success. There were later swipes that a beautiful blonde had been cast just for commercial reasons but I countered by saying you could find young women looking just as good behind the counter in Boots. The children were her own. They all knew Ray Brooks, a nice, relaxed actor, so he played Cathy's partner, Reg. Jane Harris, my assistant, and I would go down to locations, pick actors with Ken and rush back to book them for the next day. Ken shot big ratios of film but Roy Watts helped him make sense of it all in the cutting room, adding some popular music which tugged at the emotions. With Jeremy they laid the factual voiceovers and the deadly captions at the end.

At the time it didn't occur to me to fight Jeremy for more political bite in the show. What we made was a liberal, handwringing piece with no radical solution; a piece which would let everyone who was responsible off the hook. If people were moved they could give to charity. I've regretted that omission ever since. Jeremy was a sweet, liberal man of real compassion but he was not political. I should have fought him harder. I did not have the skill or the self-confidence.

In my defence it would have been a difficult task. The political class was responsible for its callousness towards the homeless, the media for its indifference and the general public for not insisting something was done about it. It was hard to show all of that. The individual housing officers may or may not have been sympathetic but they hadn't caused and couldn't solve the problem. But the homeless only confront the frontline officials so they were the ones we met in *Cathy*. Popular drama tends to be white hats and black hats in confrontation. It is a weakness difficult to overcome.

Cathy was transmitted in November 1966. I was delighted that when it was shown straight after the news it didn't look like some 'luvvie drama'. It looked as though it had been shot by a news camera, that this stuff was actually happening to these people (though audiences were more naive then, so that was easier to achieve than it would be now). Ken was feeling more sure-footed and the penny was dropping with the crew. Tony Imi, especially, loved the challenge, having previously trodden water on formulaic drama series.

I'd had to argue with Sydney about the Brechtian factual voice-overs and – especially – over the captions. These served as factual counterpoints to the fictional events on the screen, giving housing statistics to show how inadequate policy had been. For all his emotional volatility, he was tolerant and allowed me to resist him. The following day the papers were full of it, the politicians and local government officials were up in arms and the noise was deafening.

Neither Ken nor I anticipated the reaction. I've never understood audiences. How was it that twelve million decided to watch this film? I could understand a big audience for the repeat. By then everyone knew about it.

The fuss didn't fade. It increased. I was thrown. It seemed that Kenneth Adam, who was Director of Television at the BBC, was now in charge, putting on showings for MPs (who never watch TV, preferring to be on it). Jeremy, Ken and I were asked to have tea with the Minister of Housing and Local Government, Anthony Greenwood. So off we went down to Whitehall and were shown up to this mammoth office where the Minister and a civil servant were waiting. It was all very English. Tea was served in good china with biscuits and Greenwood was extravagant in his praise of the film. He struck me as a decent, concerned man. He was actually on the Left of the Party, which would make him a dangerous revolutionary now. But in the end, he was an ineffectual social liberal. He looked at us, having wrung his hands with distress at the plight of the homeless, and said, 'But what can one do?'

I said, 'Build more houses.'

He and his civil servant looked at each other and smiled in a hopeless gesture. 'Oh, if only it were that simple,' seemed to be the subtext. I didn't see why it wasn't.

We then found ourselves back on the street in Whitehall.

Sydney was delighted by the ratings and not at all put out by the fuss. This was him delivering what Hugh Greene had requested. But he too was surprised by the extent of the fallout and its apparent refusal to fade. As an actor I'd occasionally been in the public eye and recognised in the street but nothing like this. At the height of it, Sydney called me into his office. I turned up expecting a bollocking, assuming I'd done something wrong but not knowing what it was. Shades of my father. Sydney suggested we went down to the 'living room'. We settled and I braced myself. I was surprised to be offered some fatherly advice.

'OK, Tony. This is quite a rollercoaster, eh? Just enjoy it. They don't come along every week. But enjoy it quietly. If you wanna survive doing this stuff, get your head down. Get out of range. The press wanna build you up and then shoot you down. The more of a public personality you become, the more difficult it's gonna be for me to protect you. Do you want a short, glamorous life in the lime-light or a long, successful one, out of vision? Uh? Hell, let Jeremy and Ken do the publicity and become famous. You're a producer, operating inside the Corporation. Do it quietly.'

Wise man. Although over the next few years I did succumb to the occasional interview request, I mainly tucked myself away and concentrated on the work, valuing anonymity. In fact, it suited my temperament.

As soon as Jeremy had begun to open my eyes about homelessness the issue resonated with me. I'd lost my home as a boy, suddenly, and had spent my childhood fearing it would happen again. The horrors of being homeless had been exaggerated by a youthful imagination fuelled by Dickens, whose novels I had devoured. If I put a foot wrong, would I be sent to an orphanage? Would it be like those institutions in Victorian times? Would Aunty Pom's temper actually snap one day? The predicament of Cathy's children at the end of the film had been only too real to me in my infant fantasy.

Silly, really, looking back. But for me at that time, only too real.

Fact vs Fiction

[Viewers] have a right to know whether what they are being offered is real or invented.

Grace Wyndham Goldie (Head of Current Affairs Group, BBC TV)

The most accomplished fiction on the BBC is the Nine O'Clock News.

Mary Whitehouse, who thought the role of the BBC was to 'encourage and sustain faith in God and bring Him to the hearts of our family and national life', was a propagandist for the right-wing Oxford Group and the Moral Re-armament movement. She and I occupied opposing political territory so it was inevitable we would clash over and over again.

One evening at the Roundhouse arts venue in north London's Chalk Farm I debated with her on live TV. In person she was down to earth, with an attractive, no-nonsense, flat Midlands voice. Her pleasant but steely manner revealed the school teacher she had been. She was highly intelligent, a fine debater that no one could safely underestimate and she had courage, no doubt reinforced by her devout convictions. I admired her: she showed commitment to her principles. Although cruelly caricatured on the Left, she represented a sizeable group.

As the sixties revealed the scale of accelerating social change, there were many who deplored the relaxing of conventions, of deference, of sexual restraint. Even though only a minority thought it presaged political revolution, many believed that institutions like the BBC should not encourage these rebels with ideas above their station. They were ungodly and unBritish. Her National Viewers' and Listeners' Association lobby was an expression of genuine feeling.

This suburban housewife went into battle against a branch of the establishment that she felt had lost its nerve just as another branch of the same establishment was trying to cut my legs off. While she made a lot of noise she wasn't my main problem.

The bigger threat came from inside the BBC hierarchy, led by the formidable Grace Wyndham Goldie, the head of Current Affairs Group. She was an influential opponent. A determined and talented woman who had reached seniority in the BBC, she had around her a school of accomplished young turks, including future Director General Alasdair Milne, Donald Baverstock, Michael Peacock and Huw Wheldon. She was an innovator in general election coverage and modernised Talks and Current Affairs.

But she had what I thought was a blind spot. It began with her reaction to *Cathy*. She thought the film an 'early example of a new and dangerous trend in television drama'. She claimed it blurred the distinction between fact and fiction, saying viewers had a right to know whether what they were being offered was real or invented. For her it was a matter of principle so I knew that if I lost the argument with her, or lost the internal battle, I would be censored from the screen. There was no chance I would politely accept her chastisement and go back to producing what she thought of as acceptable drama. I knew I had begun another battle for survival – just when I thought I was safe.

Goldie's case rested on assumptions which were riddled with flaws but it was so doctrinally important to her and to the BBC that she could not dare to see them. She maintained that news and current affairs and what she revealingly called 'factual documentaries' were all 'an accurate reflection of the real world'. She could not accept, for instance, that her first priority was to hold the ring between the party in government and the party waiting to be in government.

The first duty of the BBC, like any organisation, was to ensure its survival. Parliament held the purse strings. Ever since Reith did a deal with Conservative Prime Minister Stanley Baldwin during the 1926 General Strike, the BBC, with typically English hypocrisy, had projected the impression of independence but quietly bowed to the reality of dependence. As Baldwin realised, if the public was under the impression that the BBC was independent, the government would benefit.

Further, Goldie failed to acknowledge that the news was not *the* news, it was merely *a* news. I – probably unwisely – goaded management at the time by claiming that the most accomplished fiction on the BBC was the *Nine O'Clock News*. To create the news, reporters retrieve facts from some sources and not others; editors choose from all the material on offer and put their unconscious spin on these facts to give them meaning; news teams are influenced, some believe too much, by the leads given in the national press and include some items for entertainment reasons, ratings being important, and others because they include good location shots. They are unconsciously affected by political lobbying groups. This influence is never acknowledged.

In the words of David Broder, then a journalist on the *Washington Post*, news is: 'A partial, hasty, incomplete, inevitably flawed and inaccurate rendering of some of the things we have heard about in the last twenty-four hours – distorted, despite our best efforts to eliminate gross bias . . .'

The 'news' is invented, skilfully created, selected from raw factual material and invested with a particular meaning according to the editors' prejudices and the political needs of the organisation.

All this is congruent with the observation that the news staff are on the whole capable people with no conscious bias, who try to achieve what they think is 'balance', whatever that may be, and who genuinely believe they are fully informing the public. What Goldie and others refused to accept was that the BBC's so-called factual output, despite its noble efforts to be accurate, was created not by those magically above the fray but by people with prejudices and deep beliefs. How could it be otherwise?

First, the BBC must go with the grain of the public's expectations or at least with those sections of the public who are articulate and believe the BBC belongs to them. The BBC tried to occupy what it thought was the centre ground. It had to occupy some territory or it wouldn't exist. What it thought was unbiased was in fact the ground occupied by those respectable, educated people, rather like the news staff themselves, who assumed the BBC would reflect their beliefs: reverence for the monarchy ('The Queen has a heavy cold' as a lead story on the main news); parliamentary democracy; patriotism; support for our armed forces (especially if in action abroad). This list extends. The point isn't whether one agrees with any of the items on the list. It's that, taken together, they reveal a particular world view which forms the basis, usually unconscious, for judging what is news and how that news should be interpreted.

This is inevitable.

I had opinions that differed from this world view.

Goldie not only wanted my version of events to be censored, she wanted everyone to believe that hers was true, factual, and balanced, while mine was offensive propaganda that would undermine the BBC. When challenged, neither she nor any of her apparatchiks would define these tricky words. But News and Current Affairs knew that fact was different from fiction, apparently, and that only they should be allowed to dispense fact.

Disputes about impartiality have scarred the BBC from its early days. Reith forced the resignation of Hilda Matheson, perhaps the most creative programme innovator in the BBC's history. She invented and ran the talks department. She started *The Week in Westminster* and introduced talks on a range of subjects. Reith thought her views were subversive, atheistic and anarchistic. She was too left-wing for his friends in The Athenaeum Club, who thought he was being run 'by a gang of reds'.

The fact that he was a crypto Fascist and an enthusiastic admirer of Mussolini clearly had nothing to do with it.

As Matheson said, 'Impartiality depends on your starting position.'

Her programme offering recipes was forbidden from mentioning fruit wines. Matheson, a daughter of the manse, was not allowed by Reith, a son of the manse, to mention alcohol.

I asked those who would engage with me what they thought of current affairs just a few years earlier when politicians were not interviewed but were politely asked if they would like to say a few words to the nation. And what did they think BBC News would have looked like in the 1860s or the 1760s? Would they have spoken favourably about the economic benefits of West Indian slavery? Fashions change, opinions shift and what seems like a fact to some is known to be a lie to others.

In 1969 I watched the documentary *The Royal Family*, an unctuous eulogy which deeply offended republicans like me. It was a public relations film for the monarchy, made not by those above the fray but by subjects on their knees. Goldie's disciples did not denounce it as fictional, politically partisan or one-sided. It was praised inside and outside the BBC. What the Palace thought remained secret but it was priceless propaganda. Not even Goebbels could have served his master more effectively.

As I write this, the BBC today needs to position itself near the political centre. After the war this was a Butskellist Keynesian perspective. There was painful confusion in the eighties as the Corporation adjusted to Thatcher's neoliberal U-turn. Now it ties itself up again, trying to fight for room to breathe while obeying Treasury dictats. It is an ideological chameleon, its news always trying to reflect where it existentially needs to be.

The test of its political independence is in its response to events, in the wider society as well as in Westminster, not in the empty jousting of daily politics.

The BBC has backed every British foreign adventure in my lifetime, being especially patriotic when British boots are on the ground and never seriously challenging whether they should be there in the first place (the only exception was Suez, which Labour opposed). It was derelict over the invasion of Iraq, night after night regurgitating what many thought were Blairite lies as if it was a government media outlet. The BBC only began asking questions long after the event, with an early-morning report from Gilligan. That led to the pusillanimous and unnecessary resignation of the Chairman and the Director General. They folded ignominiously after the report from the Blair-appointed lawyer Hutton, a proven safe pair of hands. Of course the verdict was that the BBC's checking of news stories was 'defective'.

If Gilligan was right, that he was quoting what his source had told him, then the BBC should have stood by it. If wrong, then the BBC ought to have apologised.

No one should have resigned.

So much for the BBC's vaunted independence. This is not to take sides over the Iraq adventure, just to expose the sycophancy and fear at the heart of the BBC.

It is just not true, as Goldie disingenuously claimed, that her output was 'an accurate reflection of the real world'. It was a con trick on the public, which the BBC continues to play. Its reluctance to ask questions about Jimmy Savile and its refusal to stand by those journalists on its own staff who wanted to expose him as a predatory sex offender have been a recent and shameful example of its opportunism.

Goldie had retired in 1965, before *Cathy Come Home* was shown. She attacked it in the press. She was willing to allow me to continue producing drama, which was generous of her, considering that there was already a head of drama paid to make those decisions. But it seemed I should confine myself to drama which was not politically contentious, that is, that was either 'entertainment' or 'art'. I assumed that she meant entertainment for the masses and art in the form of received culture, preferably from the safe distance of another century. She did not appreciate that all drama is political and drama claiming to be unpolitical is right-wing, establishment drama.

She was unable to appreciate that I kept faith with the public. On our films a writer and actors were prominently credited, clearly showing that we had made up the programme, that it was fiction.

Her objection to the form, the style, was a cynical diversion. Most drama, stage or screen, attempts to draw the audience into the world of the drama and the predicament of the characters, encouraging it to cast off awareness of the technique, the form. This audience involvement is called 'the willing suspension of disbelief'. An exception may be Brecht's alienation effect. I doubt she would have accepted his politics.

We enter into a conscious conspiracy with the audience. Most viewers willingly giving themselves up to it. I have always been open about the process. We spend time looking at an aspect of the world, we research it and then we make up a story, we dramatise what we've discovered. We say, this is how it looks to us. That is rather what news and current affairs and documentaries do, too.

The real objection, of course, was political. I recruited colleagues, especially writers, who were from the working class and were socialists. We offered their perspective on human experience. Goldie wanted to censor the content, not the form. It was acceptable to insert Ministry of Agriculture propaganda into *The Archers* but not for us to tug people's hearts about the scandal of the homeless or later be sympathetic to men on strike. We were respectfully exploring the lives of working people from a socialist perspective: that was the real but, of course, unacknowledged problem.

Just as Mary Whitehouse didn't object to the sexual extra-marital adventures of the aristocracy in costume dramas, so Goldie singled us out for our political engagement with the real world. The problem wasn't that the viewer might believe. The problem was what the viewer might believe. But it was complicated for her and her allies. The BBC wasn't a monolith. The sixth-floor management was split, as far as I understood it. Sydney no doubt thought I was a pain in the ass but I appealed to a naughty, rebellious streak in him. Plus, in terms of audience figures and media clout, I was delivering the goods. No doubt they found that Sydney was no pushover. I'm sure he defended Drama Group's territory and his dominion over it.

I was creating what some thought should be made, even if others didn't like it.

Yet the battles continued, film after film. Their cause descended from a principled objection over the potential for confusing 'fact' and 'fiction' to one of political calculation. Some senior management grew tired of defending the BBC, particularly from yet more complaints by MPs.

My problem was that I was fighting phantoms. The BBC was complex. It communicated in code. I knew my mission was dangerous, that to survive I had to disguise what I was planning and be ultra-sensitive to danger. I'd been in this predicament before, although it's an open question whether I projected my experience of my adopted home on to the BBC or was repeating that experience.

Certainly, I sometimes assumed opposition that wasn't there and sometimes I underestimated the dangers. It was difficult to get a purchase on reality in that subtle world of nods and winks, where what was said always had another meaning. The shadow might turn out at any moment to be a deadly enemy or merely my own paranoia. Was I paranoid? I don't think so but 'just because you're paranoid doesn't mean they're not after you', as Yossarian said in *Catch-22*. I knew that if I overestimated the danger, I would just cause myself aggravation but if I underestimated it – and overreached – it would be the end.

So I worked in secret, never telling management what I intended to produce, or I lied about it. At that time, there was no suffocating management supervision of every move. Producers were left to do their jobs. If they had a problem, they were trusted to refer upwards. I just never thought, on the whole, that I had a problem. In fact, problems only emerged when I referred upwards! The sound chaps of the BBC were expected to know how to behave. I was never 'sound'. I was pushing on an open door, but I didn't know how far I could push. I wanted to take it to the absolute limit, but not to the point of self-destruction.

Also, few in drama actually understood film so when I said, with a straight face, 'Yes, of course, I'd love you to see it but at the moment all the sound is broken down for the mix,' or 'No problem, but at the moment it's all in pieces for the neg cut,' they would nod, not wishing to appear ignorant. It bought me time. I would try to show a film only after the deadline for inclusion in the *Radio Times*, so if they wanted to ban it, the decision would be very public.

Occasionally, none of this was strictly necessary. Some in management hadn't forgotten they were once programme makers themselves. They revered and wanted to defend creative freedom and had been innovators before they went to the sixth floor. They were on my side and were happy to turn a blind eye, to give me room, perhaps to hang myself. Against those in senior management who wanted to get rid of me, there were others who were rooting for me, either on the principle of creative freedom or because I brought excitement and something different to the schedule, something modern and relevant. These allies were the modernisers, who knew that the BBC must escape the embrace of the corseted establishment. We were part of a culture shift which affected TV genres, as it had already affected theatre, film, painting and the novel.

My focus also attracted external hostility, from Parliament, the right-wing press and various institutions of the state because I increasingly devoted myself to showing working-class experience through a working-class lens. They didn't object to the sympathy and dignity in the portrait, however unusual that was, but to the militant socialist perspective.

Sydney stood firm. After a while he adopted me. I would go to his house on Saturdays and be warmly welcomed by his wife, hang out with him and learn about his early life in Canada in the thirties, when it was natural for any young person to be on the Left. I think I reminded him of himself when young. We had endless rows but I loved him and appreciated his patronage. He, and others in BBC management over the years, protected me. I couldn't have done it on my own.

Only now, thinking about it long after, do I realise that he was an indulgent father figure. He gave me room, tried to keep me from self-harm and, although capable of rage himself, allowed me to rage back without fear. I've had other father substitutes. I suppose I was unconsciously looking for them, needing them. Sydney was one. He guided me safely through.

The old accusations against all political activists applied to me. Was my work an attempt to reclaim a fantasy, infantile paradise? Was it less painful to change the world than to change myself? Was my antagonism towards authority a lack of maturity, tolerated in an adolescent but tiresome in an adult?

These accusations needed – and need – to be considered, but they are separate from ideas of socialism and democracy. These have their own momentum, their own justification, and should be debated on their merits.

I had been given about six hours of screen time. Set that against the hundreds of hours of drama and the thousands of hours of news and current affairs, it's clear some of my enemies were overreacting. What were they afraid of? But the forces of reaction in the BBC wanted to extinguish me. It went on right through the sixties and the seventies.

The few documents that have been released to me reveal disagreements about employing me at all. There are memos from Chris Morahan and Shaun Sutton, the drama heads, defending me and demanding my contract be renewed; also a memo from Alasdair Milne when he was head of TV, saying that 'Garnett is one of the most inventive producers in the business and, in that sense, enormously valuable to us'. But there are also memos questioning the wisdom of using me, demanding specific guarantees from me on the phoney fact/fiction question and correspondence between the Director General, Charles Curran and senior personnel managers, clearly nervous about having me in the BBC.

The BBC's editorial rights are clearly stated in all its standard contracts and it has the power to terminate anyone's employment. Despite this, Curran wanted to insist on extra, specific clauses on these matters in my contract. This, from one personnel officer to another: 'As you know the engagement of Tony Garnett is a subject which has been of great interest to the D G and C. Pers. Tel. has advised that before we seek DG's approval to another contract for Garnett we should submit a report on the way he has carried out his duties during his current contract.'

Eventually my clearance always came. One wonders how DG Curran could spend all this time arguing about a contract for a producer of four dramas a year. He clearly had time on his hands. Perhaps it's not a full-time job.

The Big Flame

Two years gone by but still they never
Ever cross a picket line
With their wives and children they stand together
Never cross a picket line
You must never cross a picket line

Billy Bragg, 'Never Cross a Picket Line', 1998

In the late sixties I moved to a small office at the top of the east tower, removed from the main TV Centre and as far from all management as possible. I was hoping that if they never saw me they would forget about me. I had Jane Harris, who became my long-term assistant and comrade, and an empty slate. Thanks to Sydney Newman and, possibly, others unknown to me, I was still in business.

Jim Allen had been knocking on the BBC's door for a while. No one seemed interested. He was just what I was looking for. A Marxist autodidact and trade union activist who'd been a sheet metal worker, merchant seaman, building worker, docker, miner and teacher. He had rejected the Labour Party and seen through the Stalinism of the Communist Party. Raised in the slums of Manchester, he now lived on the outskirts of the city. After reading Jack London he wanted to be a writer.

With short, bandy legs – walking with a roll as though still on board ship – he entered my office warily. It was clearly enemy territory. He had a combative attitude. Diplomacy and the niceties of conversation were clearly difficult. We skirmished for more than an hour. He told me later, when I had won his confidence, that this was potentially a big prize and he'd been determined to win a gig for a single film. He'd thought that in front of a TV producer at the BBC he should hide his politics. It took him a while to believe that his politics was the reason I was seeing him.

He was already working on *Coronation Street*. I told him he had to choose: if he wanted to be a serious writer, he must give up the *Street*. He did so immediately. That took courage. It paid well and Jim was married with a couple of kids still on the floor.

We hit it off and got to work.

After listening to various anecdotes I decided on *The Lump*. It was set on a building site and featured a Marxist activist who fought to defend workers denied protection of the law or even of a trade union. If injured, they were independent contractors and left to rot. They were subject to a blacklist, a practice which, facing exposure, the employers have only recently apologised for. The activist fights and dies in the mud, but not before opening the eyes of a student working his vacation. It was simple in construction and crude in execution. Jim was only beginning to flex his muscles as a screen-writer, but it had direct power. Jack Gold directed, showing great promise in his first fiction film.

Sydney saw the fine cut. He teased me, saying how old-fashioned it was, reminding him of the political films in the thirties made in America under Roosevelt's New Deal. But he smiled and didn't ask for changes.

During the shoot, Jim and I planned the next film. I was interested in the docks. All docks are containerised now but then it was conten-tious. Dockers welcomed the idea of cranes lifting cargo in containers, relieving them of the dangerous and filthy business of personally unloading stuff. It was not the technology itself, but the disruption that was in dispute. Who would benefit from this technological advance? What about the consequent unemployment? The history of the dockers was a brutal one: waiting each morning at the gate hoping to be picked for a day's work and always in danger of injury.

We decided to set it in the Liverpool docks. The starting point would be a recent strike, but instead of the action staying close to actual events, we wanted the dockers to stay on the dock and declare a soviet. In the end, of course, they would be betrayed, the army breaking them up and the leaders sent to prison. It would end with news of sit-ins throughout the country in factory after factory.

Jim and I saw this as an inspiration to action as well as a warning against syndicalism.

So that I could learn more, Jim took me to the 'Pool to meet Peter Kerrigan, a docker and a militant, and other comrades. We sat in Peter's tiny flat near the Canada dock and he educated me about the strike. He was an open, warm-hearted, brave Irish scouser, honest and loyal, and I became very fond of him. He ended up being in many more films that either Ken or I worked on.

After I had pushed him harder about inter-union strife and the politics behind the dispute, which was to be the factual basis of our film, he said I would have to talk to Gerry Healy. I asked who he was and he gave me a number in Clapham, which I called on my return to London.

I met Healy in a pub in Belsize Park in north London. He drank Coke and was accompanied by a young woman called Aileen, who I took to be his driver. He talked with useful authority, helping me fill in gaps. His political analysis was convincing and eloquent. I thanked him and got on with the film, not realising that this meeting would have profound consequences for many of my friends in future years.

I asked Ken to direct Jim's resulting play, *The Big Flame*, crewed up and went to Liverpool. It was delicate because unless we could shoot on the docks there would be no film. That meant obtaining permission from the Mersey Docks and Harbour Board. They were not natural supporters of the workers' control of industry. We had a ticklish, tense relationship. At any time permission could be withdrawn and we would have no film. The visual background of the docks was vital to us. I sweet-talked them into giving us full co-operation. But then during pre-production, while I was dealing with a problem in London, I was phoned with the news that the film had been called off. Permission to shoot on dock premises had been withdrawn.

Someone had let a screenplay get into the hands of the owners. I was furious and had my suspicions, but an inquest would be redundant. I went straight back to the 'Pool to try to deal with the crisis.

I booked the most expensive restaurant in Liverpool and invited the press and public relations people from the Harbour Board to lunch. The prices on the menu were high enough to make me gasp and I knew it would be a tough call to chalk this up to expenses, although by this point concerns about the future of our film had destroyed my appetite. Abandoning at this late stage would also be expensive. The BBC would be justified in demanding an inquiry. The screenplay, which no one at TV Centre had seen, would be revealed. Everything would unravel. This worried me far more than the impossibility of getting the restaurant bill through accounts, which was a non-starter. I knew I'd have to take the hit personally.

There were five of us. They ordered steak and lobster and truffles. Bottles of wine were consumed. I attempted an insouciant stance, as though this was a routine event, charming them with amusing show-business anecdotes, some of them indiscreet, about famous actors. Mostly these were invented because I didn't know much about any stars. The board members wanted scandal so I invented the most shocking tales. A good time was being had by all, except me.

Over brandies they seemed very relaxed and full of bonhomie. I asked them if there was a problem with filming. I listened to their complaints with mock surprise and laughed, although it was probably a strained laugh. 'Oh, that rubbish was rejected months ago. Do you gentlemen really think the BBC would allow such Marxist drivel on the screen? If so, you don't know them down in London. Have you ever seen stuff like that on the BBC? No. The film's as I said it was. It's a love story, with your impressive docks as the visual background, between a Catholic and a Protestant. Both families go ape-shit but the kids are in love. That's the conflict. In a way, it's one of the oldest stories in the book. You know, a modern *Romeo and Juliet*. It'll be mainly improvised using some local lads in small parts. A strike and a bunch of commies? Sure. If you want to get me the sack.'

I grinned at them. About 3.30 p.m. we parted with much drunken good feeling. I was a little mellow myself. I asked for the bill and sobered up. I paid, thinking I'd sooner do a week's washing-up there instead.

The film was back on. I emphasised to everyone we had to stick to our cover story.

Ken, as usual, conjured a feeling not of actors but of real people, of dockers in a life-and-death struggle: helped by the fact that real dockers were playing themselves. Their wit was legendary. In fact, famous comedians would hang out in their pubs, picking up material. Ken and I were taken with their nicknames: the 'ailing crab' was so-called because he was constantly off work, saying one of his nippers was ill. A stevedore was called 'the vicar' because he would look down into a hold shouting the admonitory, 'Eh, men, eh, men!' They called the boss 'the sheriff' because he's always asking, 'Where's the hold up, lads?' Or 'the surgeon': 'Cut that out, boys, cut it out.' Or the docker they call 'the lazy solicitor' because he's always sitting on the case. The cast, also including experienced actors such as Norman Rossington and Godfrey Quigley, were not only funny but moving and credible.

We were sensitive to accusations that lefties such as us tended to caricature everyone who was not working class. There was a scene towards the end which involved army officers so Ken was careful to cast real army officers from the Territorials. It made no difference. We were still accused of caricaturing posh people for our own political ends. The press did not realise – or didn't care – that the caricatures were authentic.

The film grew in power after a confusing start, but there were serious faults. The first act got bogged down in meetings, the minutiae of inter-union disputes and details of the Devlin Report which was on the future of the industry. I failed to deal with these problems. At that time I didn't have the skill to dramatise knotty exposition and Jim was learning his trade: it was the blind leading the blind. Years later I learned to apply the golden rule of Hollywood narrative cinema, the 'CIA principle': only give information on a need-to-know basis. Get on with the story and offer exposition only when absolutely necessary.

But Jim was rooted in the experience of his characters and the piece had raw energy. What I knew had largely been learned from books. I was at a remove, which was why I needed to find writers like Jim. I'd sailed into the professional, middle-class world of educated London media people. I'd disqualified myself. His was the authentic voice, his material was from the horse's mouth.

The showing of the film was twice postponed. I fought for it but began to wonder if it would be buried. There were grave misgivings at TV Centre. When it was finally broadcast in early 1969 the reaction was as I expected but the vitriol was amusing. My old adversary, Mary Whitehouse, excelled herself by writing to the Prime Minister, Harold Wilson, and opposition leader Edward Heath, urging a review of the BBC's charter, saying that the film was 'a blueprint for the communist takeover of the docks'. If only . . .

It certainly presaged future industrial disputes, as Heath discovered to his cost in the seventies. The *Daily Mail* fumed about this 'Marxist play presented as a sermon'. Various trade union leaders complained, including Tom Jackson, the postal workers' leader, who wrote to the chairman of the BBC governors. Union bureaucrats never like their sellouts being exposed. I wondered what my uncle John, the Walsall post office union officer, would have thought of that. Being a cautious Labour Party man, he would probably have sided with Jackson.

The cineastes at the BFI's *Screen Magazine* said it was impossible for a 'classic realist text' to offer any perspective for struggle due to its inability to investigate contradiction: to be truly subversive a film needed to be radical in form as well as content. I argued that they did not know my uncle Fred, the milkman, if they thought I could get his attention with any other form than the one I had chosen to use for the National Theatre of the Air. I did not waste my energy arguing with them, letting them witter on in their unreadable, jargon-filled journal.

The fallout from *The Big Flame* was serious. Our political views were clearly beyond the pale and many in BBC senior management thought it time to rein me in. I just wasn't worth the trouble. I found it even more difficult to slip political films through. Life was getting tougher and would require even more guile. It was nerve-wracking because I couldn't read the signs, which were always in code.

Mind Games

'The experience and behaviour that gets labelled schizophrenia is a special strategy that a person invents in order to live in an unliveable situation.'

R. D. Laing

'Insanity – a perfectly rational adjustment to an insane world.'

Attributed to R. D. Laing

My friendship with writer David Mercer remained strong, although his drinking tried my patience. His relationship with Dilys had ended. I had introduced him to my actor friend Kika Markham and they lived together for a while.

He was a mess when drunk. Late one night he called me and said he'd been diagnosed with cancer. I dashed over to comfort him but should have been more sceptical when I saw the almost-empty vodka bottle. He told me it was cancer of the testicles. I sat with him until nearly dawn, when he fell sleep. I went bleary-eyed to TV Centre to start my day's work and called him late morning. He was now sober, if very hungover. He professed no knowledge of cancer, of the testicles or anywhere. He had made it all up and then forgotten about it.

But he was one of the few people I knew at the time who would discuss Marx, Freud, Sartre and others. We were both familiar with the anthropologist Gregory Bateson. His double bind idea, of injunctions or emotional messages that contradict one another, had interested me, particularly its implications in mental illness. I wondered if Topsy had been struggling in double binds. I invented different possibilities and beat myself up, thinking of my guilty role in some of them. These speculations ended in frustration, of course. Her mystery was impenetrable.

Everyone seemed to be reading R. D. Laing, whose writing was creating interest way beyond the psychiatry world. It was the first step towards him becoming an international celebrity. As his fame spread it turned him into an instantly recognisable figure. He became a rock star.

David had a history of depression and had spent some time on the couch. He was avoiding real emotional engagement with analysis, like me. But we knew a lot about it in theory.

Topsy continued to drift along, only half alive, doing little, in a permanent slow motion regression. After a while I lost touch with her, particularly after she moved down to Cornwall. I saw her family, of course, because I visited often to be with little Will, who was growing into a fine boy. They were just as upset about Topsy and just as helpless. I was not only furious, with myself and with the medics, for not being able to help, I was intensely curious about treatments for the mentally ill. So I asked David to write a screenplay.

First, I had to make a deal with Peggy Ramsay, David Mercer's legendary agent. She was formidable and snobbish about television. Indeed, she was sniffy about the cinema, being an old-fashioned theatre person, representing Alan Ayckbourn, Joe Orton, J. B. Priestley and Robert Bolt. We met in her office in Goodwins Court, Covent Garden, or rather she held court there and I made my submission. She heard it with grace, although I knew as I delivered my pitch that I could be thrown out on to the street at any moment. She was not so much an agent selling the services of her client as a parent deciding if I was worthy of the privilege of playing with him. Even her clients were in awe of her.

After a tricky few minutes enduring her imperious interrogation, I began to win her over. I think she was curious about this new phenomenon, an attempt to make serious films for that coarse medium of the people, television, although she raised her eyebrows when I talked about the National Theatre of the Air. She began to trust me. When she finally accepted me I could do no wrong in her eyes. But it was a sticky audition.

R. D. Laing was formidable in other ways. He had that analyst's trick of saying little except, 'Uh-huh,' poker-faced, listening and giving the impression his X-ray eyes saw my darkest secrets. But when I got to know him and I saw behind the professional persona, I enjoyed the wit and the culture of the man.

I invited him for lunch and booked the Braganza, a fish restaurant in Soho. He turned up with Utta, his German lover. She said little but they seemed close. It looked like a new love affair. It was a convivial lunch and the wine did its work. I explained my intentions and he agreed to be the main technical adviser on the film.

Laing came from Glasgow, which could be why he outdrank David with casual ease. An evening with them, ostensibly picking Ronnie's considerable brain for our film, would carry on into the small hours with bottle after bottle of spirits emptying by the hour. I'd watched some of my uncles drink, but they could only afford Ansell's mild. Here were two alcoholics drinking like the professionals they were. I've always been an amateur so after a couple I bailed out and observed.

As David demolished a bottle of spirits his speech became blurred and soon degenerated into pompous nonsense. But Ronnie's eloquent, insightful sentences kept rolling out, seemingly unaffected, indeed lubricated, by the booze; each had a subject, verb and predicate, carrying many complicated subsidiary clauses, and I would wait for it to crash. But every time he would land it smoothly and perfectly on a full stop, the meaning intact and the style elegant to the end. The alcohol's only effect was a slower delivery.

Later I would visit him in Kingsley Hall, in east London, which he occupied and used as a residential hospital. It was, of course a famous location with memories of many great figures on the Left.

It had been a centre for suffragettes and for helping the poor of the East End of London. In the 1926 General Strike it was a shelter and soup kitchen. It was rebuilt and expanded. Gandhi stayed there, spurning a hotel, and crowds from all over the East End turned up to greet him. Some men from the Jarrow March were given shelter there. My visits felt like pilgrimages to a sacred place.

As I walked in Ronnie would wave his arm and point me to the dining table where he was having dinner with Jutta and a variety of people seeking haven from various difficulties in the outside world, including the attentions of the psychiatric profession. Emotionally unhappy people could just be, unmolested by invasive treatments, and take the time to recover. There they were allowed to express their pain.

We saw Dr Aaron Esterson in his Hampstead rooms. He was a quietly spoken, undemonstrative psychiatrist, who listened so sympathetically you wanted to tell him everything. He talked to us about his work with whole families. This formed the basis of our film.

We also spent a day with Dr David Cooper, a sweaty intellectual, intense and cerebral, lacking the calm of Laing or Esterson. He had started and ran an experimental ward, Villa 21 in a traditional mental hospital, Shenley in Hertfordshire, but in a separate space. It became a sanctuary, where people were allowed to work through their difficulties without fear of the crude interventions used by orthodox psychiatry. Villa 21 became the basis for another element in the film.

We continued to talk with Ronnie Laing, who was generous with his time.

The subject interested David and in the end we had a powerful screenplay.

In Two Minds, transmitted in 1967, is the story of a young woman who suffers from the diagnosis of schizophrenia. Although inspired by Topsy, who David had known well, it wasn't intended to be her story. The starting point actually came from Julie, a case in Ronnie's 1960 book, *The Divided Self*.

I regretted later that it might be seen as scapegoating the mother. That was not its intention and neither had it been the intention of the original research. It was not any part of the thrust of Laing's thinking. Aaron Esterson had explicitly told us that his and Laing's only aim was to tease out the dynamics within the family structure. He had spent more time interviewing mothers because in those days they usually didn't work outside the home and had more time to attend meetings with him. It would be a caricature of their collective work to take the crude position of 'blaming the mother'. I also worried that Topsy's mother would feel hurt. The film meant to suggest that the whole family dynamic was worth studying. It was never a question of ascribing blame. It was my revenge on the psychiatric establishment and its inhuman use of cruel treatments. I wanted to show the wider audience what was being done on a daily basis, in detail, and to show that there were alternative approaches to the mystery of madness.

I first thought of Roy Battersby to direct it, but he was stuck making science programmes and I couldn't winkle him out from under his blustering boss at the BBC, Aubrey Singer. Other directors were possible, but in the end I asked Ken Loach, partly because he and I shared a shorthand and partly because, even though it was not a subject he had ever shown any interest in, I knew his casting would be credible and he would push the material emotionally. He cast two seriously talented, underrated actors, Anna Cropper in the lead and Christine Hargreaves as her sister. Both were unpretentious, non-luvvy, brilliant people.

But I had trouble with David, who was proprietorial over every word. I tried to explain the technique, that we felt it was important to allow some improvisation and surprise actors from take to take, that otherwise actors will tend to hide behind the lines and not be in the moment. The chances are that the take finally chosen will be the writer's line. After that failed, I just kept him away from Ken, telling him he didn't write in iambic pentameters, so grow up. He sulked at this affront to his authorial authority but after a while sniffily accepted the reality. Why, I wondered, do individuals think they are the 'authors' of a film, when they know it is a social achievement? Ego, I supposed. I had no time for egos.

Ken, who had hardly glanced at the books I had pushed on him or even wished to engage with me in discussion about these ideas, predictably was pitch perfect, digging out heart-wrenching perform-ances, especially from Anna. He sensed where the emotional truth was and had the skill and ruthlessness to tease it out.

It didn't ease my pain, of course. But I was sure we were doing a service in illustrating that ECTs and crude pharmacological interven-tion were not the only options. I was proud to present an alternative approach and give it room to breathe before a large audience. I did it for Topsy, for her lost life, for the future we didn't have together. Irrational, of course, because the psychiatrists hadn't made her ill. But – with no doubt the best of intentions – they had abused her.

It didn't make me feel any better. I was still on the run from myself.

Sydney, however, did not approve. I showed it in a cutting room at the bottom of the east tower. The basis of his objection was that the film gave people no hope and that was irresponsible with a sub-ject which caused such distress. The film upset him and a discussion wound itself up into a row. It continued all the way to his office on the fifth floor of TV Centre. Along corridors, up staircases, past offices from which people poked their heads, we shouted and swore at each other. Sydney could curse and he did so without inhibition. We were both so involved in the disagreement we didn't notice the effect it was having. He probably didn't care, anyway. It fizzled out, partly because we had both had our say and partly from exhaustion.

On reflection some time later I thought Sydney had a point. At the screenplay stage we could have inverted the action and placed the hopeful experience with the sympathetic psychiatrist after the bleak one with ECTs, where the young woman becomes a zombie. But David and I knew that wasn't the reality so we chose to rub the audi-ence's nose in it. Also, after she was reduced to that state it would be too late for any other intervention. She was lost, existentially dead.

Sydney didn't mention his objections or our row again. He had not actually demanded any changes. I didn't make any. He had given his notes. It was our film. That was the BBC then. Despite all the battles caused by me pushing my creative freedom to the BBC's limits I was allowed to produce films which would be killed at pitch stage in today's BBC.

Topsy's fate and her experience of the psychiatric profession would keep nagging away at me. I wanted another try, this time for the cinema. David refused. He rightly felt he had done the subject. I nagged until he reluctantly gave way. Ken didn't see the point but was easier to persuade. Directors always want to work in cinema – it's where careers and reputations are made – and by the time we got to this film in 1971 we would already have done the 1969 movie *Kes*. David wrote the later film, *Family Life*, a different story from *In Two Minds*, but still exploring the same mysteries and pouring anger on what I thought was inhuman psychiatry. At the centre was a young woman caught up in double binds, confused and unhappy, who is brutally assaulted by psychiatrists and ends up as a vegetable.

I went to Nat Cohen, co-founder of Anglo Amalgamated, one of the few British distributors, knowing that his investment would bring a matching one from John Terry, manager of the National Film Finance Corporation. Their finance came from the Eady Levy, a tax on ticket sales. They were attempting the same job as the BFI Film Fund does now.

They were contrasting personalities. John was large, good-natured and Pickwickian, a member of The Savile Club, who greeted one with a sherry and turned projects down with such gentlemanly charm that one was back out in Soho Square before it had registered. He was very kind to me, almost paternal, and I loved him even when he felt he had to say no.

Nat was a small, moustached, dapper man, whose vanity made him wear a corset. He had an eye for the ladies. His office was in Wardour Street but I was often called to his apartment for meetings. This was a grand affair, in a modern block overlooking Green Park, where Rupert Murdoch now has his London home. Nat was a racehorse owner and his proudest moment was winning the Grand National. I had no interest in or knowledge of racehorses, but each time I visited him I would be played the radio commentary of the time his horse had won. After patiently sitting through that, I would tell him about the latest project. *Family Life* was not an easy sell: 'So, a mad girl goes into a mental hospital and goes madder,' he said. 'An unhappy ending. No laughs, no sex.'

I couldn't argue. To make matters worse, we wanted Sandy Ratcliff to play the lead and she had no track record, let alone star attraction. He'd never heard of her.

He looked at me with painful regret. 'You and Ken, you know, we could make a lot of money with you. If you weren't such a bunch of bloody communists.'

I thought that wasn't the moment to tease out my differences with Stalinism.

But in the end, he put up the money and we were in business. Doing a film with Nat in those days was different from making a film today. You shook his hand in the morning and could go out to spend his money the same afternoon. Over the years I got used to going to Samuelson's, the camera business in Cricklewood, and saying to Sydney Samuelson, 'We're doing a film for Uncle Nat,' mention that Chris Menges – or Charles Stewart – was shooting and add, 'and we will need . . .' I could have walked out with anything, just on Nat's word. The production and distribution agreement might not be signed until after the film was delivered but the money was always there, meeting the cash-flow estimate every week.

He made me put up the whole of my fee as first call on any over-age. Considering that represented my total earnings for the year, it concentrated the mind. But when the film was delivered under budget, he always threw in a bonus, although one had not been negotiated. London then was a handshake town, more like a village. Media law virtually didn't exist. There was no demand for film lawyers, except to service Hollywood studios in London.

The industry problem was access to finance and distribution. I begged the BBC to put even a small amount into films, offering a cinema window, but Alasdair Milne and his colleagues consistently maintained that they were in television, not cinema. The idea that a film is a film and there are a myriad ways of screening it had not yet been accepted. It would have to wait till the technology demanded it. I was delighted when founding chief executive Jeremy Isaacs and commissioning editor David Rose began to open it up on Channel 4. The BBC then fell into line and now, although still difficult for producers, there are many ways of putting even an art film together, just as co-finance from foreign sources has blossomed. All this I would have found liberating, having always despised the snobbish class distinction separating television and the cinema.

David Mercer's screenplay was barely adequate. It was lazy, perhaps because his heart wasn't in it. I wanted to do more work on it with him. He was reluctant. I probably should have called it a day then. With David on strike, but naturally reluctant to allow me to rewrite it, we had an insecure basis for a film. It was probably my fault for pressing him into it.

But Ken gave a sense that we were witnessing life rather than actors doing their thing. Ken found a suburban housewife to play the mother, a woman who could unselfconsciously identify with her character. She played her with total conviction. A psychiatrist played the psychiatrist, asking quiet, probing questions, gradually revealing the double binds at work. Ken went to elaborate lengths to create moments of spontaneity. For instance, there was a family scene round a dining table in which two little children witnessed a row. In order to evoke the emotional effect of this on them I marched onto the set, unexpectedly, and began to berate Ken angrily. I threatened to sack him and everyone else, closing the film down, if they didn't pull their socks up. This went on for a few minutes. Ken replied to me firmly. Camera and sound kept running unobtrusively. I then collapsed with laughter and hugged Ken. Everyone relaxed, grinning at being duped. But the faces of the children, whipping between Ken and me like Wimbledon spectators, showed just the concern we wanted. They weren't acting it. They were really worried. Director Roland Joffé and I used the trick in a scene from *The Spongers* in late 1977. You use anything to create a genuine reaction. Just saying to someone, 'You have a shocked expression in this scene,' doesn't cut it.

Family Life did little business, as Nat had predicted, although long afterwards he had the grace to admit it was released and marketed badly. I don't think anyone knew how to sell it or even knew what it was really about.

One good effect was that it made Ken's reputation in France, which has been helpful to him ever since. By coincidence, Ronnie

Laing's writings were just becoming all the rage among Parisian intellectuals. In fact, he was on his way to international celebrity. His fame was to spread far beyond his immediate professional circle. One can question whether celebrity was good for him but it seemed to feed on itself and was unstoppable. Or, at least, he did not seem to want to stop it. Ronnie was hot. Paris was in love. *Family Life* consequently became an instant hit in France, with enormous press interest.

Ken and I had one blissfully amusing day in Paris promoting the film. I didn't even want to go, finding French cineastes pretentious. Ken really wanted me with him and pressed me. We spent the whole day in a hotel room. Each hour yet another earnest critic wanted to discuss the meaning of the film, its relationship to the Freudian tradition, the power dynamics in the family, the new pharmacological breakthroughs and, of course, to pass everything through Lacan, the impenetrable French psychoanalyst. With the enthusiasm of those just having discovered a new intellectual game, they asked probing questions, looking for dramatic quotes about the psychiatric establishment, Ronnie's anti-psychiatry movement, the wider political implications and even the question of free will. All at a deep theoretical level.

No one wanted to discuss the making of the film itself. Each question was addressed to Ken. He would look at me with a shrug and raised eyebrows. I would give a response, using some of the jargon they craved. The questioner still looked at Ken, waiting for him to repeat my response. Ken would bravely do so, trying to remember the jargon I'd just used. I would then naughtily add more arcane stuff, just to throw him. He would look daggers at me. This went on all day. We managed to control our giggles until we were on our way home.

No critic had shown the least interest in the original casting, the mixing of actors and non-actors, the use of a real psychiatrist to play a psychiatrist, the spontaneity and credibility of the performances, the simple elegance of the framing, the rigorous concentration, the absence of all directorial flourishes. Ken's talent as a director was ignored. Instead, a different expertise was unreasonably assumed.

But he wasn't the screenwriter, nor was he an expert in different psychiatric traditions. Why not ask David Mercer or Ronnie Laing, our adviser, whose critique of psychiatry had informed our drama?

I suppose it all comes from the rigid French conviction that the director is the author of the film – *l'auteur* – which, apart from its oversimplification of a complex and diverse set of actions, revealed a devotion to individualism surprising in these socialist theorists.

A Kestrel for a Knave

'Sorry, not for us. Wrong kind of bird.'
    Wardour Street financier demonstrating his wit as he turns down *Kes*

B arry Hines had written a few pieces for BBC radio in Leeds. His first novel, *The Blinder*, was a 1966 book about a lad who wanted to be a professional footballer. Barry had played for the England grammar school team and was offered the chance himself. Alfred Bradley, the radio producer at BBC North, alerted me to him. He came down to TV Centre and we went to the bar. I liked him. His manner was straight and his frank, blue eyes shone with no hidden agenda, no duplicity.

When I asked him to write a film he said, 'No,' firmly. There was a novel going round in his head and that's what he needed to do. My opinion of him rose. A literary novel would get him only a small advance and probably earn little. He was a teacher with a mortgage and a couple of kids still on the floor. A BBC commission would have paid substantially more. I wished him well, asking if I could see the novel when he'd finished it. I then thought nothing more about it.

Around eighteen months later a typescript landed on my desk from Sheila Lemon, Barry's agent. It was *A Kestrel for a Knave*. Before the end of that day I had read it and decided it must be a film. The story was simple and direct, the dialogue rang true and Barry evoked a believable world. It was sustained by a powerful central image – the kestrel – which, rather than standing out as a literary device, was woven into the story.

I suppose also, as with *Up the Junction*, there was residual guilt that I had been arbitrarily chosen for privileged advancement as early as eleven, leaving behind most of the people I knew, including my best friend, Barry Westwood, who had gone to secondary modern when I went to the grammar school. Here was another group of teenagers with so much hope and potential having their lives crushed by an indifferent system. Why must each generation throw much of its most precious asset, the young, on to the scrap heap?

I was naive, not thinking about the practicalities: who might finance and distribute a film of this book? No sex, a loser as the lead and a downer for an ending. An impossible sell. In fact, if I'd had any experience I'd have just reluctantly passed on the project. On paper it was clearly one which couldn't be financed and wouldn't be released. Experienced producers such as Otto Plaschkes, who had recently had a success with *Georgy Girl*, told me to stop spinning my wheels.

I had never made a cinema deal, so I went to see Sheila Lemon and, thinking honesty was the best policy, said I had no idea what to offer and in any case had no money. Years afterwards she admitted to me that, used to publishing deals, this was the first film deal she had done, too. In the end we stumbled to a fee. I had to put some money down to secure the rights. Money was to be a problem throughout this adventure. I sold my house and used some of the cash left after the mortgage was paid off.

I knew that this was for Ken, not only because he shared my feelings about the waste of young people, but because the book went to his strengths. He would handle the sequences in the school naturally and, especially, would love a good performance from the boy playing Billy. The three of us took a screenwriting credit but it was just cut and paste, an editing job; the film was all there in the book.

Richard, Barry's brother, was an expert on hawks, so I hired him to find Kes and supervise the bird's training. He found a nest at Old

Hall Farm, not far from Hoyland Common, near Barnsley, where he and Barry lived. The plan was to take three chicks just before they flew away and train them simultaneously. We called them Freeman, Hardy and Willis, after a chain of shoe shops of the time. One of the birds seemed so keen on stardom he hogged the screen.

The budget was small, £164,000, but no one on Wardour Street was interested. I was told, 'Oh, we've done the north', meaning the 1962 film *A Kind of Loving* and one or two more. This had exhausted the subject. London snobbery was compounded by the dislike of the Yorkshire accents, which would not travel, apparently.

I look back with no rancour. These executives were in business to back films for a profit. It's always guesswork but they knew what had made money and what hadn't. *Kes* looked like a sure losing investment. Eventually Bob Solo, representing a large American company wanting to get into movies, agreed to finance it. His company offered to pay for me to spend some time in Los Angeles, talking with their people, so I made my first trip to America. Used to the cheapest hotels to save the budget, I was astounded when a limo met me at LAX, Los Angeles' airport, and took me to the Beverly Wilshire Hotel, near Rodeo Drive. My room was immense, with a balcony. There was a large bowl of fresh fruit that I was afraid to eat. Was it just for show, like a sculpture?

Many years later, reminiscing about our experiences, I was trumped by Albert Finney, who told me about his first arrival. An executive had met him at LAX and in the limo asked if there was anything, absolutely anything, they could do for him. Nothing would be too much trouble. Albert jokingly said he'd like a young blonde to be sent round. Thanks very much. He thought this was funny, behaving like they are supposed to behave in the movie business.

He was just settling into his fine room when someone arrived at his door. Thinking it would be room service, he opened it to find a young, very pretty blonde woman smiling at him. He claimed he was just polite with her and sent her away. Not that I believed him.

I was invited to a premiere of *2001*, the 1968 Kubrick space movie, and on the way a car took me to pick up 'my date', who had been arranged by the executive allocated to look after me. She turned out to be a pleasant, out-of-work actor hired for the night. We ended up having a drink and then I saw her home. She looked a little puzzled when I shook hands and thanked her. People laughed at me, not believing I could be so naive, but it all seemed so cold. She was a nice lass. When I told Albert I think he had the reaction I had had to his story. But it was true. I was just too shy, anyway.

One conversation should have served as a warning about Hollywood. I asked a movie executive about another movie that had just opened and he reverently told me, 'The first weekend gross was awesome.' I nodded and asked again what the film was like, what he thought of it. 'That movie will break records; it will do a gigantic gross. The projections are awesome.' Another attempt to ask about its merits as a movie was met with, 'And foreign. That sucker will travel, you know? Mammoth.' I gave up. Welcome to Hollywood.

I was taken to Las Vegas – that desert in the middle of a desert – on a private plane and watched the gaming industry fleece the willing victims. I went to the nearby Hoover Dam to see an example of Roosevelt's New Deal. I was then told to meet some people over on the East Coast in New York, so at LAX I asked where the middle of America was and bought a ticket to Kansas City in Missouri. Why not see some of the America between the coasts?

I hired a Ford Mustang and drove around for a couple of days, stopping in small towns and villages, going to the saloons and chatting with everyone. I was clearly a curiosity. The sixties had not yet penetrated the Midwest. At one point I was followed by groups of teenagers, fascinated by my long hair, shouting 'Hippy . . . hippy . . .'

When I went to the Kansas City airport to continue my journey I was told that the plane would be diverted to Baltimore. New York was in lockdown. Riots had broken out. Martin Luther King had been shot dead.

At Baltimore there was a curfew with National Guards on every street corner. I didn't want to be imprisoned in my hotel, I wanted to see the sights, so I went for a walk. Parts of Baltimore were on fire. There was smoke everywhere. The mood was tense, although the streets were eerily deserted except for the armed men. After a few minutes I was surrounded by these guys who pointed their weapons at me. I had some explaining to do. I only avoided arrest by apologising: as a Brit I hadn't understood the situation. They escorted me back to my hotel with stern instructions to stay there. I thought it prudent to obey.

In just two weeks I'd begun to experience a little of the variety and contradictions of that place of fantasy, America, which had gripped my imagination since I was a boy. I left it hungry for more.

Back in the UK we at last got into pre-production. Time was running out, because the kestrel chicks were about to fly the nest. We crewed up, with Chris Menges on camera. I met the local education committee, who gave us permission to shoot in a school during August. We chose St Helen's secondary modern in Barnsley and one of the teachers, Mr Hesketh, was our contact. Everyone in the town was helpful, honest and friendly.

What could possibly go wrong?

Bob Solo withdrew the offer of finance. No explanation. Maybe this new company he worked with was starting to learn which films would make money and had decided ours was too risky. The contracts had not quite been signed off. He was legally secure. With very little time I had to go knocking on doors again. Ken was a true friend. Never losing his optimism, he came with me, keeping my spirits up every day. But no one was interested.

I called a meeting with the main crew one Sunday evening, thinking it right to tell them of our predicament. They needed to know that time was running out, no finance seemed available and that they should feel free. I didn't want any of them to miss a summer without a gig because they were hanging on for me. I had to fight back my tears when each of them said this was the film they wanted to make; they would stick together with Ken and me in the hope it could shoot.

Richard Hines came to me with urgent questions about the birds. Should he take the chicks and start training them? No. They must be trained from the beginning with the boy, on screen. But we had no finance. I was in despair by this point. I'd approached everyone, some more than once. There seemed nowhere else to try. Then I took a call from Tony Richardson, a man I only knew by reputation. I had no idea how he knew of our predicament.

Tony's lazy drawling voice, as though everything is just too, too boring, asked if we had a problem. Ken and I went to Woodfall, his company's offices in Curzon Street, the next morning. I explained the predicament. He made no comment, giving the impression he was not really paying much attention, but told us to come back later. We spent a day wondering what all that had been about. At six that evening, we presented ourselves again. Tony just said, in his bored way, 'Well, you can start.'

'We can start?'

'Yes. Oh, no doubt the paperwork will take for ever, as it always does. But you have the finance.'

Ken and I looked at each other, not knowing if we could believe what we'd been told. I later worked out that he'd been able to find the money from United Artists because he'd given them a huge hit with *Tom Jones*, the 1963 film they initially thought would be a disaster when they saw his cut. Scripted by John Osborne, the movie had made a lot of money. He was hot. The budget for our little film was too small for them to bother with in Hollywood, so United Artists over there green-lit it without needing to know anything. It was done as a favour to Tony, although he had to cross-collateralise the one he was preparing – that is, promise any profits would cover any losses on ours.

You could say, as some have, that Tony didn't do much. It was only one phone call. Yes, but he didn't have to make it. At the time he had his own crisis, finding himself in difficulties over the rights to a Nabokov short story for what became *Laughter in the Dark* with Nicol Williamson. But he took the time and trouble not only to ask us about our predicament but to call in a favour for us. Woodfall got a credit but his deal with us wasn't onerous. He never interfered: he contributed the title, *Kes*, and he intervened to stop the London United Artists people bullying me at one point. That was the work of a good industry colleague and I never forgot it.

Years later, when things were slow for him, he fancied working for the BBC. He wanted to accept low budgets in exchange for creative freedom. I intervened on his behalf, trying to return the favour, lobbying Shaun Sutton, but to my shame no one was interested. Television and cinema inhabited different universes, even though both shot celluloid. Telling him was painful. I felt I'd let him down.

Once the new finance was in place, we raced up to Barnsley. Colin Welland had been a neighbour of Ken's. He had also been a teacher before he became an actor and screenwriter. He was an obvious choice for Billy's English teacher, Mr Farthing, but his face was well known from Z Cars. That worried me. Was Ken casting him because he was a friend? Teachers are actors by profession. Surely we could find one locally? I decided to say nothing. I knew Colin to be a good actor. In the event he did well.

All the other casting was local, such as Freddie Fletcher, a miner from Grimethorpe, who played Billy's older brother Jud; or club acts like Lynne Perrie, who played his mother. Most of the rest we had already worked with.

It was a matter of principle that Billy should be a local lad. We were convinced that although not every boy in every local school could play Billy, at least one could. If Barry had set it in Dagenham with the kestrel flying on the Essex marshes, then we would have found a boy in the East End. After lots of improvised auditions, Ken found David Bradley. He later became Dai because there was already a David Bradley in Equity. More embarrassing for me, he was an Aston Villa supporter. I later apologised to him for the confusion.

One role was left. The bullying gym teacher, Mr Sugden. Neither Ken nor I had any ideas. Then Barry mentioned a teacher he had worked with, Brian Glover. Not only was Brian perfect, but he wrestled in the evenings under the name 'Leon Arras the Man from Paris', so was in the Variety Artistes' Federation, then recently incorporated into Equity.

He was both an extrovert powerhouse of pugnacious energy and very funny, although he did piss me off. Halfway through shooting the football scene, he turned up with a bandage on his knee: a wrestling injury. We had to shoot his material again for continuity.

Brian turned out not only to be a star of the film but also to have a distinguished career as an actor and a writer. We kept in touch. His

down-to-earth attitude to show business was refreshing. Years later
he called me. 'What can I do, Brian?'

'Right. You're a man of the world. I've turned down the Royal
Court. Money's terrible, but there's another. I've never heard of
'em. Are they all right?'

'What do you mean, Brian? "All right"?'

'Are they good for the money?'

'Who are they?'

'It's for the Haymarket Theatre.' He said this as though he was
reading out unfamiliar words.

'About Nelson.'

'They want you to play Nelson?'

'No, that's that Ian Holm. I'm Hardy.' The mind boggled.

'What's it like?'

'Rubbish. But the money's not. It's put on by . . . hold on . . .
"H. M. Tennent Limited".'

'That's Binkie Beaumont, Brian, one of the biggest and oldest
producers in the West End.'

'Right. *Are they good for the money*?'

'Yes, Brian, they'll be good for the money.'

'That's all I wanted to know. Cheerio.'

I was curious and, although no longer a theatre-goer, decided I
had to see Brian in a costume drama. I finally made it on the last
night of the run. It was dire. Brian, looking dashing in his costume,
gave it his all. I went round afterwards. He looked as cheerful as
always.

'They're all miserable buggers here tonight.'

'Why's that?'

'All out of work next week. I'm OK. Wrestling Nottingham,
Tuesday.'

With Brian in place as the gym teacher we were set. I had confidence
in the crew, a mixture of fresh faces and old friends such as Penny
Eyles, who again did continuity. This was a very difficult position
with Ken as director. Under him, lines were improvised and action
changed from shot to shot. 250,000 feet of film were shot, a ratio

more usual in a documentary. Yet she calmly made notes on every detail. Just to see her contained presence, never losing her detached sense of humour, filled me with confidence. The shoot lasted eight weeks, rather tight in cinema films, but a luxury for us, coming from the BBC. Nineteen sixty-eight had the wettest summer in memory and it rained nearly every day. But it was a happy crew.

Ken and Chris Menges got on well, and Ken opened his mind to the visual element of his work. They had both admired the Czech cameraman, Miroslav Ondříček, and he became a touchstone for the style they developed. Chris, who went on to become one of the world's finest cinematographers, also operated the camera, contributing substantially to the natural quality of the action. We had wanted to shoot in black-and-white, judging that colour stock was too artificially pretty and more suited to optimistic musicals in Hollywood than social realism in Yorkshire, but United Artists wouldn't allow it. So, in our ignorance, we pre-flashed 250,000 feet of 35-mm stock, that is let some light in before it was exposed inside the camera. I didn't quite realise the dangers of partly exposing film. The idea was to desaturate it, taking the phoney colour out. Those with more technical knowledge were horrified. Luckily, we got away with it.

Barry and Richard Hines were with us throughout and the kestrels behaved. Young David trained them as we went through the shoot so they would be at the right stage each day. Under Richard's eye and with Ken's encouragement he took to it and handled them well.

Ken and I tried gently to persuade him against becoming an actor, suggesting that the film should be seen as a one-off adventure. I restrained myself after my experience with Tom Courtenay, but it made no difference anyway.

'What else would I do?' he said. 'I'm not going down pit! What's left round here? Serving at the Co-op?' He did become an actor and had a good run, playing at the National Theatre.

We tried to arrange the schedule to shoot in sequence with no one knowing in advance what would happen next or how it would all turn out. We still observed our old variation on the CIA rule: need to know. The essential goal, as ever, was to make the work as close to real life as we could. None of us know what will happen next; we merely have expectations and plans. Too much information can be confusing and makes being in the moment more difficult. If you're playing Hamlet every evening, you must know, even when confronting the ghost of your father on the battlements, that at the end of the evening you'll be killed in a sword fight with Laertes. But a film is the accretion of private moments. David was told only enough about the story to play each day's events.

Where possible, Ken and Chris shot on long lenses, a bit like taking the eye's view of the world and keeping the crew and their gear away from the action. They were especially good with the boys in the school. Barry had told us that when he was writing the novel he would take into class a scene set in school and read it. They would tell him what was right and wrong with it. He would then make changes. So that was our attitude. Ken told them that they were the experts rather than us so they should put us right. They did. Chris Menges was quietly observant, capturing moments on the wing, shooting unobtrusively, and Ken created an atmosphere where they forgot they were in a film.

It poured with rain during the shooting of the football scene with Brian Glover but it didn't show much on camera. Ken filmed in the rain. There wasn't much choice. No standing around like David Lean waiting for the right weather on our budget. It helped to convey the sheer misery of games, a memory for many in the audience.

Ken rightly felt that if we cheated the caning scene it would be phoney, so we negotiated. If I remember correctly, we used the local rate for a week's paper round and paid that for each stroke. At least that easily understood principle was the yardstick. The boys loved the money, the scene was authentic and their hands stung, at which point they all thought it was unfair. I had mixed feelings.

How far can one legitimately go? Had upsetting Carol's children for a few minutes at the end of *Cathy Come Home* – by tearing them from her arms – been justifiable? Naturally, I defend these examples but I know I'm on thin ice. Would we commit torture for realism? Rape? In fact, there's a rape scene in *Handgun*, a later film set in Dallas, but it's illusory. We don't see the rape. We fade to black

before and fade up again after it's over. People just think they've
seen a rape. The reason is that if you simulate a rape it's not believable. If you make it actually happen you're a criminal. If you then
film it happening, you're providing evidence which could send you
to prison. Who would do that? And that's without considering the
moral question. The same with a murder. The audience knows they
haven't actually seen a murder, that they haven't seen someone in
the moment of death, unless it's a snuff film, so the protagonists
must be just acting. If you have ethical qualms, don't show a phoney
simulation. One lie like that and the whole film is tainted. This, of
course, is a purist's view. But knowing where to draw the line is
difficult.

We began to notice that David was looking tired. It was a worry,
not only for the film – we had weeks to go – but we were concerned that we might be working him too hard. Then we learned he
was still doing his paper round each day before filming. Moreover,
he said he couldn't work on Saturday afternoons because he sold
programmes at a football match. I couldn't believe it. A negoti-
ation followed. We arrived at a price which would give him the
incentive to relinquish everything and concentrate solely on the
film. I won't claim it was the most difficult deal I've ever had to
do but it was delicate. Eventually we shook hands on it. He was
all Ken's.

The book's ending was a literary device which would sit uneas-
ily on the screen, so it was changed to something more direct and
dramatic. After Jud kills his kestrel, David discovers it. He opens a
bin and there is the lifeless body. This kestrel was borrowed from a
taxidermist who was working on it in Manchester. Richard thawed
it out and put jesses, the tethering straps, on it. It looked just like
Kes. I was never sure whether David was taken in by this trickery. In
a way I hoped he was not. I wanted him to believe that we wouldn't
have killed his kestrel. Anyway, according to Richard he hadn't
forged a deep relationship with the hawks. I think he was more
worried by a mean act that day. His favourite lunch was shepherd's
pie and it was on the menu. But he was told there was none, not for
him. He filmed the final scene feeling hungry and unloved. None

of it mattered much. By the evening he was fine. He did the scene memorably.

One day I was visited by Aunty Pom and Uncle Harold, who were staying with Aunty Ada and Uncle Ernie in Rochdale. They were all retired and no doubt wanted a day out, a 'destination', as they put it. They also wanted to see what I was up to. Harold had been puzzled for years and none of my accounts gained a purchase with him. I didn't actually make anything. There was a film at the end, that was tangible, but what part of it had I made? What did I actually do? So they set off early one morning over the Pennines with sandwiches and flasks of tea to find us in Barnsley.

They arrived mid-morning and stayed most of the day, wandering around. We were filming in the school so there was much to see, cables and lights everywhere, with lots of people and vehicles. I invited them to go with everyone else to the location caterer for lunch. They could just forget their sandwiches.

'We'll have them for tea,' said the frugal Pom.

They said little and left thanking everyone politely but offered no impression of how they felt. They never said anything to me about their visit but others in the family told me that at gatherings they were full of it and talked in detail about their experience – or at least one aspect of it. The filming itself was never mentioned, except in passing. They hadn't been impressed by the crew, the camera, any of the equipment or the organisation; the complications of filmmaking weren't acknowledged. All they spoke of was the work of the caterers and, indeed, this was what the other aunties wanted to hear about.

Harold would go into the minutiae: 'Seventy-two hot dinners out of that little van. In twenty minutes, couldn't have been more, could it, Ada? And a choice! And a hot pudding! Unbelievable. Three of them in . . . what do you reckon? Smaller than our kitchen, any road. Serving through a hatch. All free, according to our Tony. They don't know they're born. He said they're there first thing every day to serve breakfast. Can you believe that? Oh, yes, the full breakfast: bacon, egg, sausage, fried bread. Hot tea. The lot.

'And – you won't believe this, but we were there, weren't we, Pom? You'll bear me out – no sooner had they cleared up the dinner things, they were serving homemade sandwiches and cakes, a full tea. I've never seen anything like it. I've never heard of anything like it. Have you? Unbelievable. An eye-opener that was, watching the filming . . . Oh, yes, he seemed all right. Didn't do much, really. Just wandered about.'

So, I gathered they thought their visit to a film set was interesting.

I was sad to leave Barnsley. We had been treated with true Yorkshire hospitality. In those days we watched rushes back in the local cinema after the last house. Everyone dog-tired, we went for a pint of Barnsley bitter and a visit to a shop called Finney's for fish, chips and mushy peas. This was on David Bradley's recommendation. I consulted him for his expert opinion. He considered the matter judiciously. He knew all the chip shops and gave a knowledgeable critique of each one. He should have become a Michelin inspector, never mind serving in the Co-op. The chips were in fact the best I've ever tasted.

It was back to London. I had thought about nothing else but *Kes* for months. What was happening in the world outside Barnsley? Plenty, it seemed. It was 1968. The May events in Paris had sparked student unrest. The city seemed to be on fire, with running battles against the police. Socialist rhetoric and revolutionary fervour were everywhere. The air was filled with inchoate, dangerous possibilities. I was split. But the film came first.

The cut looked good. I always wanted less music – none, ideally – and that was something Ken and I debated but it was all in good spirit. I still think there's too much, softening the film. But although we sometimes disagreed, we never fell out. In fact, most of the time we were so in synch there was no need to debate.

The problem came when we showed it, first to United Artists in London, who made no response and then to Eric Pleskow, one of the American bosses, who was passing through London and asked to see it. I screened it in a small theatre in South Audley Street, Mayfair. He sat in the middle, with me hovering at the back by the door. When it ended he swept out and, not breaking his stride, said,

'I would have preferred Hungarian.' That comment on the dialect was the sole note and reaction from United Artists. Rank, who were their UK exhibitors, refused it. We were out in the cold. I began to fear it would never be shown. The commercial attitude was that *Kes* would do no business. Opening with all the attendant marketing and other costs would be throwing good money after bad. There was pressure to change it. I was told, in all seriousness, that it should have subtitles south of Nottingham.

This went on for nearly eighteen dismal months.

But my friend, the agent Clive Goodwin, was good with the press. He arranged showings and we gradually got a head of steam up. After some journalists pestered them, United Artists persuaded the other main exhibitor, ABC, to open *Kes* in Doncaster, just east of Barnsley, and a few other theatres in Yorkshire, no doubt hoping to dispose of the embarrassment. A week or two up there, they thought, and it would close.

One of the marketing ideas was to get Brian Glover to come down to London with some of his wrestling friends for a photo opportunity. It was thought that the stunt might make a tabloid or two. After all, we had no famous names or leggy starlets to sell. At the exhibitor's expense I took about a dozen wrestlers to lunch. I chose an Italian off Kensington High Street with a good reputation. It was fashionable with media executives and ladies who lunch. Eyebrows were raised as a dozen huge men, bursting out of their suits, took a table in the middle of the room. All conversation stopped as the regulars watched these men systematically work their way through the menu, course after course, polishing off numerous starters, a soup, a pasta dish, then some fish, followed by meat with vegetables and then cheeses. They ended with a couple of the desserts, pronouncing it a 'right good dinner, that.' The bill was astronomical. The marketing budget seemed to cope.

The photo shoot went well. The men had brought their girlfriends for this trip to London and they wanted to be photographed too. Everyone enjoyed their moment in the spotlight. The photos were big spreads in some tabloids the next day, good publicity for the film. Mission accomplished. But Brian and his friends had not thought it through. Many of their wives read the tabloids or, if they didn't, they soon had the offending pages pointed out to them. When they arrived home the men had some explaining to do.

Evening dress was specified for the Doncaster premiere, which I thought ridiculous. I've never worn a dinner jacket in my life so dealt with it by wearing an outrageously camp jacket, sending the whole thing up. The evening was complicated by the presence of various bigwigs including Roy Mason, the MP for Barnsley. He was an ex-miner, a right-wing Labour turncoat who became Northern Ireland Secretary. I despised his politics, his betrayal of his own people and his obvious desire to ingratiate himself with the posh in London. I guessed his real ambition, one shared by so many, was to end up in the House of Lords. So I tackled him in the foyer, loudly and aggressively. I didn't want him there, besmirching our film. He was rocked back. As the local MP he expected more respect. I gave him a going-over, to everyone's embarrassment, including his. I was out of order. Not for the first time, I had chosen the wrong place and moment.

Kes broke the house records in all six cinemas. It even got rounds of applause at the end. That was something in taciturn Yorkshire. At the time I said the house must have been full of Barry Hines' aunties. It kept playing. Eventually it was booked by the Academy, the prestigious art house on Oxford Street, and played seemingly for ever, breaking house records there, with queues extending down Oxford Street. We were overwhelmed. Eventually it played all over the UK and did well. This was my first experience outside the BBC. Was it always like this? I soon learned that it was not with films such as *Family Life* in 1971.

We were under pressure to dub the dialogue with voices that Americans, indeed people outside Barnsley, would understand. This would have meant posh Yorkshire, BBC Yorkshire, professional 'I'm Yorkshire and proud of it' voices, betraying the very people we had put on the screen. We were solid with the Barnsley people who had given us their hospitality. How could we then patronise them by dubbing them? It would have infuriated Barry, who hated professional Yorkshire men with a passion. We argued for subtitles in America but United Artists said that was for the ghetto of foreign language art films. We played with the soundtrack, re-voicing a few lines to show we weren't intransigent, but our hearts weren't in it. Of course, the box-office takings didn't even pay for the usherettes in the USA but it did amazing business in Britain.

On paper, *Kes* had been a non-starter as a cinema film. The experienced professionals in distribution and exhibition were justified: they thought it didn't stand a chance of earning a return, which is their criterion. I don't blame them. Occasionally, a film defies the odds and is an unaccountable hit. We'd got lucky. But *Kes* very nearly didn't get made. Only Tony Richardson's phone call saved it at the last moment. It very nearly never got shown. My ignorance of the film business paid off, this time. There was a lot of luck involved.

Protest and Confusion

Well, it might indeed be working in practice – but the real question is, does it work in theory?

A concerned French intellectual, who preferred policy-made evidence.

A typical central European intellectual believing that no idea was satisfactorily stated until it had been underpinned by an impressive theoretical substructure and been clearly placed in its appropriate position in a completely formulated Weltanschauung.

Dr Charles Rycroft on psychoanalyst Wilhelm Reich

The late sixties was a time of youthful ferment and change. If I'd been a teenager it would have affected me differently but I was in my thirties. In some ways I did live an adolescence denied all of us who had been teenagers in the repressive fifties. The music had improved, the fashion was colourful and external sexual repression was reduced, though not the internal repression. By 1966 everything seemed to relax. Everything seemed possible.

But I was not a druggy, being of the alcohol generation. For a while I drank too much. A typical day was to work at TV Centre forgetting to eat, go to the bar around six, drink there, go on to a party or two and, if on my own, arrive back home after midnight, starving. I would then make a bacon sandwich with HP Sauce and wash it down with more Scotch. Although never drunk, I continued this suicidal regime for years. I now wonder at the resilience of the human body.

I'd left the BBC to work on *Kes* and was now back in London. One Sunday I saw an ad for a house. The price was low enough to interest me so I arranged to see it. When I arrived in Brunswick Gardens I couldn't believe it. I thought it must have been a misprint in the *Sunday Times*. No. 10 was on four floors in the middle of an imposing terrace of high bourgeois houses. This was old-fashioned, imposing splendour in the middle of Kensington.

Out of curiosity, having come this far, I rang the bell and was escorted inside by an older man. I sat, trying not to reveal what I was now convinced was my imposter status. He offered a sherry and explained that he was a high court judge about to retire to the country. The price was as advertised. There had been no misprint, because the lease would expire in seven years. The rent was £6 a week. Even in the late sixties that was a steal. I took it on the spot, using my fee from *Kes*, not sure what I was to live on until another gig turned up.

It was a Church Commissioners' property and was for strictly domestic occupation. I moved in to the top of the house and used the rest as offices. We were discreet. No editing was done there. The neighbours could notice nothing more than visitors coming and going.

So there I was, broke, but seemingly living like a lord. Everyone thought I was rich, which amused me. Well, all movie producers were rich, weren't they? I could hardly pay for a trip to the super-market at first. But there was plenty of room for a film company and, as my life was my work, living over the shop made sense.

Michael White, the theatre producer, came to live next door with his family.

Soon the house became a ferment of activity, both creative and political. All day I developed material with my assistant Jane Harris and other colleagues. We had big, noisy parties, the music so loud that our Kensington neighbours sent the police round to subdue us. They were offered drinks and were tempted to join us.

The social whirl was intense and I was caught up in it. Most nights someone was giving a party. Dennis King invited me over for dinner. He was Carol White's brother-in-law. She was already in Hollywood, out of her depth, exploited and descending into depression and drugs. Hollywood has always been where girls go with dreams, where they are then commodified and, after a while, spat out. Those with talent and few defences, like Carol, are vulnerable, trusting lambs to the ritual slaughter. She had followed the false, seductive promises. She no longer had Ken's gentle guidance or my caring to protect her. By 1991 she was dead, aged forty-eight.

She had left behind in London her husband, who had been one of a big singing group, The King Brothers. The singers had followed the familiar trajectory, top of the bill at the Palladium, quickly becoming yesterday's men. At Dennis's place I would meet up with Dudley Moore and his wife, Suzy Kendall. After they broke up Suzy and I went out together for a while. We attended the opening of *Oh! Calcutta!*, a series of sexy revue sketches. It caused an uproar for its explicitness, to the delight of its producers, the critic Ken Tynan and my next-door neighbour, Michael White.

I was beginning to be social again. It was an easy time and an easy profession to be social in. Relationships seemed to come and go without serious commitment or bad feeling. Although I was involved with a number of nice women I always fell short of giving my heart. I wasn't going to do that again. My heart was still with Tops, as I remembered her.

Besides, I didn't think I was attractive, or any good at 'chatting them up', in the language of the day. I was useless at parties, being incapable of small talk, launching into a discussion of the economy or the situation in Hungary with people who just wanted to drink and gossip and pull someone for sex. I was excruciatingly shy and desperate to avoid rejection, which I thought I wouldn't survive. Marching up to the sixth floor of TV Centre to confront a senior manager was much easier than calling someone and suggesting we go to a movie. My love life was a testament to how many good women I met. They were very kind to me. I must have been a frustrating lover.

This was a pattern. I was in the sixties but not of it. I was deeply involved in socialist politics but never committed to a party. I had an abundance of close friends but I was intensely private. I was social, putting together films and attending parties and arranging meetings, but most of the time I hid on my own, immersed in books, as though I was still in the Birmingham reference library. I didn't exist. I kept up an insane momentum, working seventy hours a week as my bulwark against turning inwards. I had shut down during the Christmas of 1941. Topsy brought me back to life, but after her I closed down again. I wasn't there. There was a hole where I should have been. My act was good. But the essential me was missing. So what people were experiencing of me was an absence, someone who still did not dare to reveal to himself what he'd shut down that first Christmas; someone who offered a good imitation of himself and then, when you got too close, disappeared.

Of course, we are all puzzled by the disjunction between the self that people we know present to the world and their real – internal – self. What are they really like, we wonder?

But I was a professional at pretending to be where I was absent.

One afternoon I was in my office at the back of the house, having convened a meeting to discuss an imminent political event. I answered the phone to Ken Loach. He told me the bare details, as much as he knew, about a car accident. They had been on the M1 and another vehicle travelling in the opposite direction had broken through the crash barrier and smashed into them. He was in a hospital near Watford. They had left his mother-in-law at home to babysit. He asked me to go to their house to explain why they were late and tell the mother-in-law what had happened. Sensitively, he didn't want her to be shocked by the police giving the news. I immediately drove over and sat with her for a while. At that time I wasn't sure myself exactly what had happened except that the car crash was serious. She agreed to stay put and wait for more news.

After trying to comfort her, I went to the hospital. Ken and his oldest lad, Stephen, were injured, but not life-threateningly. They were very badly shaken up. I went to see Lesley, Ken's wife, in intensive care. I was allowed to stay just a few moments. She was unconscious and almost invisible, covered with medical apparatus, tubes everywhere. I was told she was very poorly. No one would commit to a prognosis. She didn't know that their son Nicholas, aged five, and her own grandmother were dead. It was a while before anyone knew whether she would survive. Only when they felt she was strong enough was she told of Nicholas's death and even then she was too ill to attend his funeral.

Ken asked if I would go to the police station to collect their belongings and then deal with the BBC. He was finishing a film there and was afraid of what someone might do to it. It was not one of mine. The BBC was the easy part. I went there on Monday morning and helped to supervise the film's last stages, according to Ken's wishes. The police station was grisly. The motorway cop was sensitive and helpful. He spent his life, he said, picking up items like those belonging to Ken, plus dead bodies, on the motorway. I admired and respected him but didn't understand how he could do it. The belongings were heartbreaking. Bits and pieces of clothing and the detritus of travelling with infants. A child's little shoe. All in a cardboard box. I thought of Stephen, a lovely, sensitive lad, now minus a brother who he loved, we all loved; of Lesley fighting for her life and still to face this dreadful news; and my friend Ken, who looked so composed in hospital, holding himself together, making sensible arrangements, but no doubt breaking up inside. Still, no doubt, in shock.

I went with the family to little Nicholas's funeral. Lesley, fortunately, was slowly recovering, but still in hospital.

The family stayed together and continued to courageously build their lives again.

They got through it. But you never get over it.

I've never ceased to admire their achievement, reclaiming their lives with such quiet dignity. All their children are now married with their own children. Life goes on, as Grandma said.

It continued too at 10 Brunswick Gardens, which became a social centre as well as a production base. In order to be hospitable I always had some cannabis and cigarette papers on the table, just as I had drinks in the fridge. Clive Goodwin would get pot for me in a still ungentrified Notting Hill Gate. The grand bourgeois houses were divided into small apartments where West Indians found a footing in London. The slum landlord Peter Rachman made money there and a few artists, like David Hockney, had cheap studios. On the occasions I smoked a joint I just smiled a lot in a silly way and wanted a cup of tea. It made me sleepy and not at all horny. I couldn't see the attraction. But I was in a minority. Lots of my acquaintances smoked every day and always seemed stoned.

Richard Neville, his girlfriend Louise and Jim Anderson, the Australians famous for the magazine *Oz*, lived in a house backing on to mine in Palace Gardens Terrace. One night they were raided. As the police and dogs came in the front door, Louise was busy chucking their drugs out of the back window. Unfortunately, most of them landed in next door's garden, where an eminently respectable titled lady lived. The dogs, following the scent, were soon over the wall, sniffing round her garden. She had some explaining to do. So, after her identity was confirmed, did the police. I'm not sure how it was resolved, but Richard and his friends escaped arrest.

When I had stopped laughing, I decided I was being politically irresponsible. I had nothing against cannabis. In fact, I had signed the full-page ad in *The Times* calling for its decriminalisation. But if I'd been raided and convicted on a drugs possession charge my chances of ever again working at the BBC would have been nil. Let alone the shame, which would reach Brum and the family. That would take some explaining! I immediately put my stash down the loo and from then on served only drinks.

All this sixties stuff was frivolous. Underneath there was a political ferment and we didn't know how it would turn out. The Wilson government which had been welcomed after many years of Tory rule was being revealed as moderately reforming, talking Left and acting Right. This was disillusioning for the unsophisticated. They were looking for answers and the 1968 exciting and unsettling events in Paris, with students fighting on the streets against the state, seemed to offer them. There were now not only anti-nuclear CND marches, but violent demonstrations in Berkeley Square in front of the American Embassy about the Vietnam War. Every assumption was being questioned.

The political work I and my colleagues were doing on the screen was not isolated. It didn't come out of a clear sky. The energy being released all around us was intoxicating, but unfocused. Here was a generation of young people, mainly educated middle class, who wanted political change to go alongside the social changes which were transforming society. They wanted something deeper than fashion and rock and roll and free love. But they had no connection with the organised working class, the only force the ruling class would take seriously.

I was involved, but unlike many others, didn't assume this was the start of a permanent revolution. I had the uneasy feeling that it was all froth, with no substantive base. There was no hard centre to guide change. As the seventies progressed I would become even more concerned at workers' strikes being merely a response to inflation, which was understandable with prices rising as much as 25 per cent annually. There was no credible political alternative, the Labour party accepting the market economy and the trade unions lost in economism. Various Tories on the Far Right were actually talking about a private army to fight the workers. It came to nothing, but it was an example of the febrile atmosphere of those days. Of course, I had no idea of just what would hit everyone in the eighties.

I was involved in various political initiatives. In 1967 I helped to organise the Dialectics of Liberation Congress at the Roundhouse, where Herbert Marcuse, Ronnie Laing, Gregory Bateson and Stokely Carmichael offered their radical perspectives on the state of the world and the psyche. I served on the executive committee of the ACTT (the film and TV union) and was its shop steward at the BBC, trying unsuccessfully to achieve recognition. But I was careful never to lose my main focus. I continued to work flat-out, fighting to make our films, then to get them shown. It took most of my energy. In any case I wasn't keen on marches and demos. I never spent my Easter on CND marches or fought the police over Vietnam in Berkeley Square. Although I sympathised with the protesters, I had grave misgivings about the effectiveness of street protests by groups of middle-class people. It wasn't exactly like the chartists, either in scale or composition. The police coped. I thought the only weapon which would affect policy and power relations was the action of an organised working class, its withdrawal of labour and a clear programme of change. Fat chance.

Clive Goodwin was planning a new political magazine, *The Black Dwarf.* We lamented the lack of any platform or regular meeting place for those to the left of Labour. Soon after the May 1968 Paris events, home from Barnsley after shooting *Kes*, I decided to start a Friday night meeting at my place. The main room was huge, 40 feet long, and big enough for any meeting. We invited everyone we knew in the arts who was interested in politics, plus people from various Marxist groups. Gerry Healy was also invited. I had met him during my research for *The Big Flame*, when he'd told me his group represented the Trotskyist Fourth International, in his view the carrier of the true flame of Leninism and the Russian Revolution of 1917. Tariq Ali, the activist and media darling, from another Trotskyist party, plus others calling themselves followers of Trotsky, came too. There were disillusioned Labour Party members and those just curious about politics but with nowhere to go. No matter. Let every tendency meet here and argue out their differences. I expected each evening to be lively and educational. The first was certainly well-attended, some coming out of curiosity, some thinking it would be a different kind of party. I laid on drinks.

My idea was to avoid a tight agenda. I wanted it to be a free discussion, maybe sparked by some recent events, in an atmosphere which encouraged anyone to express an opinion. I guessed we were all excited and confused by this new political energy, optimistic but unable to make coherent sense of it. To talk it through together might lead to something more organised and effective. I was a democratic socialist, but otherwise had no particular ideological axe to grind.

What happened was unexpected. Gerry arrived with Aileen, his driver and assistant. He sat down in my Eames chair, his feet in socks and sandals not reaching the floor, sipped a Coke and began almost immediately to dominate the meeting. He was like a sturdy frog, a wide mouth with no lips, wet and spitting in the full flow of debate. With an open shirt, braces and grey flannel trousers with turn-ups, he looked unprepossessing and undistinguished, as well as distinctly unfashionable, but when he spoke his rasping Irish voice riveted the room. Most were afraid to speak.

He embraced and stroked the modest and tentative. The cocky, committed politicos were mercilessly exposed. Everyone was put off balance. He always began in a whisper. No one dared even shift position, afraid of drawing attention. When anyone else spoke he would take off his thick, horn-rimmed spectacles and rub his red-rimmed eyes, then take out a white handkerchief and polish the lenses, holding the spectacles up to the light. The speaker would be thrown by this assumed indifference: it was like speaking into a void. Was he even listening? What was being said seemed to diminish in value as the eye toilet continued. The man had the quality of good actors: concentration, the ability to focus attention. Whatever he chose to do or say drew people as if he were magnetised.

One or two tried to take him on. He batted them away.

His analysis, for instance, of the reasons for the collapse of the May events in Paris seemed masterly, ending with an account of the deal between the communists and De Gaulle. Here was a consummate professional organiser out to recruit into his nascent party, in command of his brief, toying with this intelligent but politically naive audience. It was fascinating to watch. One or two who had fancied themselves on that stage went off in a huff, defeated and humiliated, because Gerry was a ruthless debater. The political issues of the day were chewed over and he would go beneath the surface of events and explain the forces at work beneath. After a week or two the meetings became his. No other group challenged him and no individual tried twice. After a month or two I noticed he'd begun to recruit among some of my oldest friends. It was an awesome professional display. I was impressed by his skewering analysis of events and his ability to make the underlying reasons for them clear. I was also fascinated by his technique, which had no doubt been honed over decades of sometimes brutal debate. He played this crowd like a violin, all the more impressive because they were probably new to him. He clearly saw it as an opportunity and he took it. Very few at those meetings had ever met anyone remotely like him.

The word got around and soon my living room was packed each Friday evening. Some, like Ken Tynan, dropped in occasionally, not because they were really dedicated to radical socialist change but because it was fashionable at the time to be on the Left: my place was like a salon. Harold Pinter would sit silently, seeming to glower but possibly he was just keenly observing. But most people were hungry for political analysis, wanted to share their thoughts and were lost without a political home.

The sixties were all ferment but no lasting substance. Social changes were achieved and they have lasted: abortion law reform, the decriminalisation of homosexuality, the fight against racism and the beginnings of the liberation of women (the last shamefully resisted by the reactionary left and many trade unionists). That there is still more work to do shouldn't take away from those achievements. But political change, based on the class struggle of working people taking power from the ruling elite – a democratic, socialist revolution – was still a mirage, a set of slogans. I remember at the time thinking that for all the excitement, those in power were not losing any sleep.

As Gerry's grip on the idealistic enthusiasm of some of my dearest friends tightened and his analysis led them into thinking it was their duty to throw themselves into his Trotskyist movement full-time, I sensed I was losing them. There was certainly an 'either you're with us or you're against us' mentality. It was as though they were joining a secret sect with its own jargon and its own loyalties.

Gerry decided to put pressure on me to join and commit myself to his movement. He would arrive late at night without notice at my front door – probably on his way back from a meeting with the car workers at the Cowley plant in Oxford – get comfortable and make his pitch. He didn't rage at me. He was charming, even chatty. I enjoyed these conversations. His historical analysis was deep and his description of current events went under the surface in ways which illuminated the class tensions. But he was in a hurry and his apocalyptic warnings of imminent oppression and disaster sounded ridiculous. 'We have three weeks and then . . .'

I had political and personal difficulties that made me keep my distance. Also, the Party seemed intellectually narrow, preoccupied with what was 'correct' and not relaxed enough to see virtues as well as objections in a range of thinkers. I was more eclectic. I was reading Herbert Marcuse, Norman O. Brown, Wilhelm Reich and Géza Róheim, thinkers of the Left embedded in Freudian theory. I was critical but appreciative. I thought R. D. Laing's ideas should not be dismissed because he was not a Trotskyist. In fact, there was one Friday meeting when Ronnie Laing debated Gerry. They were clearly from different planets. Gerry's hostility to Freud was based on ignorance and prejudice. It was all too suffocating.

However much I challenged him, he would give me no clue of what precisely they would do after taking the power or how it would work; just empty slogans. I didn't expect detailed policy but it was as though he hadn't thought about the transition. If he had, why keep it secret? He seemed so obsessed with 'taking the power' there was no energy for policy, even in the broadest terms. I wanted reassurances. I'm from Brum and we like to kick the tyres and look under the bonnet before we buy, whatever the claims in the ads. I wanted to know what the deal was. To me it all seemed to be a fantasy built on a sentimental attachment to the great achievement of the Russian Revolution of October 1917, but almost mad in its incapacity to see the concrete world as it was now, especially in the UK, a culture with a different tradition. How could he persuade enough sceptical workers? Slogans would not be enough.

I suppose in the end it was a temperamental thing. We make our choices according to our emotional needs. His group would never satisfy mine. I was becoming conscious of something which had been growing inside me since my teens: a suspicion of grand, all-encompassing continental theory and a liking for the tradition of English scepticism. It was not that I rejected theories or ideologies but I wanted them tested against evidence.

I visited the headquarters of what was later called The Workers' Revolutionary Party, in Clapham. Although liking and respecting many of the people there, I was repelled by the atmosphere. Bullying and fear were in the air. Although there was window dressing in the form of a democratic central committee that made decisions, I felt the reality was Gerry and a cabal decided everything. I've seen this in many organisations, from the Labour Party to the BFI, but it seemed suffocatingly tight under Gerry.

He rather threw me when he said I was important because he saw me as the Goebbels of the movement. I could see what he meant and was flattered but thought another phrase would have been more felicitous.

Circumstances alter cases. One can never predict what will happen, especially in politics. What seems inevitable in retrospect was never expected beforehand. The few who do predict events are usually dismissed as cranks. So could I see myself actively supporting an extra-parliamentary fight for socialism? A fight to the death for political change that would include the rejection of the con trick of 'democracy' sold to us since the Reform Act of 1832?

Can a revolutionary movement, centralised, disciplined and powerful enough to defeat capitalism be democratic? Or must it become tyrannical? The Russian experience after 1917 still haunts the West, even though ours is a different culture with deeper democratic traditions. There's no doubt in my mind that the class of land and capital would refuse to respect these traditions if its interests were in jeopardy. It would be a naked fight for power.

That could only happen in an economic crisis serious enough to impoverish the middle class. Then the Far Right would be the open enemy, not the respectable constitutionalists.

So, yes, I could join that revolutionary Left.

It's unlikely in my lifetime.

But I remember what I said about predictions.

Enriching Patron

Harold's sister Elsie was a teetotal, mature maiden lady of impeccable respectability. He would tease her. She came for tea on Saturdays and Pom would often make a trifle generously enriched with Harvey's Bristol Cream sherry. Elsie would enjoy it.

'Would you like some more, Elsie?'

'Oh, yes, thanks, Harold. This is a lovely trifle, Pom. You make a lovely trifle.'

After tea she became quite flirtatious. But, of course, she remained against alcohol. 'Not necessary!'

She had a girlish passion for Val Doonican, a singer full of Irish blarney, who performed on stage sitting in a rocking chair offering romantic ballads. His Saturday evening show on the BBC was eagerly looked forward to. One Saturday when I was home, she shyly asked, 'What's he like?'

'I've no idea, Elsie.' She frowned, disbelievingly. 'I can't say. I've never met him.'

'But you work there.'

'Thousands work there. Light Entertainment, a different department. No reason for our paths to cross. Sorry.'

She was sorry, too. She said nothing, clearly disappointed that I refused to talk intimately about my friend Val.

Why wouldn't you know someone who worked in the same firm?

If you worked there at all, that is.

I met the American director Joe Losey. His distinguished career had been interrupted by the McCarthy communist witch-hunt in America. Settled in London, he was finding it difficult to set anything up and jumped at the chance to work with me on a BBC film. He was told that he must fill in a form. The BBC had never heard of him, apparently.

I went back to Joe and apologetically handed over this lengthy form. He just sighed and began to fill it in without complaint. There was a question on the back page: 'Please state previous experience, if any'. Now I was seriously embarrassed. Joe shrugged and systematically listed his credits from the beginning, both in the theatre and the cinema, going back to the Federal Theatre project and The Living Newspaper in the thirties. The list was long and distinguished. I put it through the BBC machinery. After a while, I was told that he was unacceptable because he was 'an alien'. No other explanation was offered. I told Joe and was ashamed.

One Saturday morning in the early seventies I was woken by the telephone. It was a colleague of Dr MacDonald, the kind psychoanalyst I'd been seeing for years. I was informed that he had died during the night in hospital of a sudden heart attack. My last session with him had been three days before. He'd mentioned going in for a small procedure. He was unworried and it had barely registered with me. He seemed in robust health.

I get close to them and they die, I thought. When will you learn?

I always took calls without screening them. I was contemptuous of the self-important pomposity of those who employed assistants to vet callers. I also read screenplays submitted to me. You never know. Two people I'd never heard of, Les Blair and Mike Leigh, called me in the summer of 1971 and invited me to a screening. The theatre was empty except for a few cast members. The film was slow and lugubrious. It was called Bleak Moments and had many of them. Albert Finney had given them some money to make it, possibly because they all came from Salford. Now the pair had no idea how to get the film released and no idea how to put another one

together. I wasn't surprised when I heard their working methods. If
your proposal is to hire a group of actors and pay them to rehearse
for three months in the hope there might be a film to shoot at the
end of this improvisation, you shouldn't be surprised if there are no
takers.

Hunches are often all you have and something about these
unlikely lads attracted me. I was curious about their ideas. I saw their
principled dedication to their methods. They were serious. I was by
then back at the BBC with a contract to produce four films a year,
so I rejigged my schedule and gave them a film each. We all deserve
at least one break.

Sometime later I bumped into Gerald Savory, the head of plays, at
the bar. He was genial. 'Hello, haven't seen you for a while. What
are you up to?'

This from the man I formally reported to.

'About to start a couple of films.'

'Ah, jolly good. Who are the writers?'

'No writers. The directors put a bunch of actors together, improvise for two or three months and shoot the results. Hopefully.'

'Interesting. So, who are the directors?'

'You wouldn't have heard of them, Gerald. They've done nothing before.'

'Ah . . .' Now clutching at straws. 'The cast?'

'All unknowns.' This was true. Mike Leigh's film – *Hard Labour* –
featured Bernard Hill, Alison Steadman, Liz Smith and Ben Kingsley
– all unknown in 1973.

He looked puzzled, as he had every right to.

'Well . . . Jolly good luck.'

I then heard nothing from him until I showed him the finished
films. I don't think he was overwhelmed.

This was management by benign neglect. Something we might
recommend to the management consultants like McKinsey. Only
the BBC would take that chance. Who would risk funding a cast
and director without a track record for months on the small chance
of a film worth shooting at the end? These directors, whose work
subsequently enriched our culture, could have been abandoned

– depressed and ignored – at the starting gate. I often wonder if the BBC of today is of a mind to do the same thing for the next young, untested, uncategorisable talent. I suspect that at best they would have their originality ironed out of them on *EastEnders*.

Mike Leigh is short and bearded. He's like a garden gnome, very contained and intense, with a wry humour on the edge of black. He is bright and self-confident. I was fascinated by this confidence. It seemed to be based on nothing. How, I wondered, could this physically unprepossessing man, broke and unknown, with ideas so difficult to sell he would be shown the door all over town, seemingly be so coolly, arrogantly sure of himself? In the eyes of the world I was doing OK yet I was a bundle of insecurity, alert to the probability of it all crashing down, with constant doubt about my worthiness. How does he do it, I wondered?

Of course, I didn't know what was going on inside him, any more than he knew what was going on inside me. For all I knew, he thought I was self-confident, with the world at my feet. Each is a mystery to the other, let alone to himself.

But there was Mike, seemingly with an almost messianic belief in himself and his method. Although its elements were not unique, he has made them his own. This iron-clad belief was as serenely evident when he was unemployed, unknown and broke as it is now when his work has given him a place in world cinema.

Such single-minded determination and refusal to dilute one's beliefs is rare. An element is necessary to do original work but most people also have some flexibility. Usually, such rigidity is a sign of brittle and unconvincing certainty. Truly emotionally secure people are more relaxed around the edges. So it's a high-risk strategy, not least because such focus cuts you off from other valuable ideas. When it pays off, it does so handsomely. But we don't hear about those who get nothing for it but years of neglect and little appreciation; the withering of original talent on the vine; the slow, unmarked death, in angry disappointment. Of course, too much compromise is another death and one which carries with it self-contempt.

The outsider may think this results from a choice but mostly it doesn't. It's about personality, not talent. Some are gifted with original talent, believe in it with imperial arrogance and yet disguise this with a manner which seems friendly, flexible and collegiate. That's the way to rise easily to the top and stay there. Many of the most successful people I have known manage this trick.

It's been pleasing to see Mike's career develop so well. But having seen his method at close range I was not tempted by it. I suppose we were both single-minded. We had little interest in the other's ideas. But his voice deserved to be heard.

Les Blair is as talented as Mike, but his personality is different. He is a relaxed man who has never seemed driven. He is easy-going, enjoying life in a balanced, live-and-let-live way. For Les the working method was not a religious dogma.

Mike set his film in Salford and began his three months of improvisation. I did nothing but provide the means – encouraging and empowering. Then I observed. His cast was so large and the canvass so broad that *Hard Labour* took up most of the budget, leaving just enough for Les to direct a chamber piece about a handful of students in London, *Blooming Youth*.

Both films were original, slow and quietly riveting once you had given yourself up to them. They drew you in, refusing all the conventions of plot and incident which usually command an audience's attention. The improvisations gradually built complex, rich characters and then relationships. Mike and Les would find a narrative arc strong enough to carry them. It was an education for me. These were people of genuine talent who were enriching our culture and deserved to be funded. David Rose, then producing at BBC Pebble Mill, was a sympathetic facilitator. He took Mike under his wing and gave him room to continue.

Radio Times (Incorporating World-Radio) February 28, 1963. Vol. 158: No. 2051.

MARCH 2—8

Radio Times

FIVEPENCE

SOUTH AND WEST EDITION

BBC

tv

Sound

The Birth of a Private Man

Pauline Letts and Tony Garnett in David Mercer's television play

SEE PAGE 47

Me with Pauline Letts on the cover of the *Radio Times* for *The Birth of a Private Man* (written by David Mercer). *(© Radio Times)*

Topsy with Dame Edith Evans on the cover of the *Radio Times*. (© *Radio Times*)

(*above*) Me on the right talking to Carol Wright in *The Boys*. Carol was also in *Up the Junction* and *Cathy Come Home* many years later. (© *Ronald Grant Archive*)

(*left*) Me with Dudley Sutton, Jess Conrad and Ronald Lacey in *The Boys*. (© *Ronald Grant Archive*)

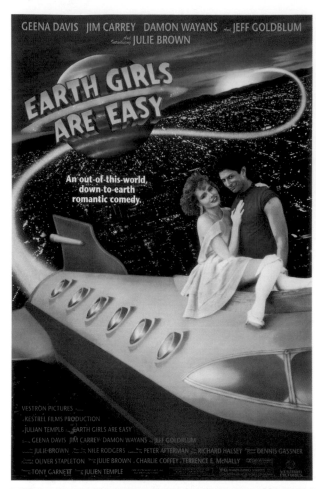

(*left*) *Earth Girls Are Easy* poster.
With Geena Davis and Jeff
Goldblum. (© *20th Century Fox/The
Kobal Collection*)

(*below*) Paul Newman as General
Groves in *The Shadowmakers*.
(© *Paramount/The Kobal Collection*)

Handgun. Karen Young on a Dallas shooting range. *(© 1982 Studiocanal Films Ltd. All Rights Reserved / The Kobal Collection)*

Sesame Street: Follow that Bird. Big Bird on the road. *(© CTW/HA/WARNER BROS/The Kobal Collection)*

Ruby's backstreet abortion, my main motivation for making *Up the Junction* happen. (© *Moviestore/REX/Shuttersock*)

This Life regulars. (© *BBC Photo Library*)

Kes. Dai Bradley with the kestrel. (© *Woodfall/Kestrel/The Kobal Collection/Barnett, Michael*)

The film poster for *Kes*. Objected to, especially by London Transport, for obscenity and bad taste. (© *Woodfall/Kestrel/The Kobal Collection*)

Carol White in *Cathy Come Home*.
(© BBC Photo Library)

Ray Brooks and
Carol White with
her children, Sean
and Stevie, who
were also in *Cathy
Come Home*.
*(© Moviestore/REX/
Shutterstock)*

Days of Hope

One day, chatting to Uncle Fred on his milk truck, I asked him about the General Strike in 1926. At that time he had been working in an engineering factory.

'What did you do?'

'It was a nice break from work. We went up the pub. What do you think we did?' I looked puzzled, so he elaborated. 'We had a few drinks then we passed a resolution. Nem con.! As soon as this pub shuts, we'll have a revolution.'

His face was impassively serious. Was he joking? Teasing me, as usual? His eyes seemed to give him away. But you could never be sure with our Fred.

I'd been talking on and off with Jim Allen about labour history and was reading more deeply into trade union growth after the Taff Vale case that encouraged the growth of the Labour Party.

Eventually the shape of 1975's *Days of Hope* emerged. It wasn't a single idea. The form, four films about different strands of the Labour movement, from World War I to the General Strike, came out of long discussion and argument. We dug deep into the research and it started to take up much of my time. Jim, with no formal education, was not an academic, either in experience or temperament, but his practical immersion in labour disputes at the sharp end and his personal experience of betrayals gave him an invaluable map and compass, helping him to find his way through the maze of detail. I sent him documents, memoirs, biographies and historical papers. We argued it all through for months. Ken was down to direct this one from the start and I kept him informed.

Jim would come to my place for a few days and we would talk into the night. He moaned about everything. I'd meet him off the train at Euston in my Triumph Spitfire, a low sports car, and he'd look at it with contempt. 'I'm not sitting in that fucking canoe.' He'd complain about food, although at the same time maintain that it was just fuel and should be provided by a central caterer. He'd look at whoever I was seeing at the time and say, 'What do you see in her? There's more meat on a butcher's apron. You need a lass with summat to catch hold of, lad!' He thought the fashions were laughable. In fact, London was a joke.

He'd complain about his son's latest japes, but with a grin. He loved his wife Claire and his kids. I discovered his dark secret: he secretly cooked, making a mean stew.

I would often stay in his house in Middleton, near Manchester. Claire made me very welcome. She was a school teacher, very bright, with no side to her. But I dreaded going because it meant a re-acquaintance with his vicious Bull Terrier. It terrified me. I couldn't go for a pee in the night for fear of being mauled by it. As soon as I arrived, it growled. This just amused Jim. One day his dog was discovered eating the pedigree Persian cat belonging to the woman over the road. Jim was proud.

I was frustrated by a bedroom scene with two of the leading characters, Philip and his wife Sarah. It was another problem of information and exposition in a static situation, just a place arbitrarily chosen to convey some political facts. There was no dramatic reason for it. I wanted to see if we could find another way and made suggestions. Jim didn't want to bother, thinking it adequate to set out the politics as an exchange between the couple before 'he then gets his leg over'.

I said, 'This isn't a scene.'

'Ken'll think of summat. He likes the actors making it up, doesn't he?'

'Jim, Ken is as inhibited with sex scenes as you are. Neither of you is Anaïs Nin.'

'Who's he, for fuck's sake?'

Eventually we cobbled together four screenplays. Some sequences were undramatic. The decision not to betray our sources meant there were dull and indigestible patches. Ken Loach did well disguising them but the films are only a partial success artistically. We were proud to stand by them politically. The historian E. P. Thompson's ambition to rescue working people from 'the enormous condescension of posterity' was constantly on my mind.

This was a big, expensive project. Featuring scenes of trade unions and class war required crowds of people all dressed in period costumes. World War I demanded uniforms, horses and explosions. I was aware that everyone was being taken to their limits. I was used to asking crews to squeeze a quart into a pint pot but I knew we needed more than my usual budget. Chris Morahan was doing a stint as head of plays. He got behind it and lobbied Paul Fox, Controller of BBC One. Their vote of confidence was important.

Even so, it was a big ask. We made the four films together with the same crew, shooting all over the UK, from Rochdale in Lancashire to Masham in Yorkshire, to Durham in the north-east and down to Bristol in the south-west. The working day of the costume department – on location first thing to dress two hundred extras and then late at night doing the laundry for the next day – was punishing. The tensions stretched our tolerances.

Ken and I clashed but each time we would talk it through and one of us would give way. We never fell out. He was calm, unperturbed by disaster, even when the whole day's shoot of a large, expensive crowd scene was ruined in the bath by the laboratory. Through the long months he never lost his concentration and managed to develop with John Else, the cameraman, a visual style which deftly evoked the period. This got me into more fights with the BBC technicians, who received with alarm from the Prince of Darkness yet another sequence lit by one candle.

There were a few difficult moments. When Jim visited and started muttering, 'I'll kill that bastard Loach,' I'd take him for a walk round the block, trying to explain that he was just giving the actors room to breathe and that his words would be used. I was an unconvincing physical protector of Ken, being as small and frail as him, but Jim's threats remained just that.

Feelings occasionally ran high. Once I arrived at the location in Durham from the production office to see Ken still shooting at 2.00 p.m. Lunch had been waiting since 1.00 p.m. and was nearly ruined. The crew were not complaining but clearly needed a break. I walked to the camera and told Ken this was his last shot and then it was lunch. No argument! He put up his hands in despair, saying, 'Well. . . if no one wants to make a film . . .'

We broke for lunch. Ken didn't mean what he said. There was much to achieve that day and he was absorbed in getting it right. He'd forgotten details like lunch. Our crew were loyal, but needed to eat.

Near the end, shooting in Bristol, I was given a challenge when the camera crew looked over to me and grinned. Their loader had his hands inside the black bag, loading a magazine. Film had to be inserted into the camera magazine without any exposure to light, so loaders did it by touch. The crew challenged me to do it. Everyone was looking, Ken smiling mischievously. I accepted. With all eyes on me, I had no choice.

I was given time to practise. I took a black bag to my digs with a magazine and some old film and worked on it every night. As my Uncle Harold had told me, I had five thumbs on each hand. Learning to do this blind, just by feel, was frustrating. I thought I'd never get the hang of it and the day of the test loomed.

I arrived on location like a man going to the gallows. The camera crew were silently watching as I changed the magazine, sweating, nervous and concentrating like mad. Then John Else asked for the loaded magazine and inserted it into the camera. To my horror a scene was actually shot using my handiwork. I've never dreaded a technical report from the lab more. Fortunately, I was lucky. No problems were reported. I could face the crew, sadists that they were.

It reminded me that the loader, one of the most junior members of any crew, must always get it right, must really know what he or she's doing, or there's no film. Like writers, they have nowhere to hide. A producer or a director can get their credit and be paid much more yet only know how to hustle, knowing nothing about film-making.

By the end of production we were all exhausted. My most difficult task had been telling Ken time and again that the unit must wrap a location by the end of that afternoon. We must move, say, to Bristol this evening and shoot there tomorrow. This hurt me as well as Ken. He obeyed because even in his anguish he knew I would only make that decision if I had to. So our relationship was stronger than ever.

Ken and I knew, whatever the quality of the drama buried in that footage, we had made a statement on behalf of organised working people.

It was good to have it at last safely in the cutting room and I drove back to London feeling knackered and relieved. I'd been invited to a party and almost didn't go but decided to pop in, having said I would. There, Clara, someone I knew a little, introduced me to her daughter, Alex. It was all so proper, we might have been in a Jane Austen novel. We left after a few minutes, talked for hours and started to live together a week or two later. It lasted thirteen years and we have a son, Michael. Days of Hope, indeed.

Everyone on the film was buoyed by the comradely support of trade unionists all over the country. They gave of themselves generously. Many acted historical figures with confidence and authority, showing us yet again that creative talent is around us in abundance.

Our motive throughout was to warn about the future. I never had any interest in making period films in which aspects of the past were decorously set in aspic. The classic BBC costume drama left me cold. Fine clothes, carriages and aristocratic houses do not make an end in themselves. This chocolate-box view of history is reactionary. For me, history is contemporary.

Each generation invents its own history. It is fought over because the powerful ideas in the present are built on the interpretation of the past. The ruling class has always known this. History is a class issue. I had become interested in the oral history movement. I devoured Christopher Hill's work on the English civil war and E. P. Thompson's 1963 *The Making of the English Working Class*.

We wished to warn that when a crisis erupts, the Labour Party leadership always sides with the employers and the TUC bureaucracy betrays its membership. We showed this process in detail, as the miners were left hanging out to dry, isolated and near starvation, until they were forced to crawl back to work, on worse terms.

Before the films were transmitted I was alerted that the Controller of BBC One was unhappy. This was Bryan Cowgill, who had succeeded Paul Fox as Controller. He was an untypical BBC mandarin. Leaving school at fifteen he entered provincial journalism rather than university. Huw Wheldon said he wrote the best prose of anyone in the BBC. 'His memos are literature,' was Huw's flamboyant judgement. He made his name running *Grandstand*, the Saturday afternoon sports show, smoothly integrating outside broadcast live reports from all over the country. No mean feat in those days, when the technology didn't quite meet the ambition. Bryan had a fearsome, choleric temper. Grown men quaked when Ginger Cowgill was displeased.

The news came down that he didn't like episode one and demanded cuts before he would transmit. There was a scene in Ireland involving the discovery of the body of a British soldier, the victim of an IRA explosion. His mate discovers the remains and, in shock, murmurs, 'Oh, fuck.' Jim, Ken and I thought that entirely reasonable. Bryan did not. So I went to see him on the sixth floor in an attempt to change his mind.

Bryan was not a man who changed his mind. He refused point-blank and didn't wish to waste time discussing the matter. I did. The discussion quickly escalated, neither of us giving an inch. Sydney Newman in a rage was nothing compared to Ginger Cowgill. In the end, his face red with fury, he spoke a line which at the time I was too angry to find funny. 'If you think you can fucking well say fuck on my channel, you've got another fucking think coming.'

I was dismissed. He was intransigent.

We reluctantly cut the line.

This happened at a time when attitudes to language were relaxing. Years before, in 1965, Ken Tynan was the first to use the word 'fuck' on BBC television, though if he'd said it on Bryan's watch he would have feared for his life.

Back then we usually negotiated by means of memos and management would often use them to say things like, 'We will allow one only of "bugger", two of "God almighty" and three of "bloody". "Jesus Christ" will not be allowed and nor, of course, will "fuck".' Sometimes I would adopt the old trick of putting in a redundant oath so I could trade it.

All these memos, of course, were dictated to nicely brought up secretaries, from Roehampton or wherever, who then went off to type them. I hope they were not morally depraved as a result. Did their fathers know?

Reactions to the series were interesting and varied. The BBC management were put on the defensive and as usual played a straight bat. Many were furious that I had been allowed to produce it but all blandly held off the critics. The head of Westminster school, Dr John Rae, launched an angry attack on the historical accuracy of our treatment of Conscientious Objectors. He had written a book on the subject and clearly felt he was the authority but we had consulted with another expert. I felt his attack rested partly on ideology and partly on pique that his book had not been our major source. It was difficult because he made a noise in the press and his prestigious day job gave him a platform. I could hardly accuse him of pique and, anyway, it was probably unconscious. Our expert argued with him and I withdrew. It was a draw.

Some of those who hated our view of the war used the old trick of finding an inappropriate badge on one uniform to declare, 'If they can't get one small detail like this right, surely the whole film is a distortion.' We had been as assiduous in these details as in the screenplay research and our crew had done an impeccable BBC job. There were few mistakes, each tiny. One reason all this mattered to me was that I had listened often to my relatives, who were pedantic about practical items. If a drama showed a car, for instance, it had to be accurate, not a model from, say, 1926 in a drama set in 1921. It would ruin the whole thing.

'Switch this rubbish off. Bloody useless.'

Venom from all sides poured over the General Strike film: defenders of the Tories, the Labour leadership, the TUC bureaucracy, the

Stalinist Communist Party – each behaved as though they had suddenly joined Mary Whitehouse's campaign.

The BBC remained silent about the deal between the Prime Minister, Baldwin, and Reith, with good reason. We had invented a scene – in the sense that there was no independent evidence that it took place exactly as depicted – set in the garden of No. 10. Everything said in the scene had been verified and was on the record, either in official documents or detailed in the memoirs of those present.

Churchill, realising the power of this new device, the wireless, was itching to take it under government control, the better to control the message. He realised the importance of winning the propaganda war. Baldwin, a much cannier class warrior, refused. Instead, a deal was done with Reith. In exchange for the government not expropriating the BBC, Reith would promise to follow the government line on the strike and refuse airtime to anyone in favour of it, thus allowing the BBC nominal independence in exchange for giving up real independence. Baldwin knew that the public would be more likely to believe what it heard if it wasn't from a government source.

Reith justified this deal to himself by reasoning that the government was on the side of the people, the BBC was on the side of the people and, therefore, the BBC was on the side of the government.

This encapsulates the arrangement ever since. If the opposition – a future paymaster – has another policy, the BBC achieves 'balance' by giving it airtime.

We quietly refused to budge, allowing the films to speak for themselves: Baldwin's Tory government was an agent of the coal owners; Baldwin was a class warrior who later refused to even meet the Jarrow marchers; TUC leaders schemed against and abandoned the miners; Ramsay MacDonald and the Labour Party leadership washed their hands of the dispute, in indecent haste, and the Communist Party refused to offer leadership, choosing to sabotage the work of its militant membership.

Despite the lacunae in the films, Jim, Ken and I were proud. The films put ordinary working people at the centre of the story. They gave a clear and detailed warning: not only could it happen again but we provided the chapter and the verse.

Later, we would be horrified at the events of 1984-5, the effects of which are still being suffered today. Again the Labour leadership distanced itself and the TUC bureaucrats wrung their hands – or, more accurately, washed their hands. The miners were once again left out in the cold for the police to attack with impunity.

I fear it could happen yet again, to some other group. Those who don't learn from history are condemned to be passively buried by its repetition.

'Has he got any side on him?'

One day Pom and Harold were invited to my school to see the headmaster, Sir Rodney Paisley. Not knowing what it was about, Harold joked to Pom they'd both get six of the best. She was not amused. They were shown into his study by the school secretary, with me fearfully bringing up the rear. Sir Rodney, resplendent in his gown, rose and greeted them with a handshake. When they sat down he opened his cigarette case, offering it to Harold but, of course, not to Pom. Harold looked at it and got out his own pack of Woodbines, then his cigarette of choice.

'No. Have one of mine.'

Sir Rodney put his case away and accepted Harold's offer, allowing him to light both.

Soon after I was asked to leave the room. They never told me what was said but they didn't look too pleased when they left.

That moment was a revelation. It not only showed Sir Rodney gracefully putting a parent at his ease but, more importantly, it demonstrated Harold's deep assumption of his equal status, despite his acceptance of the status quo in those deferential times.

Harold would say calmly of the royal family and Conservative toffs, 'They're born to rule. It's in the blood.' Yet he never seemed to be socially intimidated. Time and again I saw him being exactly the same with everyone of whatever class, with men and women of great power and of none. Always courteous. He wore a trilby hat and in the street, on seeing a neighbour, he would raise it as he greeted her. If it was Christmas time, he would say formally, 'Compliments of the season, Mrs Edwards.'

I didn't know the source of this but I admired it. Oddly enough, the combination of social confidence with courteous charm is something I've noticed since in old Etonians.

Although with them, it's a class weapon.

Even my illiterate Grandma was the same. If the Queen of England had walked into her kitchen there would have been no simpering or awkwardness. She'd have told her to sit down and then put the kettle on.

One morning a pleasant woman from BBC radio called, asking me if I'd be free to appear on the following Friday's *Any Questions?* This was an important show, attracting cabinet ministers relishing its large audience. Each of the panellists was compelled to answer questions from the audience. To say you had no opinion, were unqualified or didn't have enough facts was not allowed. That had always struck me as silly, turning the show into just unenlightening entertainment and a mere parade of prejudice. None of us can say anything useful about everything.

I realised that the invitation was a red-light warning. I had occasionally given interviews about the work, offering information and responding to criticism. I sort of enjoyed the attention and felt guilty at the same time. But I had mainly followed Sydney Newman's wise advice.

This invitation crossed a line. It would be a step towards seducing me into what later was called celebrity but was then more selective and subtle. Now, one has to work harder to avoid celebrity than anyone then had to work to achieve it. But I knew if I performed well, it would lead to more invitations and more temptations which the performer in me would find hard to resist.

So I politely declined and have continued to decline similar invitations, the infant refusing to tap-dance. I'm more relaxed about it now but for decades I scrupulously hid myself away, putting others up to be interviewed as the publicity machines became hungrier.

I've speculated, of course, about this. My Dad's suicide and the trial of Mom's abortionist were reported in the newspaper. Suicide and abortion were 'immoral criminal offences against God and the crown'. This resonated in a low church family that was not looking for publicity. In addition, our kind of people, people we might know, only ever appeared in the *Birmingham Mail* in shame. The 'kiddy fiddler' scoutmaster or vicar, the man in the next road caught coming off shift at the BSA with a 'foreigner' (that is, a personal item made in the firm's time with the firm's metal on the firm's machine). Notoriety and shame went with fines and prison sentences. The last thing anyone wanted was to be in the *Birmingham Mail*. Other sorts of people were in it and were admired. That was fame. We avoided it.

Latterly I've wondered if coming from Brum – or perhaps my kind of Brum – was also a factor. Making an exhibition of yourself in public was frowned on. Boasting was scorned and pushy people disdained: they were dismissed as mancunians or, worse, cockneys. Their response to my adolescent pretensions was a level, 'Oh, ar,' neutrally delivered from an expressionless face. I had always been too clever by half and so full of words I 'must have swallowed a dictionary.' Little boys should be seen and not heard.

The more successful and well known I became, the less Pom and Harold, in particular, offered me any praise or even took much notice. What happened in London, happened in London. What was he like in Brum? Getting big-headed, is he? I knew I was constantly being inspected and reported on.

When a letter arrived inviting me to appear on *Desert Island Discs* I guessed it was my son Will sending me up. He worked at Broadcasting House so had access to the headed notepaper. He'd have to get up earlier in the morning to catch me, I thought. But I was assured by colleagues that it was genuine. I politely replied, turning it down. My sons were disappointed, having hoped to be involved in the choice of music. I couldn't believe that anyone would want to hear my choice of records, which would probably be all John Lennon anyway. That's what I said.

But the real reason was that I didn't want to lie. I would have had to talk about my parents and there were still some of their siblings alive, people I loved who would not want that painful story rehearsed. I would also be upset about Topsy and I feared some tabloid hack seeing an opportunity and harassing her for a 'Where are they now?' story.

But I still don't know why I turned down *Who's Who*. I wrote back to say thanks, but I knew who I was and didn't need to be in a book to find out. Some years later they asked again, wondering if I'd changed my mind. I wrote back, politely telling them that I'd looked at their book and didn't like much of the company I was being asked to keep.

Maybe I didn't know who I was.

So my attitude to personal publicity is only partially explained. Maybe it's changing. I couldn't have written this book before now.

Maybe it's just a hangover from the fear of the family sadly shaking its collective head. The biggest question ever asked was, 'Has he got any side?'

I needed the answer to be, 'No'.

Law and Order

When in Brum one weekend I thought I'd pop over to see my Aunty Minnie. She lived in another district, Kingstanding, and I'd not seen her for a while. When she opened the door she looked relieved.

'Oh, thank God you've come.'

'Hello, Minnie. Just wondered how you were keeping.'

'Terrible. My telly's on the blink.'

'Oh, sorry to hear that. I've got the car. I'll nip down to Kingstanding and see when the shop can send a lad up to fix it.'

Her head pitched to one side and her eyes narrowed suspiciously. 'I thought you said you worked at the BBC.'

'Well, I do, Min, but I don't know anything about televisions.'

'Mmm . . .' She nodded, staring at me, clearly disappointed. I don't think she ever believed a word I said after that.

Troy Kennedy Martin introduced me to G. F. (Gordon Frank) Newman one Saturday evening at his house. Troy was a generous host and I would often pop in for a drink and a game of ping-pong, which I played with more enjoyment than skill. It was a case of one writer being generous to another. I didn't know Gordon but on Troy's good word I read a novel of his about a bent Met detective.

It rang true. We met and talked, strolling round Hyde Park, hour after hour. Gordon is taciturn, shrewd and immensely knowledgeable about cops and villains. He once told me that at school there were boys who he knew would become either detectives or villains but he could not tell which of the two any boy would choose. He had kept in touch with old friends in both careers. Because he wrote fiction and was obviously a man of discretion they trusted him enough to be frank.

We did not set out to make a four-part mini series but gradually *Law & Order* (1978) emerged as my curiosity about the whole judicial process increased and his knowledge was revealed. Of course, Gordon was up for it. He knew so much and wanted to dramatise what he knew. This would be his first opportunity to write for the screen. But my issue with the law – detectives, the judiciary and the actual laws themselves – goes back to my infancy. I wanted to investigate, to expose the secrets behind the public facade of probity.

I remembered Uncle Fred's patience under my interrogation, as if I was a detective sergeant and he was a witness, possibly an accessory. Reliving those dark days of the war when he'd lost his Ida, a sister he was very close to, raking over the details yet again for a sceptical lad, must have tried his tolerance. But he did not turn on me. 'Well, Christmas was out of the winder, that was for sure. All over the end of December there was a cop stationed outside your house. Whenever he left the house, they followed him.'

'I said to Jan, "You'd think they'd have more to do. You'd think Tom was bloody Hitler, the way they're carrying on."'

'A detective, plain clothes, kept coming round. We couldn't get much out of your Dad. Tom was in on himself but by all accounts the plain clothes cop kept at him, trying to break him down. I think they were looking for the woman but your Dad wouldn't talk to them. They threatened him, I think, but I wasn't there. It all happened in your house. Anyway, this cop didn't crack the case. Not then. But they got her after.'

He looked at me as though hoping that would be the end of it. I stared implacably back, not giving an inch. 'It was a bad time, Tony, you understand and, whatever the rights and wrongs, I felt sorry for your Dad. What was done was done. I don't blame him, either. It was just bad luck, really. The poor bugger looked like death's door.

I don't know any more. I'm sorry. I'm sorry. I'd tell you if I did. Come on, it's just morbid.'

The cops were no doubt doing their jobs, trying to extract a secret from Dad, to crack the criminal case of an illegal abortion. I too wanted to crack the case. I hated secrets.

The great institutions are the most secretive of all. The Met is an example of an institution assuming a right to know your secrets but ruthless and devious in guarding its own.

What I refused to acknowledge about myself was that my own life was built on secrecy. The very thing I vowed to destroy in others was the foundation of my own life. Few knew about my parents' death, particularly the circumstances. Topsy's illness was still too raw to talk about. Only a handful were aware of my arthritic spine and my daily pain. I worked in hiding at the BBC at the top of the east tower, not revealing what I was planning. It was odd that this secretive man, who wouldn't even talk to the press, was so dedicated to revealing secrets. None of this occurred to me at the time.

Law & Order told the same story from four different points of view, one in each episode: the villain, the detective, the solicitor and the prisoner. Gordon's style was low-key, with detailed observation and complex narratives. These screenplays were laconic and under-stated, an insider's look at a private world. I realised that the most shocking element was the corruption of Met detectives that was not merely endemic but, indeed, a qualification for advancement, even of membership, of this elite squad. Potential recruits to Detective Branch were tested. If they refused to join the others on the take they were sent back on the beat or to traffic.

The traditional TV police procedural would show a corrupt cop – the 'bad apple in the barrel' – being arrested and expelled by honest coppers horrified by his actions, vindicating the boys in blue and reassuring the public. To underline just how different our angle was I decided that the corruption should be shown without comment or emphasis. It would be part of the natural order of things and depicted with a shrug. So standard that it was not worth noting. This normalising of police criminality was what made it shocking to the public and caused outrage in the Met and among the establishment.

I needed a directing style which would go with the grain of the writing. My hunch was that Les Blair's laid-back personality would naturally fit the style we needed. His work had the quality of not insisting.

He had only directed two small chamber pieces using the technique of long weeks of rehearsed improvisation. This would be not only his first scripted film, but a big mini series. When I offered it, he was thrilled but shaken to learn he was to direct all four, back to back. It had to be shot by the same director and crew; I wanted it to be seamless.

With Gordon's help we put the word out. As usual, we didn't want recognisable faces that would undermine the credibility. Two of the leading parts were played by Derek Martin and Peter Dean, at that time unknown. People came in from all over east and south London claiming to be actors. When I reminded them that we could not employ them unless they were members of Equity, they would shrug, 'No problem, Tone.' I still don't know how they managed it but everyone we made an offer to flashed a new Equity card. We combined the newcomers with experienced but unknown professionals and divided them up between villains and detectives, following Gordon's revelation that they all came from the same communities and often knew each other.

Early one evening, Les and I were casting in an office at TV Centre and some men who had been sent up from reception failed to arrive. We assumed they had got lost in that confusing building. But en route they had met two BBC security men, retired Met detectives, who had years earlier nicked one of our hopefuls and seen him sent down. The would-be actors were stopped and questioned. When they said they were about to audition for a BBC film, the security men thought this a pathetic alibi and laughed. It took some time for the matter to be resolved. I've forgotten whether we cast any of them.

A few serving Met detectives came on board, moonlighting for cash, to advise us and one took Les Blair and the designer, Austen

Spriggs, round Scotland Yard one weekend afternoon to check the layout. 'If we get stopped, I'm bringing you in for questioning.' That information allowed Austen to dress the offices accurately in a new building we used by Euston station.

A senior man from the production staff, a BBC lifer, told me that having read the screenplay he could not in all conscience continue: he felt the films unfairly traduced the Met, which he respected. I rather admired him for being prepared to stand up for his beliefs. It showed character. But it posed difficulties. For him, it would be a black mark. BBC lifers did shows as they were allocated. They didn't pick and choose. For me, if he went into detail as to why he was coming off the production it might attract dangerous interest and scrutiny. I could not ask him to lie.

So I offered a compromise. I would quietly arrange for an exchange with another show so no one would comment. He was happy. He didn't want to make a federal case of it. We shook hands and I asked him to just do one more thing, that evening. He was to take an envelope to a certain pub. I gave him instructions about who he was going to meet. He did so willingly. The next morning I told him that the envelope had been full of used notes, of mixed denominations from our budget, and the recipient had been a serving detective in the Met. He was so shocked, he said he would stay with us.

This was the extent of the naivety that existed in nice, educated middle-class people who wanted to believe police and media propaganda. Poor people had for ages been at the sharp end of their practices and had no such illusions.

Les Blair, like all good directors, has an in-built bullshit meter. The performances were as a result honest, low-key and authentic: no acting on display. His laconic, deadpan, unexcitable manner infected everyone and the result was just what the films needed. It was a challenge for him. He came through.

There was an explosion in the press when the films went out, with politicians and the Met in apoplectic denial. We prompted questions in the House of Commons, of course, and a debate in the House of Lords. Eldon Griffiths, MP, my old adversary Mary Whitehouse and the usual suspects complained. The BBC refused to sell the films abroad because it would be bad for London's image. We had obviously drawn blood. It was clearly necessary to preserve confidence in the Met even if it meant not facing up to its corruption. Eventually, *Law and Order* was repeated, but only after opposition from some senior management.

A while later a Met commissioner, Robert Mark, said that it was his ambition to arrest more criminals than he employed. That, we thought, would at least be a start. No politician or journalist apologised to us or even said that, after all, we had been correct, even though one corrupt cop after another was exposed year after year. It seemed that the one bad apple in the barrel doctrine was an essential part of the ruling ideology.

As usual management was divided, undecided whether I should be expelled or encouraged.

Gordon's world of cops told the truth, but television's lies about them continue to this day.

Scotland Yard top brass knew the truth. Indeed, some of them were a part of the problem. How do you reform an institution which is riddled with corruption? Cops on the take, brutality and racism have tainted the Met way back into Victorian times. Denying or minimising the problem doesn't solve it. It just preserves the status quo ante.

The Spongers

When I feed the poor they call me a saint. When I ask why they are poor, they call me a communist.

Oscar Romero, Archbishop of San Salvador,
El Salvador, assassinated in 1980

Uncle Harold was a royalist who always demanded silence and respect for the Queen's Christmas message. Every year he would give the same judgement. 'She speaks well, doesn't she? And she's not as young as she was. They work hard. Though I don't like all the hangers-on. Well, Pom, I doubt she had a better dinner, I say, if she's had a better Christmas dinner than us, she's a lucky woman.'

I knew this Silver Jubilee would be encouraged by the media, led by the BBC. It made me angry, not just because I was a republican but because of the contrast between this ridiculous confection and the suffering all over the country made worse by the Labour government cuts in welfare provision. Even Labour councils were making hard decisions to balance their budgets.

The atmosphere was febrile. It was the first sign of the conflicts to come in the eighties that would fundamentally change the country. I was nervous, without knowing quite why. Thatcherism was not even on the horizon but something I couldn't grasp was threatening.

I did know that the BBC, being nauseatingly obsequious to royalty, would give the Jubilee the treatment so I thought we should make our own contribution to the celebrations. I naturally turned to Jim Allen, who was as firmly republican as me, and we thought we would set our drama in the middle of a Jubilee celebration. Jim did some research and came up with the story of a single mother of four children, one of whom has Down's syndrome. It was based on a case in Salford.

In our film *The Spongers*, which went out early in 1978, a girl with Down's syndrome, Paula, is taken away from a home where she is thriving and put in a different borough in an old people's home to save money. Pauline, the mother, is in rent arrears and appeals to a tribunal for help. Her father speaks for her. We cast my old friend, Peter Kerrigan. He spoke from the heart and was very moving.

Christine Hargreaves played Pauline. I remembered her from *In Two Minds*, in which she played Anna Cropper's sister. I'd always admired her. She approached this role in the right way, living with the children before the film, making a bond with them. One of them, a charming little girl, Grace, was Jim and Clare Allen's daughter. Christine also spent time in the community, becoming part of it.

We filmed in Oldham and, as usual, depended on local people's goodwill and help. They made us welcome. Bernard Atha, who had appeared in *Kes*, played a local councillor; he was a councillor in Leeds, so didn't have to 'act' it. Bernard Hill, who had been in *Hard Labour* for Mike Leigh, was an experienced actor and Gertie Almond, a wonderfully coarse and warm local club act, was in her first film. They both fitted in credibly.

I was introduced to the film's director, Roland Joffé, by Clive Goodwin. On the form book, I shouldn't have even considered Roland. He was a theatre director who had done a bit of television but never a film, let alone a big one and one for which he would be asked to adopt my particular style. I couldn't explain many of my decisions rationally but as the two of us chatted I felt there was something about him, something I couldn't put my finger on. It was just a hunch that he could do it.

His contract didn't come through. Clive harassed me on Roland's behalf, saying there was a theatre offer waiting that he had to take. He needed to work. I couldn't get an answer so eventually went

to see Shaun Sutton, the Head of Drama. He was a pleasant, conventional, liberal-minded man who never looked for trouble. He'd
once told me that when Sydney Newman had asked him to give
up producing children's drama and become a head of department,
he had said, 'I don't know anything about management. Could you
give me some advice?'

Sydney just said, 'Don't sleep with the help.' Good advice but
redundant for a respectable, uxorious man like Shaun. He seemed
shifty when I asked about Roland and his answer was mysterious.

'There's a problem. He hasn't got BH [Broadcasting House]
clearance. I'm afraid there's nothing I can do.' I pressed him for an
explanation. All Shaun could say was, 'It's the man in the mac in
BH.' I was by now furious at this nonsense. I picked my people,
not some obscure man at Broadcasting House, and I wasn't about
to lose this one. I could have given the gig to someone else. There
were plenty of directors to choose from. But now it was a matter of
principle, so I marched up to the sixth floor to see the Controller
of Television, Alasdair Milne. We had always got on, even though
he was an acolyte of Grace Wyndham Goldie. He was one of those
urbane Scotsmen with a cut-glass English accent, a Wykehamist who
had served in the Gordon Highlanders.

Alasdair greeted me warmly. It was the end of the day and his
secretaries had gone home. As I sat, he poured what I assumed to be
a fine single malt and offered it to me neat. I sipped as we exchanged
small talk. It was all very polite.

I got down to business.

'Alasdair, you – the BBC – may hire anyone you wish and refuse
to hire anyone you wish, of course, but I want to hire Roland
Joffé to direct a film. If his contract doesn't come through I will
resign. That will mean questions from the press. Why suddenly
resign in the middle of a contract? I'll be forced to say what I know
about Roland's rejection and be tempted to say what I suspect.
I'm not threatening you, Alasdair. I've nothing to threaten with.
But we've known each other for a long time and always got on.
I thought it only courteous to tell you in advance. It's not a problem if you're prepared to go into all you know for the press and

give them your reasons for refusing to hire this man. Just to direct a drama.'

There was a pause. He offered me a thin smile. I remember thinking it could go either way. I half expected to be thrown out.

He picked up the phone, looked for a number, dialled and then said, very quietly, 'Put Joffé's contract through, will you?'

We then finished our drinks as though this had been a mere social visit. I complimented his Scotch although my palate was not informed enough to judge.

He stood up, we shook hands warmly and I left.

It was not an isolated case. Some time before I had been offered an extension to my contract and I had agreed. But it didn't come through. I asked about it and was met with embarrassed silence. They were doing their best, apparently. I said if it didn't come through, I was leaving. I had other options. Eventually, it did, with no explanation, although with a few nods and winks. It was clear that my ability as a producer was not being questioned. Drama Group wanted me. At a senior level – up to and including the Director General, the question mark was over my politics and the content of my work, even though the BBC had full rights over editorial matters in all contracts, including mine.

Roy Battersby was treated worse. He was blacklisted for years, presumably for being a member of the Workers Revolutionary Party, a legal organisation. But Roland Joffé's case was silly as well as unjust. He may have attended a few meetings or demos, as most young people did, partly out of curiosity, but I was around political people throughout that period and he was an intelligent, concerned Liberal. For that he was to be prevented from earning his living directing dramas.

Senior management went along with this intrusion from MI5. In Drama a fight was put up and sometimes the MI5 apparatchiks backed off. As far as I know there were no principled resignations. So much for the BBC's independence from government, for its embrace of balance and for its claim to be politically neutral.

The security services also gave News and Current Affairs 'background briefs' on strikes and subversives in trade unions. No matter that these activities were within the law; they were treated as enemy action and the BBC senior management colluded. I've no idea what the state of play is now and would be cautious of believing any BBC attempt to clarify it.

I gave Roland an experienced cameraman, Nat Crosby, and my old friend Bill Shapter as editor, arranging for Bill to be with us during the shoot. It was a big challenge for Roland. He came through brilliantly. Like Ken, he was calm and sympathetic, never shouting or throwing his weight around. He was good with the little children, especially the one with Down's syndrome, Paula, turning every scene patiently into a game. I encouraged him to just shoot, giving the actors room to breathe, trusting Nat to follow them with the camera.

There was one scene in the council chamber that Bill Shapter and I suggested he shoot in a way that would not have been recommended, say, in Karel Reisz's classic book, *The Technique of Film Editing*. Roland said, 'But it won't cut.' Bill and I said in unison, 'It'll cut. Don't worry.' He looked at the producer and the editor and nodded doubtfully. It cut.

But above all I respected Roland's courage in throwing the dice on his big chance, going out on a limb and risking everything. I was very pleased for him when I saw his later successes such as *The Killing Fields* in 1984 and 1986's *The Mission*.

We didn't know how to end the film, discussing possibilities right through the shoot. In the end we decided that Pauline could see no future and no escape. She uses a prescription from the doctor to make up drinks for the children, puts them to bed and drinks the same drink. None of them wake up. Some criticised us for 'defeatism', saying she should have continued to fight. We decided that it was the audience who needed to respond politically. It was our task to make them want to fight.

It affected me, of course. I didn't mention to anyone that suicide resonated with me.

The Spongers was a film meant to move people. How can we treat our fellow citizens, our children, so cruelly? But it also had another political edge, opening with big cardboard cutouts of the Queen and

Prince Philip, the real spongers, being treated with casual disrespect by some workers and it ended with a Jubilee street party, heard over the preparations for the deaths.

Jim and I were pleased the film had a large audience. It was a big talking point. It clearly struck a chord.

But I think of it now and am ashamed that the situation for people like this family is worse, just as fifty years after *Cathy Come Home* there are more homeless than ever.

Clive Goodwin

Clive Goodwin was launching the political magazine, The Black Dwarf.

Gerry Healy was dismissive. He was starting a daily Trotskyist newspaper.

'Could we be your colour supplement?'

The laughter would have drowned Gerry's crushing reply.

But for once, he had none.

It was early one morning in November 1978. My wife Alex and I were still in bed and I took a call from my friend, Irving Teitelbaum. He said he'd just been told that Clive Goodwin was dead. He knew it was in Los Angeles but had been told little else. I was shocked and deeply upset.

Roger Smith had introduced me to Clive and his wife Pauline Boty in 1964. She was a warm, attractive personality, very welcoming and full of life. A painter and actor and activist, she lit up a room. When I first met her she was a big-boned, healthy beauty with a hearty energy. She became pregnant. Then she was diagnosed with leukaemia. Chemo would have killed the baby. She wanted the baby, thus sentencing herself to death. Her daughter, Boty Goodwin, was born healthy and normal. Pauline's health deteriorated. I hardly knew her but it was awful to see her, still exuding good spirits, languishing on a chaise longue in their vast room on Cromwell Road, week by week thinner and paler, clearly disappearing in front of our eyes. I can only imagine what it must have been like for Clive, let alone her. This woman, so alive, so promising, with life ahead of her, being cut down at twenty-eight years old like this, cast a shadow over those who loved her. She died in 1966, when Boty was a few weeks old.

Over the years Clive and I became good friends, growing closer as our children grew up. Will was with his grandmother in Brum. She would put him on the train at New Street station and the guard would keep an eye on him, handing him over to me at Euston. He naturally met my friends and also their children. Marsha Hunt and I have been friends since the sixties when she was in the musical *Hair*. We are like siblings and she is part of my family. Her daughter Karis and Will, when children, would look at each other nervously. Sometimes he would play with Boty. A little, wary boy observing these girls who seemed so different from the kids in Brum. Clive would slip a pound or two into his hand, reminding me of the gestures of my uncles when I was a lad. Boty lived with Clive when she was older. He never married again.

At Roger and Troy's suggestion Clive started an agency for writers and directors. He'd worked with Ken Tynan on *Tempo*, an early sixties arts show and been an actor, but this new venture was perfect for his talents. As the sixties progressed he became a pivotal figure, meeting and getting to know everyone in the arts and left-wing politics, making connections and nurturing careers. He was an important cultural figure. The agency grew quickly and the list was impressive. Indeed, after his death, his clients, as they matured into big stars, formed the basis for the success of a number of London agencies.

We became firm friends and saw each other every few days. I employed many of his clients and sent him new ones. But I think what drew us together was a sadness and underneath that a depression, which we never discussed. We were too busy fending them off.

I admired him for all those qualities I didn't possess. He gave the best parties, strolling around nursing the same wine glass, seemingly doing nothing, but there was always a buzz in a room full of the most engaging people.

Any meeting he called would be fully attended, effortlessly, as though he just had to snap his fingers. On one occasion, his room was packed with activists and hangers-on wanting to meet Daniel Cohn-Bendit, one of the leaders of the uprising in Paris in 1968, known as Dany le Rouge ('Danny the Red'). He arrived directly from a television interview. Clive, of course, had gone to Paris as soon as it erupted, and, of course, had got to know him. The political discussion was heavily underway when someone alerted the meeting to a stranger. He was discussed and despite his protests was evicted as an MI5 or special branch infiltrator on the dubious grounds that he looked like one. His large black boots were the clincher, apparently. It later turned out he was from *The Times*. These were paranoid days (although, as someone pointed out, being from *The Times* does not preclude one from being MI5). Clive was a magnet for everyone vaguely on the Left and in the arts. He had social élan.

I knew he'd been in Los Angeles to close a deal with Warren Beatty for his film *Reds*. As each day passed I was given new details about what occurred. Apparently he had been in the lobby of the Beverly Wilshire Hotel. His head ached. Then he collapsed. The staff concluded he was drunk and called the police. He was thrown into the drunk tank, where he died, alone and unattended, some hours later. The London press, no doubt taking the official version as true, were full of stories about his dissolute drinking. It was an ugly ending to a sad story.

It then appeared I was an executor of his will, along with the poet Christopher Logue and Irving Teitelbaum. Clive had omitted to tell us. Irving's view was that he hardly knew him and he withdrew, quite reasonably. Christopher had many virtues but he wasn't the most practical of men. So I took it on. As it was, Clive's estate was simple to administer. Little Boty was his heir. Eventually, the poet Adrian Mitchell and his wife Celia, who had daughters of their own, took the twelve-year-old Boty lovingly and generously under their wing. The agency broke up, to the enrichment of other agents.

What remained was the slur on Clive's reputation that had to be refuted for Boty's sake. Clive rarely drank alcohol and only occasionally smoked dope. He was not drunk, he was suffering from a brain haemorrhage overlooked by the negligent Beverly Hills police.

Luckily, I was frequently in Los Angeles and was soon to move there. I met a high-powered lawyer in the Century City area, recommended by Warren Beatty, who agreed to take the case on a contingency basis. Together we embarked on a five-year battle. Everyone told me it was impossible to win against the Beverly Wilshire Hotel and, especially, against the Beverly Hills police. I knew I couldn't give up – partly for Boty and partly for my dead friend.

I lined up agents and famous writers in London who were ready to appear in court in Los Angeles, plus producer Elliott Kastner, who had suffered a similar attack but was saved by being taken straight away to the Middlesex Hospital. The clincher was to be the appearance of Boty herself, defending her father's reputation. I guessed the prospect of an attractive young English girl in the witness box speaking about her dead father would be a risky prospect for the other side. At this point, when we were at the door of the court, both parties – or rather their insurance companies – caved in. Boty won substantial damages. But the real victory was the restoration of Clive's reputation.

I continued to see Boty as she grew up. I still have a precocious little storybook full of her own illustrations that she presented to me. Her mother's talents were clearly coming through. She went to California and graduated as a star pupil at an art college. Having been through a drugs phase, she was by then clean. She had a brilliant future opening up. A fellow student offered her some heroin at a graduation party and in her euphoria she accepted. It was too pure for someone clean and she died, aged twenty-nine.

So, this whole family was wiped out in their prime.

I still miss Clive.

The Walls Close In

*Life was hard for Auntie Minnie in the thirties. She was a widow
and the sole provider for her daughter, Eileen. Work was scarce.
She asked for help. The means test men came and made a note
of her possessions. On seeing the piano, they said, 'That's got to
go.' Minnie said Eileen was learning to play.*

'Still got to go.'
Minnie threw them out. 'We'll manage.'
They did, just, with help from the family.

I'd been working so many hours for so long it was no longer sustainable. The idea was to leave no time for introspection, no space
for my internal reality to win a purchase on my thinking. I worked,
or invented work, seven days a week, from early morning until well
into the evening and then used booze and the social round to fill in
before bed. This vain attempt to fend off what I had to eventually
face was exhausting. I was on the edge of collapse, leaving me running on empty.

Externally, the rapid moves to the Right by the Labour government were infuriating to watch. The economic difficulties caused
by the Opec oil price increases in the seventies seemed a signal that
the Keynesian post-war boom was stuttering to a stop. The capitalist
system, facing this crisis, was about to show its teeth. In response,
the Left was suicidal. The prospects for the UK seemed particularly

bleak. These were years before the North Sea oil boom. Of course, I couldn't predict the future, but there was danger in the air. I failed to put my finger on what it was.

The atmosphere inside the BBC was oppressive and there seemed to be less room for me to breathe politically. It was subtle at first, but I sensed pressure to find work closer to the mainstream, both in form as well as content. There was a feeling of the end of a chapter of opportunity. More worrying was my own reaction to the gathering political clouds. I was running out of ideas. I feared repeating myself. I was bored by the riffs we had used in the past, both in the style and in the message.

I had four films a year in my gift. There was little chance of doing anything interesting in the cinema at that time. Many directors and writers saw me as their only hope. I could only work with a few of them. This was resented by directors who expected me to magic their careers when I had few opportunities and no magic. I dreaded going to parties for fear of being pushed up against a wall with demands I offer a film. I understood the frustration but it made me uncomfortable. It was as though I had a brilliant future to offer them and I was perversely withholding it.

Above all, I was depressed at losing some of my best friends into the Workers Revolutionary Party (WRP). These were fine people who had sacrificed their careers to dedicate themselves for little money. I felt isolated and rejected. The more I observed the more impressed I was by the political analysis, but the WRP seemed to behave like an extreme religious sect, with its charismatic leadership demanding obedience and its conviction that it and only it had the truth. It used sacred texts like weapons. It had followers, not members. Some were bullies, others seemed cowed. There was a menace, a subtext of intellectual, if not physical, violence.

I tried to keep my friends but I failed with one or two important ones. It took a long time for those relationships to be repaired. I kept a distance, admiring the dedication and principles of those comrades who gave their lives to the struggle. Like members of the Communist Party I met in my teens, they were some of the finest people I've ever known. But I held to my differences despite

considerable hostility. It was uncomfortable, isolating and exhausting. I was not a fellow traveller but I tried to remain cordial and
continued to engage.

The psychology of it fascinated me. What do people reveal about
themselves when they join or refuse to join particular political
movements? This is a question about the people, not the movement.
I was struck by how many Communist Party members had been
brought up as Roman Catholics. It must have been easy to exchange
one set of certainties for another, one promise of heaven after death
for another of heaven on earth and the obedience to the dictates of a
leader and his apparatchiks. Healy's Trotskyists were angry, not just
with the class enemy, but within.

Of those I knew who joined, some had fine ideals, some were
disappointed with their lives outside the Party and some were suffering from unresolved difficult emotions, finding relief in a cause
which could use their feelings of hostility. Some were all three.
The hostility to Freud in revolutionary parties of the Left is not
just theoretical: if you dissolve your anger by reconnecting with its
source and then working it through, there is no anger left for the
Left to use. The result is that, among the fine idealists, there was an
unhealthy atmosphere of bullying, cold anger and intimidation in the
WRP.

William Reich is the only person I know of with the distinction of being expelled by both the International Psychoanalytical
Association and the Communist Party (of Berlin). He also made
an attempt to reconcile both sets of ideas. The leadership of both
organisations were hostile to each other.

Political activism on the Left is often an attempt to reclaim the
fantasy of infantile paradise, the paradise before temptation in
Genesis, if you like. With me, activism represented the old fantasy
that changing the world would be easier and less painful than changing myself. I really did think for a while that we could make a film
and change the world. A fantasy indeed! But it meant I could avoid
the need to change myself, a pyrrhic victory of no permanence.

For a dozen years I'd dreamt of making films by the people, for
the people and of the people; and of opening the eyes of a new

generation to a particular approach to film-making, an observed, distilled naturalism. But these ambitions were being swept away by changes that were gathering momentum, changes in the ideological basis of society.

I was clearly swimming against a tide.

People now might find it difficult to understand but a generation with more energy than analysis had experienced enormous optimism in the sixties. Not just a relaxation of oppressive attitudes to sex and drugs, but a liberation of wider social conventions and the beginnings of a feminist revolution. The collective buzz of anti-Vietnam War marches persuaded many in that generation to confuse form with fact. The Left achieved nothing substantial and lasting, politically or economically.

The serious unrest that followed in the seventies, that generation's first recession, was also their first experience of working-class militancy in strikes. The talk of army intervention, the hardening of the political debate on the Right, all gave the impression that a final political showdown was imminent. Many in this generation felt starved of answers. Organisations like the WRP seemed to have those answers, both in their coherent and persuasive analysis and in the form of an organisation that claimed to be ready to enter decisively into the imminent fight. This was difficult for some to resist.

Ken Loach, like most directors, wanted cinema, but in those days it was almost impossible to raise money for our kind of film. His young son, Stephen, had a 1968 book by Leon Garfield, *Black Jack*, an adventure set in the eighteenth century. Ken said he wanted to do it. I liked Leon and thought it was a good children's book but had no interest in it. Yet I was close to Ken and didn't want to let him down. My mind had dried up and I had no alternative to offer him. I reluctantly said I would produce it.

I should have said, 'No.' I was acting in bad faith. I was bored. I produced it badly. Ken said he wanted to adapt it. I just said, 'OK.' I gave few notes. The money was raised, partly from John Terry at the NFFC and partly from France, after Ken had cast a well known French actor. I was bodily present on the location but might as well not have been. In not wanting to let Ken down, I let him down badly. Whenever I have behaved like this it has been a mistake. The film finished and opened in 1979 to little business.

For years I had been asked why I wasn't directing myself. Huw Wheldon even gave me carte blanche to direct whenever I wanted. I had never understood this because directing had never attracted me. Others saw it as an aspiration. If I'd wanted to I'd have done it years before. But now, casting round for something which might bring me to life again, I wondered about it.

I had written a screenplay based on research I did into prostitution. It contrasted the different lives of street girls (their word) in Brum and expensive, upper-class call girls in London's West End. It looked at them unsentimentally, as workers hiring themselves out on a freelance basis. It didn't make them sexy and none of them had a heart of gold or left the business because a client fell in love with them. It was an attempt to look at work and refuse the clichés of the prostitute genre.

During the research my wife Alex would answer the phone for me with, 'He's not here. He's with a prostitute.' The subsequent awkward silences amused her.

The research was fascinating. The girls in Balsall Heath, Brum, were suspicious and only saw me after the intervention of a social worker. They then became friends. The London call girls were easy if I paid the rate: so what if I got off on talking to them with a tape recorder? I learned that the street girl would do a client in the back of his Cortina and then be free to meet her kids when they came out of school. The hours were better than working on the checkout at Tesco and so was the pay. She could do the trick thinking about something else and then leave it all behind her. Not so the high-fee call girl. She had to pretend things she didn't feel. This psychological pressure led to stress and drug abuse.

So, on the basis that a change is as good as a rest, a cliché remembered from my childhood, I decided to try this directing business. I'd see if everyone was right.

The budget for *Prostitute* was small and I was lucky to raise private funding so decided to take the opportunity to test some ideas to their limits. Living dangerously had worked for me in the past, making me feel alive and on the edge.

How far can one go in rejecting traditional narrative structure, the familiar riffs of, 'How will it all turn out?' How far can one go in observing natural, spontaneous behaviour, rejecting all aspects of 'performance'? Can one observe on film what doesn't seem observed? I crewed up with old colleagues Charles Stewart and Bill Shapter and plunged in. Some in the cast were professional actors or aspiring professionals, although none were known. Others were prostitutes appearing in a film for the first time. I have never said which were which.

There was one difficult moment. Money enters a film's account in accordance with the submitted and approved weekly cash flow analysis. One week, Bobby Blues, our production accountant, told me it hadn't arrived. Not only must we stop shooting but, because the crew were on two weeks' notice, we couldn't pay them. I asked him to continue to investigate why the cash had dried up and to arrange a bank loan to see us through. This he did with the local NatWest.

Then I had to go to the NatWest branch with him. I finished the shot and discussed the next set-up with Charles before going to the bank. There I put my house up against the loan. It would see us through for a while. Eventually the glitch was resolved and the cash flow resumed. They say you're not really a producer until you've had to put your house up. That certainly was not a boring day.

The film caused a problem at BBFC, the censor's office run by Jim Ferman, a director I knew who had worked at the BBC years before. It was a mystery why he had given up poaching for game-keeping but there he was telling me that an erect penis was unacceptable and unnecessary. My reply that it was central to a film about prostitution and its excision, if he would excuse such a painful term, would undermine the film's most powerful and necessary image, did not impress. Neither did the argument that without at least one erect penis the film would lose its *raison d'etre*. It had to be cut. It would deprave the population, apparently. Unfortunately, I was contractually obliged to ensure distribution, so the penis was painfully cut.

Prostitute played out of competition in Cannes and did some business around the world on its release in 1980 although the distributor was disappointed that it wasn't more titillating. Sex sells tickets but this film made men uncomfortable.

The experience taught me more about the nature of performance and story; it didn't convince me about directing. Aspects were fascinating: working with the actors and in the cutting room. But the main impression was boredom. It was just waiting around. Waiting for costume, waiting for lights, all day one is waiting for something or somebody. It was sufficiently engaging to leave little room for other activities but not engaging enough to keep me interested. I concluded that it was a temperamental matter. Most of the good directors I know are obsessive personalities. I have to kick them off the set into the cutting room and then lock them out of that. They home in on detail and never become bored as they polish. I've often been in a final mix where they obsess about two different sound effects, both of which sound the same to me or at least are equally acceptable. A few days of that and I want to scream, begging to be released, losing the will to live. I needed to be involved in many projects and dart between them. I'm the same now, always reading five or six books, skipping from one to another. I decided I should leave directing to others who might be more talented and certainly were more suited in personality to its demands. It wasn't the answer I was looking for.

Of course, when the full impact of Thatcher's eighties hit and we saw the implications of the ideas of Friedrich Hayek and Milton Friedman as they drove policy, I was as stunned as anyone. I had no excuses, having dipped into their books and followed with interest key Conservative MP Keith Joseph's tour round the universities, glad that he was being met with derision. Well, the joke was on me and people like me and it wasn't funny. But all this was in the future. I wish I could claim to have predicted it all. I didn't. What I did continue to feel was an unanswerable unease.

I decided I needed a spell away. What I couldn't admit was that I actually needed a spell inside my past, not running away from it. I ended running six thousand miles, but still unable to escape. Fear of self is powerful.

But where? My background was films and I only spoke English. Then it occurred to me that during the sixties and seventies there had grown in the USA an interesting independent, low-budget film industry, separate or at least semi-detached, from Hollywood. I made a couple of trips and my interest grew. American culture had fascinated me ever since I was a boy during the war. Why not make some American films and learn about the real USA? If I saw my own country from a distance that might renew my understanding of home and provoke some creativity. The more I thought about it, the more the prospect energised me.

Go West, Middle-Aged Man

My family, especially the younger ones, took a view of my life in America. I was, after all, in 'Hollywood'. They knew about that.

'Just sits in the sun by the pool. Starlets in bikinis giving him Bacardi and Coke.'

'Ar. Not the only thing they're giving him, either.'

Apparently.

Nothing I said shifted them from that conviction. That's what producers there did.

They knew.

For the first time in years I was scared and exhilarated. My work had always been wine that didn't travel, so I'd be starting from scratch in my early forties, in a strange country, knowing virtually no one. It would be a cold shower. Just what I needed. Certainly better than a slow death staying where I was.

Harry Ufland, a Los Angeles agent, had seen *Prostitute* in Cannes and offered to take me on. I went to see him in Beverly Hills and he told me I had three pitches the following day. He gave me a list. I only had a vague idea what a pitch was; I had no idea how to construct one. In London people just came in for a chat. But I bought a map of LA and drove off in my rented car to find Paramount on Melrose Avenue, Fox in Century City and EMI, near Rodeo Drive.

Invited to sit down and faced with an expectant expression, I knew I was on. The actor must have kicked in. I told my story as simply and as clearly as I could. Months later, sitting on the other side of the desk, I witnessed Hollywood pitching at its flamboyant best. It seemed that screenwriters had to be performers. I was offered so much overacted drama in the pitching that I couldn't concentrate on the idea. So I surprised them by quietly suggesting we chatted a little about what they wanted to write, making their carefully rehearsed performance redundant.

Harry was a tough New Yorker representing Robert De Niro and Martin Scorsese, among other talented and established people. Through producer Sandy Lieberson I took a gig under Gareth Wigan, who'd been an agent in London. He was now an executive on the lot of Warner Bros at the Alan Ladd Company. I had a foothold. It would buy me time while I researched and wrote a screenplay.

On my first day I negotiated my way onto the Warner lot in the San Fernando Valley. It's a large complex of offices and studios. The main building, where the senior executives worked, was a lovely late art-deco evocation of pre-war movie dominance; though not as wonderful as the old MGM, now occupied by Sony. I eventually parked and found the Ladd Company, occupying some bungalows on the lot.

Gareth took me in to meet Laddie. He looked eerily like his actor father. When I arrived, he and his right-hand man, Jay Kanter, were chuckling. I asked them what was so funny. Clint Eastwood's company, Malpaso, had bungalows next door. It seemed that some-one had parked his car in one of Malpaso's spaces. So a production executive had strolled out with a baseball bat and smashed all the windows. 'He won't park there again,' said Laddie. It was clearly a very amusing incident. I wondered if I'd parked my little Toyota in the wrong place.

Welcome to LA, as they say.

This was the end of 1979. I observed the train wreck of Thatcher from a distance, but walked straight into Reagan. Almost overnight, the independent film movement shrank. Interest rates soon went sharply up. The Fed were determined to kill inflation. Easy money was over and finance difficult to raise. Hollywood moved sharply to the Right. It only wanted shoot-'em-ups, usually an American killing foreigners, with lots of special effects.

The marginalising of narrative, character-based cinema accelerated. I was energised and fascinated by American life but had no idea how to get anything made. I was starting over in a hostile environment. I was 'Tony who?' It did indeed feel like a cold shower. Of course, it did me good although I didn't appreciate it at the time. I knew too many people at home who at my age had slowed down, taken an executive job and rested on their laurels, waiting to be sent to the House of Lords to bore for England.

My physical health improved. The dry weather and constant sunshine eased my arthritic spine and lifted my spirits. I had a new world to negotiate. I may have been scared, but I wasn't bored.

But how to get a film made?

I went to Dallas to research an idea about America's obsession with guns. I realise now it was prompted by the crazy murder of John Lennon, shot by a stranger outside his home in Manhattan in 1980. I remember watching the news reports on television, sad and puzzled.

My project turned into a rape revenge story about violence. Texas seemed as good a place as any to shoot it, as it were. I learned more than I ever wanted to know about guns.

I had wondered why such an open, friendly and hospitable people chose to settle so many disputes by shooting each other. All of us must find ways to deal with our anger. Prolonged effort is required for us to kill with our bare hands and even real calculation is used to kill with a knife, but a finger just has to press a fraction of an inch on the trigger of a gun. That is power.

The American empire is even bloodier and more complacently in God's grace than the British empire was. That is not the product of a few crazies in Washington. It goes deep into the culture.

America was created through genocide, on the corpses of an indigenous people, and has been continuously at war all over the world since it became a great power. I was interested in the heartland, not in the liberal West and East Coasts. Deep in its psyche is the constitutional right to bear arms and to use them: a profound perversion of the original sturdy assertion of individual freedom in opposition to the power of the government.

I wanted to explore this psychology and link it with the predicament of someone who has been deeply hurt and has no available means of redress. How can she deal with the desire for revenge and the need to forgive? To avenge, to expunge anger and self-inflicted guilt, but also to forgive, to put it behind her, to stop it festering? Guns are not the only means of male domination. So is rape. The two are natural allies.

EMI came through with the tiny budget for *Handgun*. I left the Ladd Company and moved to Dallas. Just to be there evokes and jars. We opened the film in Dealey Plaza, where one thinks of the murder of John F. Kennedy, a location burnt into all our memories. Walking downtown one passed lawyers and oil executives strolling among the vast office buildings, wearing suits and cowboy boots, reminding one of the TV soap *Dallas*. Everything was on a vast scale. Texas was Yorkshire, I felt, thinking itself a different country and a superior one, operating with a grand flourish, self-conscious directness and a scarcely hidden chip on the shoulder.

I cast in the lead an unknown young woman, with little experience, Karen Young, after weeks seeing people in New York. While auditioning there, talking to many young actors, I was fascinated to discover how many were army brats or had fathers who worked all over the world for oil companies. I wondered if the rootlessness of the life – going to different schools, each time having to be accepted by a different subculture – made them actors before they even knew they were. No wonder, I speculated, they took it up professionally. They'd been doing it all their lives.

At the time I failed to see it might apply to me. I was uprooted early in life and had to become the young dog who did learn new tricks.

I went back to Dallas to cast Texans. Some were local actors, some were members of the gun club, one the manager of the gun shop. It was a smooth shoot and I enjoyed the hospitality of the Texans. No doubt being a white, Anglo-Saxon male helped. I was shocked nearly every day by local attitudes.

A colleague took me to a steak house where the steaks were on display in a cold cabinet. They looked huge. I don't eat much red meat and have a small appetite so I politely asked if I could have the children's portion.

'No!'

My colleague noticed a nasty red weal on the waitress's cheek. He asked her about it.

'Oh, my daddy shot me,' was the insouciant reply.

My first assistant director was a retired Dallas detective who knew everyone and could get us in anywhere. He was loyal and helpful but a good old boy. On visiting his house, I saw it was an arsenal of guns of all kinds. He took my shock as an expression of interest, not being able to understand any man who didn't like guns and proceeded to explain them to me with obvious pride. The gun shop where Karen's character buys a gun was where former president Lyndon B. Johnson used to buy his, I was proudly told. It was immense. You could start a war against Mexico just with the guns there. But everyone was affable, talking about the stock as they would in a home electronics store.

It was a hot summer and got to over 100 degrees on the gun range. Charles Stewart, the cameraman, was initially regarded with some amusement by the macho Texans. He's an upright, well mannered Englishman, who at all times wore a formal jacket. This was because the padding protected him as he operated the camera from his shoulder. Also, he thought it helped him more easily merge into his surroundings, although it looked distinctly odd out there. At four each afternoon he would politely ask for tea and when iced tea was understandably brought, he asked for hot English tea. Who was this mad Englishman, the Texans thought. They wondered how long he would last in the midday sun.

But after they had witnessed Charles, with a 35-mm Arriflex camera on his shoulder, day after day do tracking shots walking backwards as steadily as if the shot had been on rails, they reversed their opinion. He was revered. The whole crew would do anything for him. He was now macho.

Bill Shapter came over to edit, although he was also with us on the shoot. This was fortunate, because he and Charles made me do things I wouldn't have been interested to do. For instance, in the middle of a night shoot, plagued by insect bites and bored out of my mind, they insisted that we needed yet more shots – of the gun, of the rapist running away, of a close-up of Karen, of a wide shot of the gun range. This was simple film grammar and all shots we might need in the edit for narrative clarity. I knew this and even had a list but had to be forced to shoot them. I just wanted to go to bed. It was mechanical and boring.

Editing in Los Angeles, the assistant brought in a kid, Amy Pascal, who had just graduated from UCLA. She was looking for a job. I offered her one answering the phones.

The problems started when we showed the film. Everyone had an opinion and wanted changes. They expected, and thought they'd financed, an action film with sexually threatening overtones. Plus a rape, which would titillate the male audience. We'd made a character study and a detailed observation of Texas mores with a rape that made men uncomfortable. In the end we managed to lock off a version of *Handgun* that didn't satisfy them and yet made me unhappy, longing for our lost film.

I was financing my own office overheads and trying to find a way to develop projects and get distribution finance for the kind of films which no one understood or wanted to understand. Detailed social analysis and close character observation were not on anyone's agenda.

There were some offers to distribute *Handgun* in the USA, the most interesting from the Samuel Goldwyn Company, which I should have taken. But Warner asked to see it. Why would a big studio want to see a small art film? Lucy Fisher asked for a meeting. She was from New Jersey, Ivy League educated, and now an executive at Warner. I liked her. She was also effusive about the film. I was thrown when she said Warner wanted to distribute it and also to give me an indie producing deal, give me offices on the lot and pay my development costs. This was too good to be true and I should have smelt a rat but the offer would buy me time. I said, 'Yes.'

So began an unlikely time as a producer at a major studio.

Lost in the Hollywood Desert

Life's like a movie. Write your own ending.

Kermit the frog

I moved into a swish, air-conditioned office opposite the Warner executive building with Amy Pascal, who was showing promise. I promoted her and took on more staff.

No one at Warner mentioned *Handgun*. Eventually I became impatient. I demanded something must be done about its distribution and lobbied Terry Semel, the head of the studio. After more delay I was told it would be released. My relief turned into dismay when, instead of opening it at Sundance or the Toronto festival and then booking it into a few art-house cinemas, trying to build interest, they eventually opened it in 1984 with no publicity in a couple of cinemas in New York that were wrong for the film and then washed their hands of it after a few days, saying it was doing no business. No discussion. They had fulfilled their contractual obligations. Period. Move on.

The explanation I was eventually given, unofficially and non-attributably, was that Clint Eastwood had a rape revenge movie, part of the *Dirty Harry* franchise, *Sudden Impact*. He had made a mint for Warner over the years and they naturally wanted to protect one of their most prized assets. Even my little art film, so different in style and audience reach from anything Clint Eastwood would offer, had to be neutralised. So they got hold of it, waited until Eastwood's movie was out and then buried it. This was a business decision. Nothing personal. I was unable to confirm this: no one was likely to admit it. But those who told me, did so with a, 'What did you expect?' shrug. It's Hollywood. Get over it.

That's easy if a film is a commodity you trade. It's difficult if a film is part of you, like a child who, for all its faults, you love. When that umbilical connection is at the mercy of a commercial world you are at a disadvantage.

But as Grandma said, life goes on.

Working with Lucy was congenial, though Warners never wanted to make anything which interested me and I couldn't accept their suggestions, all of which were conventional right-wing pap with big stars and special effects. It was an unlikely marriage. I was miserable. I needed another film so I spent my spare time writing in the hope of getting something up that I wanted to make.

I watched Jerry Falwell and other fundamental preachers with cable television shows and I was fascinated by their power as well as their deeply reactionary politics. They reminded me of Elmer Gantry in Sinclair Lewis's novel.

So I went to the Carolinas to investigate. I drove around for days, starting in the Appalachians and working south, dropping into small communities to chat, staying in motels, where the cockroaches clattered away as the light was turned on. Some places were suspicious of me, a stranger reflexively assumed to be up to no good and as I left one community the whine of a cop car stopped me. I was told to get out of the car with my hands visible. As I turned, I saw a gun with a cop behind it. Afterwards I would think how much incidents such as this were like the movies although as they happened I was too scared to think about anything. When the cop courteously asked for my details I became overly polite, a caricature Englishman, until he released me with, 'You go well now.' Guns everywhere.

I found a fundamentalist preacher, without a television show, who had been in an altercation with his town's librarian. She had resisted his demands to remove a list of immoral and unchristian books on the grounds that they were literature and that it was her duty to protect free speech. She lost her job. I tried to talk with her but she wanted no more trouble, especially from an outsider. I attended his church and sat at the back. He pointed me out. Everyone turned round to stare. He questioned me about my religious beliefs. In an attempt to provoke him I said I had no religion but I was a socialist which, as I understood it, every Christian should be. I added that I'd read much of the New Testament and thought some of the King James version was profound literature. Had he read volume one of Karl Marx's *Capital*? His eyes narrowed. He announced to everyone that the devil was all around, even penetrating their place of worship. I innocently said we were just recommending books to each other.

He was very smart, using me as a butt as he addressed his congregation. It was a lively hour or so. The next day he met me in his office, saying I must have been led astray and offering his ministry to bring me to Christ. He defended his actions over the library as those of a man preventing his congregation from being poisoned.

I had my story and went back to Los Angeles to write it. I was optimistic when Harry Ufland said he had an offer for finance. But it fell through because Harry held out for too much. I said I didn't care about the money – not a smart thing to say in Hollywood.

Meanwhile, I was developing projects at Warner. I was occasionally indulged and allowed to pursue an idea. Like most studios, Warner was profligate in the number of projects it took on at screenplay stage, perhaps because no one knew what might make money. Better to cast the net wide at the front end when costs are low, pick a few to send out and see if they attract A-list talent. But my projects were not thought profitable and most were politically distasteful, even though executives thought their decisions were not based on ideology but rather on hard-headed business. They might have been right. Creative freedom is a complicated idea.

Fashion dictated much of what was made. Executives tried to guess the zeitgeist; difficult when your green light may be two years ahead of the premiere. But some areas, or at least some ways of looking at them, were taboo. The situation behind the iron curtain in Stalinist countries was approached in the same way.

It was difficult to know what decisions were made by executives as a response to the anticipated audience prejudice, what was an attempt to guess fashion and what was outside the executives' frame of reference.

In the fifties even a married couple hadn't been allowed to be seen occupying a double bed and until very recently movies featuring a black leading character fighting white racism were not green-lit on the grounds that they wouldn't play in the south of the USA. Until the sixties casual prejudice against black culture was common but antisemitism was taboo. I painfully discovered that my preoccupations, my wish to explore American culture, were not shared by Hollywood.

I also took meetings with whoever Lucy Fisher wanted me to meet. One morning I went over to the main building to spend an hour with Dolly Parton, who I vaguely knew of. Why she was being burdened with me was a mystery but I was supposed to hear her ideas and give her mine in the hope we could find a vehicle for her at Warner. She was short and busty and all hair, just like her professional image. I supposed that each time she left home she was 'on'. This perfect image of a dumb, sexually available blonde was the exact opposite of the woman underneath. Within a few minutes I saw she was a razor-sharp professional, intelligent, canny and tough as old leather. She was also a very successful businesswoman. Her business was 'Dolly Parton'. We talked at length and I found her really interesting. I've no idea what she made of me. Nothing came of it, I'm glad to say.

I did agree to produce one movie Warner offered, a kids' movie by the people who did *Sesame Street*. I said I'd do it because I thought it would thrill my little lad, Michael. He was about four, going to a local nursery every day, but still mainly playing at home. Often I would drive him to his school, playing John Lennon in the car. He loved 'Beautiful Boy (Darling Boy)' and we would sing it together. We were living in Ojai, seventy miles from my office, a small town surrounded by mountains and avocado bushes. The rent was reasonable. We had a spacious bungalow with a pool and little Michael would go out the back door and pick an orange or a grapefruit off the tree. Will, now a teenager, would come over for the summer and the two of them would spend most of the day playing in the pool. To avoid the commute, I worked three days a week in LA, staying at a motel, and then spent the rest of the week at home, working on screenplays. I was getting a daily kicking in the Hollywood snake pit, but it helped to see the boys splashing and laughing, living in the moment, enjoying the sunshine.

But I could barely deny the truth: it was idyllic misery. Alex didn't want to be there. She needed to be nearer the London School of Economics as she worked on her Ph.D. She was lonely. I was miserable and frustrated, still manically fighting losing battles and blindly in flight from my past.

We were growing apart. The situation couldn't continue.

The Childrens' Television Workshop had begun talking to Warner about a movie. I have no idea why I was asked to produce one for little children. I'd never worked on anything like that, except *Black Jack* with Ken, and that didn't do any business. But Michael was entranced by *Sesame Street*. The offer to produce this movie was too seductive to resist. I had a vision of him actually meeting Ernie and Bert and Oscar the Grouch. What a thrill for a little boy.

I accepted. It would be a small movie with nice people. What could possibly go wrong?

Plenty.

Terry Semel, the boss at Warner, had doubts, partly because the film could only play afternoon matinees, so he insisted on a small budget. Warner thought the Workshop were a bunch of TV amateurs. In turn, the Workshop thought they were about to be raped by vulgar Hollywood. An album deal would help the film commercially, but in Nashville they only thought about their artists and songs, which often worked against the film. So, everyone was suspicious and pulling in different directions. I was too far in before it dawned on me that I was supposed to deliver a road movie musical with puppets that made money for Warner, sold albums and yet preserved the integrity of the Workshop. Plus, I had only five million dollars to do it.

We went to Toronto, where the people were warm, the winters were freezing and the summers were full of mosquitos. But it was a cheap place to shoot. Warner wanted star guest appearances so I asked that every big name be offered a thousand dollars for one day's work, which in Hollywood is an insulting pittance. Those without children – like Jack Nicholson – said, 'Sure, one day, but for big bucks.' Those with children rearranged schedules to make sure they could appear and didn't even question the fee. That was the power of those puppet characters over children – and children over their parents.

I asked a cool pro, Pat Churchill, who had worked on *Handgun*, to run the shoot day to day and hired a young director, Ken Kwapis, who was sweet and right for the material. The cast included Chevy Chase, John Candy and Sandra Bernhard.

Muppet creator Jim Henson saved my sanity. I went to see him in his brownstone in Manhattan. He courteously interrogated me for half an hour. Then he promised full co-operation. This he gave with impeccable professionalism. He and Muppet performer and director Frank Oz performed brilliantly, of course, but it was Jim's imprimatur and support which lifted me. I was sad to hear that, just a few years later, he died so suddenly and unnecessarily.

Terry Semel was right. *Follow That Bird* bombed in cinemas on its release in 1985. But its VHS and, later, DVD sales were enormous round the world. Above all, my Michael met Ernie and Bert and Oscar the Grouch and all the characters from *Sesame Street*. It was worth the aggravation just to see his face.

Amy Pascal, the kid who'd started by answering the phones, continued to thrive. She was ambitious and energetic. She rose in the company and eventually became Head of Development. I encouraged her and gave her room to follow her instincts, which were much more popular than mine. She was a young Californian and in touch with the audience. One of her projects, which I'd done no more than keep an eye on, was a mad musical set in the San Fernando Valley called *Earth Girls Are Easy*. I could see its charm and the screenplay was very funny but it was miles from my interest or expertise. My plan was to try to get it green-lit and then share producing with Amy, giving her another step up in her career. But development takes time. She was ready to move on and broaden her experience by the time the screenplay was ready. This she did, with my blessing. She's done very well since, her roles including Head of Production at Sony, running Columbia, TriStar and MGM.

With Amy gone, I was left with a project I was bad casting for.

I asked Julien Temple to direct. His *Absolute Beginners* was about to open and there was an enormous buzz. He was hot and everyone wanted to work with him. Then it opened in spring 1986 and bombed, both with the critics and the public. Suddenly, he was untouchable. I thought both reactions were barmy.

In Hollywood, where nothing is secure or predictable, people indulge in magical thinking. They believe success and failure can be communicated, like a disease. If you touch someone who is successful, that success can transmit to you. You can literally catch it. So when you're hot, everyone wants to have lunch. But you must keep clear of a failure, in case that person's failure travels to you. This practice even extends to making and returning phone calls.

Absolute Beginners, starring David Bowie and set in 1950s London, was badly flawed but had moments of real imagination and daring. Was a young director to be treated like a leper just because he didn't live up to the hype? In any case, I'd already offered *Earth Girls* to him. True, nothing had been signed. But I was brought up in a tradition where you keep your word. A handshake was a contract.

Warners' interest cooled. Jeffrey Katzenberg at Disney would go with it but not with Julien, so I walked away. Although it would have been a tempestuous ride with Jeffrey, I liked him and respected his professionalism. People couldn't understand why I was behaving in such a self-destructive way. They thought I should ditch Julien, accept Jeffrey's nomination of director and enjoy the experience. Instead I was alone, without finance or distribution.

Then John Heyman came in using his contacts and financial expertise.

In the seventies I'd had an affair with Suzy Kendall after her marriage to Dudley Moore had ended. When that fizzled out we remained friendly and I'd sometimes go up to her house in Hampstead for some shepherd's pie, her specialty. John Heyman would pop in. When living in LA I would see him on trips to New York. I'd help him on a screenplay and he'd help me on a business deal. He was entrancing company, astounding me with amazing anecdotes about the famous. He could persuade anybody of anything and seemed to have nerves of steel. His memoir would be a sensation but it will remain unwritten. He has always preferred to be anonymous – pulling the strings, putting the elements together.

John came to the rescue of *Earth Girls*, calling up finance as though by magic. No sweat. We were in business.

I gave Julien his head and he did well. I'd reasoned that his music videos were stylish and witty – he'd worked with bands such as the Sex Pistols, Culture Club, the Rolling Stones and many others – and as a foreigner in the San Fernando Valley he would notice stuff, rather like someone from outer space. Casting was by Wally Nicita, who secured Geena Davis, Jeff Goldblum and the unknowns Jim Carrey and Damon Wayons. An amazing cast when you look back on it.

It was shot in the Valley. I let them all get on with it. What did I know?

Then the fun started. The financiers Credit Lyonnais and De Laurentiis Entertainment faced bankruptcy. Vestron picked the film up. It opened in 1988 and got a general release the following year when it did big and increasing business but then the marketing push abruptly stopped. Later I found that Vestron, too, were going bust. I thought, After this no one will go near me for fear I will bring bankruptcy!

It was a weird experience.

I was gradually getting the hang of Hollywood, how it worked and what could get made. The problem was that it offered nothing of any interest for me. I needed money, of course, like anyone with a family. The romance of poverty can only be enjoyed by those who've never been threatened by it. I knew plenty of young aristos in London who despised money, choosing to forget they were trustafarians. But money ceased to interest me once I had my house nut, my basic needs covered. Director Alan Parker joked I was the only person he knew who could produce four movies in Hollywood and not make any money. But I never got into debt: Uncle Harold was always on my shoulder.

The typical newcomer to Hollywood rents a nice house in Brentwood and leases a new Mercedes. Front is everything. I was horrified when my business manager said I had to borrow the money to buy a little Toyota or he couldn't get me a credit rating. I reasoned that if I was in debt the studio would own me. I knew I could take a plane on a Friday and be free to start at BBC TV Centre on the Monday. It was beginning to tempt me.

I was still fascinated by America and learning about it each day. It appeared more and more horrifying and wonderful as I peeled back each layer of its history and uncovered its complexity. I realised that each time I hit on a generalisation about America, the opposite was also true. It was not wall-to-wall McDonald's, as tiresome London snobs assumed. I longed to explore this on film. But I was failing.

I don't feel bitter about this. Hollywood has more psychopathy, is more machiavellian, more narcissistic and has more people dissociated from their true feelings than most places. This is because enormous rewards of riches and power are dangled daily and the fight for them is ruthless. It offers sun, sex, celebrity and wealth. Winners take all. But the casualties are many. Look closely at most faces, look behind the tan and deep in the eyes you will see fear. Just beware of those whose fear you can't see. These are the socially functioning psychopaths and they're dangerous. London is now trending that way. The individual isn't the problem. It's the system which offers fertile opportunities for them to thrive. But the sticking point for me was my disinterest in embracing the only kind of success on offer. In turn, they showed disinterest in what I needed to make.

Despite this, I learned many professional lessons there. Some very bright and talented people are drawn to its opportunities, especially writers. I worked with and admired some of the best, brilliant technicians lost to rewrites, their original screenplays taken from them and given to another to improve. Warner had around 130 movies in what it called 'active development'.

One day I took a project from the library and read the first draft submitted by the original writer and then the sixth draft that resulted after two other writers had worked on it. This last draft was like a Swiss watch, perfect in its structure. It was also lifeless, dead on arrival. The first draft was a structural mess, with action occasionally ending in a cul-de-sac, but it was alive, bursting with energy and the characters came off the page. There was a lesson there. I never forgot it.

I'm grateful for all those pros in Hollywood who taught me the tricks of the trade. Our early films would have been better if I'd had their expertise.

But losing the fight with Hollywood was not the real problem, the one I still refused to face. I needed to disinter what I had buried and denied. I was now a man who thought he was still running like mad when he was really sinking; his little legs had no purchase.

My marriage was slowly winding down. Alex, my wife, moved to London to be near the LSE. Her Ph.D. was nearly done. She took Michael with her. I flew there for one week a month, desperate not to lose touch with him. I was also flying to New York frequently and began to feel that a plane was my second home. I was permanently jet-lagged, not knowing what time of day it was or even what day. I knew it couldn't go on but I was stubborn. Hiding in the present solves nothing but I preferred it to facing the past.

You can't be a parent six thousand miles away. You have to be there. So it was Los Angeles or Michael: no choice. Will, my son from my marriage to Topsy, was now a young man working permanently in London. So that was where I had to be. I had to face up to a very different professional climate, which would throw up more challenges.

Then Roland Joffé called to say there was a movie he wanted to direct. Would I produce it? I said, 'Yes.' It was my last desperate attempt to escape reality.

Bad Faith

Fred Zinnemann was granted a courtesy meeting at the studio by a young executive. He smiled at Mr Zinnemann and nodded encouragingly.

'Now, Fred. Tell me what you've done.'

The director of High Noon, Day of the Jackal *and* A Man for All Seasons, *smiled thinly back at the boy.*

'You first.'

The small private jet dazzled in the hot sun and the dust clouds rose as it hit the runway. It was isolated in the middle of a nowhere that looked like a moonscape, dry and barren.

Paul Newman emerged. He was easy to recognise. Movie stars usually are. He removed his sunglasses and revealed his piercing blue eyes. They shone bright. He gave his familiar smile, the one that says, We're up to mischief together, and shook hands. He had a relaxed charm but was all business. That suited me. Shorter and slighter than I'd expected, he had thin legs that he was rather self-conscious about. No matter. On screen in full military uniform he would be the Paul Newman the audience expected. An idealised person. A movie star.

What was I doing here with him and an assortment of other, minor, stars like Laura Dern and John Cusack? Spending twenty-five million dollars of Paramount's money? Feeling the dust and heat in Durango, isolated in the middle of Mexico?

I was doing what I'd been doing all my life: busily evading myself.

Hollywood was drowning in projects. Few would ever be made. That's why so many writers were sitting by the pool of their nice houses contemplating suicide. They are paid well to write, or rewrite, screenplays which will never be made. Roland Joffé had been taken with a project, *Fat Man and Little Boy*, about Robert Oppenheimer and General Leslie Groves at Los Alamos: the making of the atom bomb. For many years it had defeated a long list of writers, directors and producers. Many stars had been attached. Roland had attempted yet another draft.

I had given Roland his first film to direct, *The Spongers*. He had risen to that brilliantly. I felt invested in him and had been proud for him during his subsequent successes. He was a friend and I didn't want to let him down. That is always a bad reason. If you take a job or make an offer out of friendship or even allow the fact of friendship to enter into a professional judgement, the odds are it will be a bad decision; and probably let down the friend you wanted to stand by. I have rarely made that mistake, having been consistently ruthless, often risking close friendships. But this time, as with Ken Loach on *Black Jack*, I did make that mistake.

I should have turned down the project. I was in no emotional or physical shape to give it the professional attention it deserved. I was in turmoil over my marriage that was in the process of divorce and its consequences. I had grave doubts about the viability of the project and my suitability for it. I was so depressed it was an effort to face each day. I was not thinking straight. My mind was elsewhere. It would all hit home when the test screenings of the film in a mall revealed that a large part of the audience did not know which war it was or that Japan was the enemy. They had never heard of Hitler. So we had to shoot extra, clumsy exposition.

Warner passed on making the film. Ned Tanen at Paramount said he would take it. But his green light was for a budget squeezed too tight for comfort and he wanted a star name. Paul Newman was free (well, rather expensive), so was miscast as General Groves. He was a good and serious actor but did not have the physical weight or the coarse, brutal energy of Groves. In any case, by then he was not a star with enough box-office clout to carry a picture on his own. Roland was keen to cast an unknown actor, Dwight Schultz, as Oppenheimer. He was physically right and had suitable nervous energy. He evoked Oppie visually, even down to the detail of how he smoked his cigarettes. But he lacked charismatic magnetism, the quality which made Oppie irresistibly attractive.

The conflict between the sophisticated intellectual wizard and the crude imperatives of a bulldozing general lacked a vital spark. Without this to generate dramatic excitement, all the fine film-making in the world, even on a grand canvas, would not fly.

Years later I taught MA students at Royal Holloway College, London University. One of my exercises was to make a list of the criterial attributes of a movie and of a film, showing the differences between them. Not as a quality exercise: there are some wonderful movies and some wretched films. But because the distinctions are important. *Fat Man* should have been a film. But it needed a large, expensive canvas: a big budget and two box-office stars. It ended being neither a film nor a movie.

We shot in Durango, Mexico, a place with a long movie pedigree. It was the base camp for countless Hollywood westerns. The production manager was a tough old pro who had worked there over the decades and knew the ropes. A virgin mesa was chosen. It looked like New Mexico in the early forties. We recruited locally and over a hundred carpenters plus other trades started to build Los Alamos from scratch.

I had heard scary stories warning me that nothing gets done in Mexico without cash bribery. I decided I could not work like that so everyone we dealt with was told that whatever deal we negotiated would be honoured in full, in cash, on time. There would be no other payment to anyone for any reason, without exception and, yes, that included the police. I was anxious because all this was new to me. We were not in Doncaster with the miners now. But people must have reckoned I was serious and wouldn't back down. In fact, I think they were relieved.

We were all billeted in El Presidente hotel. It was a large, traditional low building set around a courtyard pool. The staff were warm and helpful, a characteristic of Mexicans generally. They treated us well. I inspected the kitchens. They were spotlessly clean and well ordered. One LA actor, on being shown her room, asked for some drinkable water. She was not going to drink Mexican water. I went to her bathroom sink, filled a glass from the tap and drank it down.

'There's your water. Any more questions?'

There were none. She drank the water, as did everyone else. No one died.

One evening I went out to a restaurant. I wanted a change from the hotel but wherever I went they offered just a variation of rice and beans. No matter. I'd spent my life on film locations eating what was available locally. A cab dropped me back to the hotel. I handed the driver a note. I've never been good at foreign currency: it was a family joke that it took me five years to get used to dollar bills. I said, 'Thanks,' and got out of the cab.

'Señor?'

He handed back the note. I had given him a hundred instead of a five. He could have just driven off. He earned little and probably had a family to feed. I have never forgotten his honesty and recall it whenever I hear ignorant prejudice against Mexicans. I found them to be hospitable and hard-working. Most of them were dirt poor.

But '*mañana*' was a problem. A movie runs by slotting together many elements on a rigid schedule. Timing is everything. Next Tuesday at 10 a.m. means just that, to the minute. To my Mexican friends it meant some vague time in the future. They also didn't want to disappoint, so would make unrealistic promises.

My boy, Michael, joined me for some of the shoot and the young actors generously played with him. They threw the little lad in and out of the pool and he ate platefuls of rice and beans, his favourite. However many platefuls came his way, he was never bored. He was in heaven. His presence reminded me that life might be worth living.

Paul Newman was an exemplary professional except for one problem. He was passionately involved with race cars and no mean driver himself. So his insurance excluded him from driving. A car with a young Durango driver duly arrived at his rented house on the first day to take him to the main location about forty minutes' drive away. He sat beside the driver. On the second day, Paul told him to move over, settled behind the wheel and drove himself, arriving in, I was told, twenty-three minutes. Those who saw him weave the car at speed through the slow traffic of the town and then put his foot down, taking bends like an F1 driver, were impressed. I was pissed. This was serious. An accident to an uninsured leading actor could cost the movie millions of dollars. I talked it through with Paul, who nodded amiably, seeing the problem. The next day he drove again, arriving, I was told, in twenty-one minutes. What was I to do? Handcuff him? What I did was ignore it and hope for the best. He didn't even scratch the car throughout the shoot. I had other worries.

The fax machine in the production office was kept busy with aggravation from various Paramount executives or wrangling letters from divorce lawyers in London. I remembered my Uncle Harold's advice: never get involved with a lawyer. What a wise man.

The movie limped to the end of the shoot. At least, I did. Roland's optimism and sunny temperament never faded. Uncle Harold also used to say, 'If a job's worth doing, it's worth doing well.' I did not do this one well. I let down my colleagues and I let myself down too.

Perhaps Ned Tanen thought *Fat Man and Little Boy* would be a worthy *succès d'estime* and win awards for Paramount. At the time it was green-lit, in the middle eighties, the whole world was afraid of nuclear conflict. It was five minutes to midnight, according to the scientists' doomsday clock, and the terror was real. By the time the film opened late in 1989 there was a thaw in the Cold War and the Berlin Wall was soon to be just rubble. It was yesterday's news.

The movie did no business.

I not only felt a failure, I felt numb, like an engine finally spluttering to a halt.

It had all caught up with me. I was unable to run any longer. I needed to face what I most dreaded, what I'd used every device to avoid. But I couldn't do it on my own. Who could help? I'd run rings round psychoanalysts before, avoiding facing what ostensibly

I was there to face: too clever by half, again, and not wise enough. Who could help a man who knew he needed help but would use all his guile to avoid help, or at least the pain that went with the help?

I fell off the plane in London, frail, dangerously thin, exhausted and a washed-up failure at fifty-two.

Facing the Past

After they had retired all my aunts and uncles would go off together. They even plucked up their courage and went on a plane to Spain. But they preferred the English seaside.

Aunty Floss cooked in a works canteen during the war. After Uncle Terry retired from the plastering they tried running a boarding house in Cliftonville, Margate. But most of the guests were family.

'Let's go down and see our Floss.'

So Floss and Terry didn't make much of a living, but they all had a good time together. It was like being children again.

Floss would glance at the football on the television, all the uncles in a ring around it. She watched disapprovingly as the players fought for possession of the ball.

'I'd give 'em all a ball each. That'd cure it.'

My uncles would say nothing. They wouldn't even look at her. Their expressions said it all.

Pom and Harold had been born in 1901. As old age overtook them and they became more vulnerable, we became closer. He had retired and their life was good, their prudence allowing them to just keep the car going and enjoy an outing. I wondered how he would react when he became too old to drive.

But they retained their steadfast independence. For years I had tried to have central heating installed, but he would have none of it. I persisted, selfishly, because I wanted it for my winter visits. I had been thirty before my first winter with it and after that I became soft and never wanted to be without it.

As a boy during the cold spells the ice would form even on the inside of the bedroom windows and getting out of bed to get dressed in that freezing temperature called upon all the willpower so admired by Pom. You could see your own breath. The only warm bit of the house was a space in the living room just in front of the coal fire and then the shins would burn red and the calves would still be freezing. My final plea was to remind Pom that without a coal fire she would not need to rake out the ashes every morning or set a new fire with rolled-up pages of the *Birmingham Mail*. It would be automatic heat, all over the house.

'Dries the air,' was Harold's final dismissive judgement.

Discussion over.

My suggestion that they install a phone line was dismissed without discussion. I suggested the practical reason that as they were getting older, it would be useful, maybe life-saving, in an emergency.

'Don't need that. Wouldn't use it.' And the final clincher, 'Waste of money'.

They were starting to look very old and frail. Pom developed a shake in her hands where her veins stood out, just like Grandma. I felt closer to her and in the years before I went to California we would sit together and talk about family news. They were both very tired. They lingered for a while.

But the day Harold really died was when he was forced to give up driving. Its inevitability had been masked by denial, which is what most of us do when faced with death. He thought he would drive for ever, unable to contemplate life without a vehicle. The petrol shortage in the war had been trying but so had other things and he knew that had been temporary.

Since his first motorbike there had always been an engine to tinker with. He had been driving since 1929, years before the driving test was introduced. When he first got behind the wheel there were no impediments. Just the freedom of the open road.

Now there was no open road. There were traffic jams and the Highway Code and a loss of road courtesy. The end of an era.

At last he accepted what others had been telling him. His reflexes were too slow. His mind was no longer sharp. He was now a threat to himself and those around him. He was deeply sad. He said little as he hung up his car keys but the sight of him looking longingly at the Ford Prefect, sitting sadly in the garage, was moving. He kept the tyres inflated and methodically checked them with his pressure gauge. He regularly started the engine, as though he needed to keep it in working order in case he was given a reprieve.

He would sit in the driver's seat for a minute or two listening to the music of it. Then he would switch off and get out, giving a wing a caress as he left it to sit in lonely estate in the garage.

They died when I was in America, Harold in February, 1986 and Pom in the following July. She had suffered a stroke.

The divorce had to be faced. No one in our family was divorced. It was unthinkable. I was glad Pom and Harold were dead. I'd given them enough trouble without this. Harold used to point at his head full of grey hairs and say, 'You put every one of these in.'

The other practical problem was how to earn a living. Two homes cost money. I found a place nearby. Alex and I had agreed that Michael was our shared priority. He would stay with me for half the week. We wanted to minimise his disruption. We were cordial and we trusted each other as parents, working harmoniously to share Michael. Will came to live with me.

Mark Shivas, who ran BBC TV drama, kindly invited me to return. I spent a couple of weeks at TV Centre, the first since the late seventies. It was demoralised, sullen and negative. The atmosphere was uncreative. I saw fear and bullying, which I hadn't seen much of before, and a cold, hierarchical atmosphere: Thatcher's 'management's right to manage'. It was a world where my ideas would die. You could smell the anti-creative air as soon as you walked into Drama.

I'd noticed a change in the atmosphere as soon as I returned to London. I was yesterday's man, so I expected kids to come in full of passion and anger, telling me I was full of shit and asserting their view of the world. Instead they were on their best behaviour, watching me closely, trying to work out what they thought I wanted. They were there to sell, but had no idea what. They were waiting to find out what I wanted to buy. They seemed to have no convictions of their own and no confidence. They had been Thatchered. Others, of course, came in as hustlers, confidently selling the sizzle rather than the steak. The worst, oddly enough, was a middle-aged man, the former manager of the Sex Pistols, Malcolm McLaren. He came to see me out of the blue with a pitch that was no more than a bare idea. He expected me to do all the creative and organising work while he did the publicity, took ownership and sole producer credit. He thought selling the idea to me was all he had to do. I sent him packing. It was a thin idea anyway. Even good ideas are ten a penny. The art is in the execution.

While I was thinking about the BBC offer, John Heyman, the man who had put the deal for *Earth Girls* together, approached me. He lived in Manhattan but had a house by the beach in the Bahamas and one of his neighbours was Chris Blackwell, the founder of Island Records. Philips wanted to buy it. At that time no one quite knew how to value the future earnings of pop stars like Bob Marley and U2 and therefore how to put an appropriate price on Chris's company. John solved the problem, ingeniously, in a way which looked simple in retrospect.

What to do with the money that resulted?

They decided that a little of it should be spent starting up some production companies and I was asked to run one in London. So-called independent production companies were now part of television's ecology. I had always thought it was a petit bourgeois delusion. But the lobby was winning more and more programme territory.

I accepted his offer and we started World Productions in 1990. At least now we were all financially secure for a while.

With producer Margaret Matheson we moved into offices in South Audley Street at the top of Lew Grade's building, with an empty slate. I had decided to forget cinema, which was just as chancy and arbitrary as ever and still largely a tiresome waste of time.

TV controllers were buying renewable one-hour series, the easy industrial way to keep an audience. I had never produced one or even thought about them. I set about learning a new trade.

My main work went on under the radar. Few knew about it. It took over five years, the hardest work I've ever done and the most painful. It is the work I'm most proud of. As with my career in films, I couldn't have got through it without help. When I look back, I see it as my life's work and the only real accomplishment. Everything else is minor.

If Freud was right, adults are people who cannot recover from their childhoods, people who don't know themselves. In my case it was a traumatic forgetting and I'd devoted my life to not remembering. I'd spent years pretending on stage to be someone else. Then further years telling stories on screen in order to excavate truths about other people. As an adolescent I'd pestered my family for the truth about my own story but avoided my own emotional memories, my own feelings. I had kept a safe distance, as though anaesthetised.

Only now, knowing there was no escape, was I ready to be an actor in retelling, or recalling, my own story. Or would it be reinventing? Is it possible to invent the truth?

However I managed to tell it, that story could be my salvation. Why then had I refused to tell it? Why did I feel nothing? Why was I so detached? Was it because there was a secret buried by me, of guilt, of something I had to bury? A truth which I had good reason not to face?

I embarked on an autobiographical exploration, dreading what I might discover and the anguish it would evoke. It occurred to me that if history is our way of concealing the past, what if my suspicion of my guilt was a way of concealing my actual guilt? What if this need to discover the hidden truth actually did reveal that underneath I was guilty of unimaginable crimes? Crimes I couldn't fully imagine because I'd protectively repressed them? What would I discover? Did I dare?

It wasn't courage that finally drove me to dig into my life, though. It was existential necessity.

Who could and would help me? Alex suggested Charles Rycroft. He was a distinguished psychoanalyst, famous for his books and reviews. I was, of course, familiar with *The Innocence of Dreams, Anxiety and Neurosis* and so on. I admired them. His English style was lucid and elegant; this man could write a sentence. I thought he had probably retired. In any case, why would he want to see me? At Alex's urging I wrote to him. To my surprise he invited me to his rooms in Wimpole Street for a consultation.

He was reassuringly old. From impecunious minor aristocracy, like everyone he was partially a product of his class and time. Worryingly thin, courteous, quietly spoken; always impeccably dressed in a conventional three-piece suit, a crisp shirt with a collar that knew how to display a tie; kind, with an impish love of irony; widely and deeply read beyond his specialty, particularly in novels and poetry; sceptical but not intolerant. He had left the British Psychoanalytic Association, finding its cliques and testy disagreements tiresome and he disapproved of its intolerant treatment of Donald Winnicott.

In his 1985 book, *Psychoanalysis and Beyond,* he wittily describes his brief flirtation with Stalinism in the Communist Party of Cambridge in the thirties. He told me how instructive this experience was in his dealings with the psychoanalytical establishment. He didn't even call himself a psychoanalyst. He preferred the simple 'therapist'.

We couldn't have been more different, yet we were alike. I was temperamentally an unbeliever, a Brum sceptic who always had to kick the tyres and look under the bonnet, who took some convincing. We both loved ideology, this side dogma. Charles was courageously his own man. I knew immediately we would get on. I trusted him. I could work with him. But would he care to work with me?

Miraculously, he took me on. He went on to practise in the basement of a small house in a Chalk Farm terrace where he and his wife lived. There I would go, walking up from Chalk Farm tube station, three times a week, for a fifty-minute session, facing him without an idea of what would emerge. It was a small room, warmly appointed, with a comfortable chair for him, beside and just behind a couch. Another chair faced him. He would greet me each time in exactly the same courteous way, whatever the emotional climate.

At the end of our fifty minutes he would murmur, 'It's time.' He would then rise and go to the door, formally shaking my hand as I moved past him. Sometimes I would be heaving with tears, struggling to get a grip. At other times I would try to brush past him, angrily ungracious. His manner never altered. Nothing could unseat his even temper.

Thus began five years or so of terrible anguish, wonderful release and a deep paternal friendship.

The atmosphere in Charles's consulting room changed with my mood. Some days it was a balm just to be there, cocooned in his kind embrace; other times it felt like a prison and he seemed like a sadistic torturer, indifferent to my anguish. Then I would leave and beat myself up. Aunty Pom, long dead but still on my shoulder, would be contemptuous of my self-absorption, saying, 'Huh, pity about you!'

Charles was relaxed and informal, not caring whether I was on the couch or in the chair facing him. But he strictly applied the basic rules. However artfully I tried to engage him in ordinary conversation, trying to elicit details of his life, he would refuse, always bringing us back to me. This infuriated me. I was bored with me, I would lament. He always recognised my ploys, my wriggling attempts to avoid myself. In his quiet manner he was immovable.

He did not let me get away with anything. This very bright man just refused to play any intellectual games. He didn't even use any jargon. Sometimes I let fly at him with a venomous anger. I abused him, using language as my weapon. Then I gave him the silent treatment, spending session after session saying nothing. I threatened to walk out, telling him he was a waste of my time. I tried to seduce him by making him laugh or at least engage in chat.

He just sailed on, never rising to the bait, never retaliating, always in a quiet good humour, always listening and remembering, never making a note.

I hated him. I loved him. I thought he probably knew everything. I patronised him, deciding he probably knew nothing. I said, or tried to say, anything that came into my head, although not everything. That would be impossible. Much of it was detritus, although he was panning for therapeutic gold, so every speck of detritus was given equally grave attention. My repetitions, going over the same ground over and over again, embarrassed the entertainer in me. They were just unprofessional. But somehow I couldn't avoid it.

My early memories triggered violent emotions, usually displaced on to him. My rehearsal in this book of the early traumas are a mere echo of the intense dramas enacted in that calm consulting room.

Meanwhile, I was trying to live a life outside. My professional life was a challenge, as I tried to win orders for new shows and establish the company. On many days I would leave Charles and I would still be fighting back sobs, shaking from the intense session. On the tube I would be unable to swallow them back. By the time I reached the office I would have gained control again.

The work for the screen needed to harmonise with my domestic life so there could be no long spells on location. I needed to be home with the dinner ready for Michael and some on the hob for Will when he got back. So I recruited likely talent and gave it room to develop, worked up ideas with writers and supervised green-lit shows. I would go briefly on location, just to keep an eye on a show. I saw all rushes.

Maybe my role would have changed anyway because of my age. It was a shock to realise that in the screen business one can make the transition from being an enfant terrible to an eminence grise overnight. I enjoyed this paternal role now. It felt right, although I knew I must discourage dependency. Those who allow others to be dependent, to be stuck in infantilism, are often those who need others to be dependent on them. I made sure that while I supported and encouraged, I also reminded them, 'I'm not your father.'

My aim was to find cracks in the managerial concrete and encourage flowers to grow through them. The creative spirit has always had to struggle to find expression.

I took up a neat police idea from John Wilsher. That made me watch examples of drama series from the USA and Britain. I discovered that US series expressly did not develop character: *Kojak* was the same character in episode twenty-three as he had been in episode two, revealing just a few personality traits set in aspic. I guessed this was to give freedom when the show was stripped across the week in syndication. Maybe it was a fear of confusing the audience who did not see every episode. But the more I thought about the possibilities of long-running series, the more I warmed to the challenge.

Films are about creative vision and picking the right people. They are also about organised delivery. I had World Productions to build and future shows to develop. I could not afford to spend time immersed in every detail of any one series. I hired producer Peter Norris to be in daily charge. He was a good pro. Straight and honest with me, he was a grown-up who would take responsibility but know when he was out of his depth. He was experienced in physical production. I had a good time with him.

Between the Lines had been submitted to BBC's Drama Series Department. Silence. I knew the BBC was slow but I was in a hurry. I asked for a meeting with its head, Peter Cregeen. He was polite but told me that it was a pass. They didn't need another police series. Thanks, but sorry.

Disappointing. But fair enough. I have never questioned, appealed against or tried to second guess a buyer. If you don't want it, that's your decision; if you do, then let me make it for you, don't interfere. But something didn't feel right. I called Jonathan Powell, Controller of BBC One and a distinguished drama producer in a previous life. I asked him if he was sure he didn't want this cop show. He said, 'What cop show?' It had never been submitted to him. Drama Series had their own cop shows in development and didn't want one from me jostling them to one side. I didn't blame them. It just showed the BBC in denial. They had refused to reorganise to adapt to the new reality of outside submissions; not difficult in itself but impossible if you refuse to accept the reality. It would be a few more painful years before it adapted. They were grudging years which caused confusion and distress.

Poor management – in this new temple to management.

Jonathan read it, bought it immediately and we were in business.

I was worried about the lead. Neil Pearson, who I had seen briefly in Channel 4's news comedy series, *Drop the Dead Donkey*, was a candidate. His age made him young for the rank of detective super-intendent, but it was possible at a stretch.

Yet the character is not only a smart investigator, he is a flawed romantic, incapable – as they say – of keeping it in his pants. Was this actor crumpet? His character is attractive to women. The actor must be able to play that convincingly and naturally or the series wouldn't work. I had no idea. So I asked if he would pop in to see me and alerted the women in the office to clock him in and clock him out. Neil and I chatted. I liked him. After he left, they all said, 'Oh, yes, he really is crumpet.' He was cast.

We became good friends. He has since taken sadistic pleasure in inviting me to White Hart Lane to see his beloved Spurs humiliate Aston Villa. Again and again. Perhaps because he was cross, I auditioned him in a crumpet test.

But he was brilliant in a very good cast and held it all together.

So we were up and running. I started work early but I could never beat Lew Grade, even though he was now well into his eighties. His chauffeur would deliver him in the Rolls-Royce at the crack of dawn and Lew would be in his office, a cigar almost as big as him in his hand. Each day I tried to creep up the stairs to my office without him noticing but I never succeeded. He would put his arm paternally on my shoulder and offer confident advice.

'Tony, what you 'ave to remember is, you 'ave got to 'ave the stars.' He would point his cigar for emphasis and then speak very slowly and loudly to make me understand.

'You. 'ave. To. 'ave. The. *stars*.'

'Yes, Lew, I'm sure you're right.'

He was an example of someone with no hinterland, with no other interests, who could not gracefully withdraw. People like Ted Turner in America were throwing him scraps, but his day in the office was empty. It was all show. His ITV company, Associated Television, had been slyly taken from him and he was lost.

He was the great showman who didn't know that you have to leave the stage while the punters want more.

Between the Lines was about the department in the Metropolitan police which investigates corruption. I bought the idea because its premise meant we could show bent coppers every week. Being the Met, there would never be a shortage of material.

The Met's media people were now more sophisticated than their blustering ancestors, who had responded angrily to *Law & Order*, the earlier series about corruption in the 1970s. Then their response to our criticism was taken up by the press and the result was to give the series extra publicity. It would have been wiser to keep quiet. In 1992, they coolly said *Between the Lines* was enormous fun and good entertainment but, of course, complete fantasy.

So it amused us when sometime later the Met announced the creation of a new department. It was set up to investigate corruption in A10, which was the department originally set up to investigate corruption. They seem to chase it but never catch it.

The press and some politicians have often accused me of being anti-police. I'm not. The questions I raise are always about democratic accountability. Who shall police the police? The Met is a state within the state. It exercises arbitrary power daily. All attempts to control that power have only led to impotent bureaucratic excess. There is probably not a major urban police force in the world which is straight: the temptations are too great. But who and what will minimise this corruption and make police accountable? This is an important question to ask in a democracy. So much arbitrary power is exercised secretly; the consequence might be unlimited corruption festering below the surface.

In my lifetime we have seen exposed the fitting-up of innocent Irishmen for bombings carried out by the IRA in Birmingham in 1974 and elsewhere; the brutal physical attacks on the miners at Orgreave during the strike in 1984, followed by the contamination of evidence; the egregious slander of Liverpool fans after the criminal incompetence and cover-up that followed the deaths of supporters in the Hillsborough stadium disaster of 1989; wholesale corruption over many years among West Midlands detectives; every year suspicious deaths in custody, but never a cop brought to justice; the scandal of cops working undercover in legitimate, law-abiding lobbying groups in the 1980s, secretly fathering children and ruining innocent women's lives; the deliberate incompetence of the investigation that followed the racist murder of Stephen Lawrence in 1993 and 'Operation Tiberius', a 2002 report leaked in 2014 that revealed senior Met detectives were actually employed by gang leaders to sabotage criminal investigations. These are just some of the scandals we know about.

Why criticise me for shining a light on the police and their lack of accountability? One of the tests of a free society is whether its police serve the public or whether they are above the law. Another is whether or not the media has freedom to expose and criticise. If the BBC cannot shine a light on dark authority it becomes just state propaganda. I thought I was merely doing my job.

The highlight of the second series in 1993 was the relationship between Special Branch, MI5 and MI6. Our research told us that, after the good cold war days, when there was plenty of work, they were exaggerating the 'terror' threat and scrabbling around competing for ownership of that lucrative territory. Their turf war was taking up energy they should have spent co-operating. They did not trust each other, indeed bugged each other's phones, treating each other as enemies of the state. Tony Clark, Neil Pearson's Met cop, found himself in the middle of all this. He was perplexed because they all refused to talk to him. When he did get to the bottom of it, he was summoned to Whitehall and viciously threatened. He would serve time in prison, his career ruined, if he breathed a word. He understandably kept his mouth shut. The crime, a cold-blooded murder, was covered up. One hopes the audience was as shocked and amazed as he was.

The show was humming along. It was in good shape. But I was bored. My boredom threshold is low and that has always led me into trouble. I later learned to do a maximum of two series of each show and then hand it over completely to someone else. But I tinkered with this one and the audience were furious. It took weeks to recover its balance.

My first experience of renewable one-hour series left me thoughtful. My colleagues had helped me learn new tricks. My mistakes had chastened me.

My life was full and gradually becoming easier. I spent time with my sons, which was satisfying. World Productions prospered as I recruited young talent and gave them room to develop while I worked up ideas with writers and kept an eye on productions. A big 8 p.m. Sunday night show for BBC One, *Ballykissangel*, began in 1996 and financially underpinned all our work for six years.

Life was beginning to feel enjoyable.

But at its centre was the work with Charles Rycroft.

When I was a small child people would say, 'Oh, he's got over it.' I hadn't. You never get over it. Why would you want to? My parents will always be with me. But you can get through it and come out the other side. I, belatedly, had to go through all the stages of mourning that I'd spent my life fighting to avoid. Deep down I had not accepted they were dead. I remembered that in the days after Mom died I'd said to myself, 'She'll be home by Christmas.' She wasn't and neither was I. No wonder every Christmas since had been so bleak.

As soon as this little boy within me truly accepted their deaths, he would know why he was so lonely. Then, of course, came the impotent speculation, 'If only . . .' I beat myself up for months, wallowing in the fantasy that I could have saved her and then him. After all, although I was only five Dad had said, 'Look after your mother.' Clearly I had failed.

After that came open fury, a fury that had been repressed all this time, a fury that scared me. Fortunately, it didn't scare Charles.

Finally, through the depression, came mourning, that process of such wrenching emotional pain I thought I wouldn't survive. But when you mourn you accept the fact of death.

Weak and trembling, I was left with regret and acceptance. I was left without inappropriate guilt. I was left with memories and experiences that nourish me.

My life's work has not been the public one, on the screen. It has been the struggle to get myself back, the me I lost that terrible Christmas. Truths are easy to repeat. They are difficult to feel. If you can feel them, you understand them in a way you can use.

I realised I had not caused Topsy's illness. Her existential death, her unlived life, was a terrible loss for her and sad for those who loved her. But it remains a psychiatric mystery.

I did not murder my first analyst, Dr MacDonald, the kindly man in Hampstead. He suffered an unexpected fatal heart attack. That happens. I did not cause it. It had nothing to do with me.

At five I had no duty of care. My mother's death was not the result of my failure.

I was not such a terrible person that my parents preferred to die in order to escape me.

At five you naturally think you're the centre of the universe. Everything revolves around you. You cause everything.

If you think that at fifty, you're barmy.

So, I realised that the deep feeling of being evil, that people died from being near me, that I murdered them, was just me stuck in a magical infantilism. It was a load-releasing relief to realise it was a mirage.

You are not evil, you are not exceptional. Get over it. You're just a normal human fuck-up.

What a relief!

I could relax for the first time since I was five.

To atone is to be at one with oneself. Free of internal conflict, I became more relaxed with others. I was able to view the world a little more realistically now I projected fewer bad feelings on to it. So my politics shifted. I understood and judged with a more tolerant understanding. My work became less of an exhausting war. I fought but didn't look for a fight. Life was fun. I felt more secure.

I still feared a black swan, though. I doubt I will ever stop expecting the unexpected disaster smashing down from a blue sky.

The change happened gradually, imperceptibly, in the sessions. Two steps forward, one step back, as Lenin famously said. In fact, the changes were so slow one couldn't detect them. Then there would be a movement, what felt like a real shift. It would disappear, only to reveal itself more robustly months later. It was frustratingly elusive.

The endless repetitions continued. I just couldn't stop endlessly repeating myself. I was like a little lad picking a scab or a stuck vinyl record. I bored myself and was embarrassed for Charles. I despaired. Maybe I just wasn't any good at this work, I thought. But if that's so, I'm stuck forever in no man's land.

Very gradually I realised I was taking for granted the most profound changes in my personality. My attitude to myself and my feelings about the world had shifted. I was not afraid any more. This at first felt as though there was something missing. I'd spent my life in terrible, lonely anxiety, whistling in the dark, simulating insouciant self-confidence. As I got used to it, I felt it to be normal.

Shouldn't I be anxious? If I relax, won't something terrible happen? Isn't it too much of a risk to relax? Gradually I dared to let the sentries stand down.

I woke up to myself, connecting to the me of infancy, before the trauma of my parents' deaths.

Eventually my relationship with Charles changed. I began to see him as he was.

He reckoned we had done our work and to my surprise I agreed with him. So this is what it feels like? I couldn't have imagined it.

I'd finally faced my past rather than find fresh ways of hiding in the present.

The Kids Are All Right

In the early seventies Pom and Harold came to spend the day with me in London. I took them out for a stroll on the Saturday afternoon. Pom had her best frock on. Harold wore a yellow jumper, an M&S Christmas present. They looked round the shops on Kensington Church Street with curiosity.

Pom saw a dress and fondled it. Simple and short, it was dark blue, printed all over with lots of little flowers.

'I had one just like that in the twenties,' she said, amazed to see such an old-fashioned dress in such a fashionable shop. She then looked closer.

'Shall I tell them? I think I should tell them. They've made a mistake here.'

She pointed to the price, which she thought impossibly high.

'No, Pom, there's no mistake.'

She looked shocked.

Harold was inspecting some trousers. Looking closer, I saw that they were cut wide and had turn-ups, just like the ones he was wearing. I had given up turn-ups years before. Only old men wore turn-ups.

But here they were, these trousers in cool Kensington, in a shop which sold only the latest thing. Harold was a dedicated follower of fashion, evidently.

You just have to wait long enough and you're back in fashion again.

Working in my office in Golden Square, Soho, a call came from Michael Jackson, Controller of BBC Two. I hardly knew Michael. When we first talked, he rather threw me. Here was this lad, who looked like a student, telling me stuff about my working life that I'd forgotten. Impressed as I was by his erudition, it made me feel like a museum piece. But we got on. I admired his qualities. He knew his TV history and was an analytical thinker, methodical and intelligent.

We clashed ideologically. He was from a generation scarred, as I put it, by the end of ideology, which was itself an ideology. I would tease him that his embrace of postmodern irony was just a way of excusing himself from caring about anything or anyone. I assumed he thought I was an interesting specimen of a nearly extinct species, 'sixties' leftie'; although he would have been wrong. I was a leftie long before the sixties.

We had got off to a bad start. I'd turned up for a meeting in his office at TV Centre, at his request, and saw him through the open door on the phone. I thought nothing of it. I was a few minutes early, obsessive punctuality being, I hope, the only Prussian thing about me. He would finish his call and we would begin our meeting. But he then made another call and it went on. I gave him ten minutes and then left. His assistant came down the corridor after me but I went back to my office. He called, apologised, and we had a convivial lunch. He asked me to do a turn for him at the Edinburgh Festival, which I'd never attended, having been busy in Los Angeles whenever asked to give the MacTaggart Lecture.

This phone call years later was a surprise.

'Would you be interested in doing a series for Two?'

This is not a question one expects from a Controller. It was redundant as there was only one sensible answer. 'Yes, Michael,' I said. 'Tell me what you have in mind.'

'It must be forty minutes.'

That was an odd length. We'd have to rethink the structure.

'Young people. Starting their first jobs.'

'OK.'

He must be worried about BBC Two's demographic compared

with Channel 4, I thought. Overpaid marketing wizards were at work again, but it made no difference. When the series – *This Life* – began in 1996, friends would call and say they were enjoying the new show about young lawyers on Channel 4, not realising or caring it was actually BBC Two. The shows viewers fancied, not the channels they were on, guided their viewing. In fact, some shows, like *Coronation Street*, are bigger than any channel.

'Could they be lawyers?'

He had recently seen a documentary series about young lawyers.

'They could be anything you want, Michael.'

'Oh, and it's very low budget.'

'Really? What a surprise.'

A low-budget series on BBC2 Two at that time meant opportunities. An eight o'clock Sunday night slot on BBC One demanded a show which would attract a large, traditional audience. No experiments in narrative, camera or acting. It must be conventional. But this was an open door. We could frighten the horses.

Being twenty was so long ago for me it was irrelevant, even if I could remember it. I knew nothing about the new generation's perception of the world. So I recruited a young team and asked them to tell me.

I didn't care whether anyone, in front of or behind the camera, had a track record. Their experience was not essential. I wanted contemporary knowledge, talent and the willingness to take risks. With this series we had the opportunity to try things, to go too far, to discover limits; for people to discover their own creativity without inhibition.

It was also an opportunity, rare in the atmosphere of this BBC's management, for me to put some ideas into practice. My starting point had always been that gardeners don't make plants grow. Plants grow because it is in their nature. But they grow better, truly become what they can be, if the conditions are right. That means leaving them alone, not constantly digging them up to see how they're doing.

Producers must do this for everyone. They must organise, surely, but also create a soil of encouragement and a feeling of love, trusting in people's inherent potential. Directors, indeed the whole crew, must have this relationship with the actors, who are the main carriers of the drama to the audience. Producers must believe in everyone. Then everyone will truly believe in themselves, feeling secure and loved. Any work based on fear becomes mere technical pretence. Insecurity leads to defensive self-protection, the enemy of creativity.

So it is all, in the end, about belief in the material offered by the screenwriter and in the inherent capacity of everyone to respond creatively to it. Good producers are critical – they are not afraid to weed, even prune – but from a basis of love and approval. They need to earn the right to be listened to. Not rely on authority.

I tried to reward success with a smile of encouragement and praise. I did not punish failure by making people feel worse: they felt bad enough without me rubbing it in. The aim was to create an atmosphere in which everyone can dare to be childlike. That is the source of all creativity.

This generation had been competing in a different atmosphere. After a while, though, they forgot their fears and I began to see just how original and creative they were.

That was beautiful to me.

The most important decision was who to appoint as a lead writer to set the tone for the series in the first couple of episodes, someone who would create the outlines of the leading characters, give the series 'attitude' and a baton other writers could grasp and run with. Get that right and we'd have a chance.

In my office we read and read and we discussed endlessly. No one jumped out at me. Weeks passed. Then a junior kid learning the ropes found something by Amy Jenkins. I'd never heard of her and the screenplay was unproduced. I read it. She could write. I asked if she would care to meet me.

Within a few minutes I knew we were in business. Amy was in her twenties and had read law at UCL. She told me she couldn't stand my generation. We refused to retire and we still had sex. Why didn't we just get out of the way? She hated the sixties and couldn't stand the Beatles. This was fighting talk. You criticise John Lennon in my presence and you're in trouble. She was fearless, opinionated and sharp. She'd do.

I gave her some parameters and freedom within them. I then hoped for the best, hiding my own nerves. This was to be the template for the whole series. Everyone had the same brief. I told them what they mustn't do, what the limits were. That liberated them to do anything they wanted within those limits, to surprise themselves as well as me. The sonnet form, I reminded them, has strict rules, but there are no limits to what it can express. If you tell people what they must do, you imprison them, crushing the creativity neither they nor you know they have.

Amy delivered just what I needed. I was so pleased I left in a line about not being able to stand the Beatles. Who was I? My voice was irrelevant. My job was to listen to her and others, to use my experience to guide them and to bolster their courage, to help them express themselves.

The crew shaped up well. The directors were young and had little experience. That meant they had not settled into bad habits. I told everyone that we would do as little lighting between set-ups as possible. The production would be generally lit. Actors would not be on marks and would be free to go where they wanted. The camera's job was to find them; it was not part of the actors' job to pose for the camera. The camera didn't exist. We would try anything to see if it worked. We experimented with maximising close-ups, in which just one eye filled the screen but we decided this was too extreme after a while, so we pulled back. The film editor was invited to throw away the rule book and play with the material. The only rules were to seek clarity and explore character.

The casting was, as usual, a long and difficult process although in the end I was happy. They were all as fresh and inexperienced in acting as they were in life. We got to the point where our only uncast character was Anna. No one got near to this complex person. Even good actors only caught one dimension and flattened her. There were just days to go. A decision had to be made. We had to keep our collective nerve and carry on looking. Di Carling, our casting expert, continued to search for possibilities. None were right.

Then, at the last minute, Daniela Nardini walked in. She seemed full of self-confident hauteur but there were revealing nervous tics she couldn't quite disguise. She took on Anna as though it were a fight to the death and everything fell sweetly into place. We knew Daniela would take what was on the page as a starting point. She was cast. She turned out to be a huge hit with the audience. It had been close.

I tried not to let on how relieved I was.

I still knew we might have a disaster on our hands but I also knew it would be an adventure. If you want to learn anything you have to risk going down in flames. Playing safe is treading water, which is in itself a failure. This is something television management has forgotten. I wish they would think more about nurturing young talent through creative failure. That's how talent finds itself. Its absence is the reason for so much drama being boring and predictable. Very low budgets on the internet would be an obvious way to give people room to breathe, to prove themselves and to show what might be possible. It would be a safe means to fail. Others, like Amazon, are experimenting in this way. The BBC has been slow to do so.

Thanks to Michael Jackson, we now had the chance to hang ourselves on network TV.

My concerns were for the kids I'd gathered around me. I knew this experience might be the making of them. But the business had become a ruthless one with no second chances. I'd asked them to go out on a limb with me. I shall always look back with pride and admiration, not just for their talent, but for their courage.

One achievement of the writers, week after week, was their ability to illustrate the general by use of the particular. I remember one episode was almost entirely about the question, 'Who stole my yoghurt?' Intrusions on private property and differing ideas as to its importance are central to the difficulties faced by those sharing a flat and a fridge. It's also a key complication in the wider political debate. By exploring this one question we were able to lay bare character and the politics of that community.

One of my golden rules was that the show must never, ever, set foot into a courtroom. I was severely pressured but remained immovable. Precisely because they were all solicitors and barristers we had to stay outside. This series was about young people who just happened to be lawyers, it was not a legal series. Once we allowed even one scene in a court the whole series would be there. Courtroom drama is too easy to write. We tantalised the audience but never succumbed.

Because the budget was cripplingly small, we set most scenes in a composite set representing their shared house. This was constructed in a larger building also housing the production base. I hired a bright young producer just learning the ropes on *EastEnders*, Jane Fallon, knowing she could handle the pace and the constraints. One day she asked me about the music. I said there would be no musical score, just source music. As it was music I now knew nothing about, I wanted no part in choosing it. She suggested Ricky Gervais, who I'd never heard of. He was very knowledgeable, she said, but there was a problem: she lived with him. I thanked her for her honesty and he was hired. He chose and produced the opening music but more importantly, selected a long list of music tailor-made for each character. His knowledge was indeed encyclopaedic. I liked him and trusted him.

The series began transmission in March 1996 and was met with vitriolic criticism from the press, especially outside the television reviews. I paid little attention and rarely read any of it, but was puzzled. Why such hostility to a small BBC Two series? My guess was the young journalists recognised themselves in the characters and didn't like what they saw. The ratings were indifferent.

This Life had few friends on the sixth floor. There was no hint about a second series, no word at all, either of the show's renewal or its cancellation. Maybe management hadn't made up their minds or even noticed that a decision had to be made. My neutrally expressed enquiry was not answered.

When we wrapped I suggested that all the costumes and props should be stored pending a decision because it would be impossible to preserve continuity for a second series if they were dispersed. I was told that the BBC had no plans to do this and in any event wouldn't pay for it. So I decided to keep the stuff and my company would pay, just in case, although we were under no contractual agreement to bear this expense. I don't know if the decision on storage by the BBC was just a crude way of showing their indifference to *This Life*. I suspect it was an innocent, unprofessional cock-up. The new, efficient BBC was falling over itself and no one was taking responsibility. At that time it was amateur night out on the sixth floor.

The end credits asserted that *This Life* was a Pebble Mill production. The BBC's Pebble Mill studios were in Edgbaston, Birmingham, and claiming the series was based there helped to bump up the quota of regionally-made programming, the BBC having promised to be less London-centric. But our show wasn't set in the Midlands, had no cast or characters or crew from Brum and none of it was shot there. True, I was brought up there but that would be a thin reason. It was a cynical internal accounting ruse to create the appearance of a quota which didn't exist. I thought they should all be ashamed of themselves for this deception but I decided not to waste energy on it.

Eventually the show was renewed. Perhaps Michael had nothing else. We were now told to make 26 new episodes. I should have insisted on fewer. It was too exhausting for everyone, considering what we were attempting to do.

The second series went out the following year, with transmission just ahead of shooting, and about halfway through the run articles began to appear in the tabloids. The first series was being repeated. The tone of coverage was suddenly shifting and we discovered our show was either sexually disgusting – if you were an older, eavesdropper viewer – or a cult hit, absolutely necessary viewing – if you were the age of the cast or even early teens. It all reinforced my conviction that I'd never understand or be able to predict audiences. I urged everyone to ignore it all and stick to the show itself, not to start believing in their own publicity.

By the end of the series the BBC, hitherto indifferent to the point of ignoring the show, suddenly decided it was unthinkable to cancel it. The audience was demanding more. But, as always, management didn't understand drama production. Our cast were now stars and

there had been no options to renew their contracts, indeed no planning for the series' future. Plus, I was bored. I had other shows in my
head; I wanted out.

In the management game of musical chairs, Michael Jackson had
by then been succeeded by Mark Thompson as Controller, a stage
on his inevitable journey towards being appointed Director General.
I was adamant, but said he could take the show and produce it
in-house if he wished. He said he wouldn't do it without me. In the
end, he accepted the inevitable and handled the rumpus in a calm,
unflustered manner. It was clear he was head-boy material.

We got on well. I respected his opinions, always happy to nick a
good note from anybody. Jane Root followed him as Controller in
1999 and started to handle outside companies and she was encouraging. The BBC was showing signs of getting its act together.

Trojan Horse Drama

Uncle Harold would put a little aside each week to pay for a summer holiday. It was a matter of pride. A small boarding house would be booked somewhere, Dawlish in Devon or the Mumbles in Wales.

At Snow Hill station we would all board the steam train. Perhaps my love of the rhythm of trains began then. On arrival, Harold would walk me to the front of the train to where the driver and stoker would be wiping sweat from their dirty faces. Harold would greet them and then say to me, 'Thank the driver.'

I would do so and the driver would beam back at me, saying, 'You're all right, son. Safely here, ain't we?'

It pleased me to do this, although I never knew why at the time. Remembering it now, I do know. For Harold it was an exchange of respect from one skilled man to another and he was introducing me, teaching me good manners and not to take people for granted.

I love his memory, now, for that.

I was asked to pitch directly to Controllers and others on the sixth floor. Another sign that the management pyramid was narrower and power was being concentrated higher in the hierarchy. I knew I mustn't blow it. This is a competitive business and getting an order for a new show is precious; the attempt usually ends in delay and disappointment. Orders are elusive. I had to adapt.

I knew exactly what I wanted to do: a series set on a sink estate that used to be respectable and hard-working but had started to go downhill in the seventies when local industry died. Too many of its residents went on to rely on welfare and the only career path was in the one remaining growth business: drugs. The Labour Party had taken over from the 18-year Conservative administration more than a year earlier and I wanted to show the despair on the other side of Tony Blair's paradise.

The series needed regular characters who could knit it together, would know the estate intimately and take the audience from house to house, from one troubled family to the next. But I knew if I'd said, 'I want to do a series about some social workers,' the reply would be, 'Are you mad?' or, at best, Mark Thompson, Controller of BBC Two, would have screwed his face up sympathetically, pretended to consider and said, 'Interesting. I wonder if there is an audience for it, though?' In other words, 'No, thanks.' So I said, 'I want to do a cop show.' Their eyes lit up. Audiences love cop shows.

I didn't really want to do one. This wasn't another example of me wrestling with the idea of arbitrary power and the role of the police, questions which had haunted me since childhood. It was tactical. I'd realised since returning from Los Angeles that television had narrowed its focus and tightened its management. Now it was about what they wanted to buy, so I decided we must do Trojan horse drama, delivering what they said they wanted but hiding my show inside.

The Cops finally went to BBC Two and Mark suggested we omit episode one, which was just setting the series up. It was a good note and I readily agreed, although I didn't relish telling the writer Robert Jones his opening episode had been cut.

Our uniform bobbies spent their days round the housing estate that they knew so well, being called here and there, revealing the lives of people as they dealt with problems, fulfilling the same dramatic function as social workers. We also had the opportunity to examine these foot soldiers doing our dirty work, usually with good humour and well-honed diplomatic skills. We also saw some who were high on their power and abused it. We were able to ask sympathetic questions about just what society should demand of its police force.

The Greater Manchester police offered co-operation which they withdrew after seeing the first series. They had every right to behave as they saw fit. There was no problem. We relied on off-duty cops, out of uniform, for technical advice and paid them in cash.

For the first series we recruited a team of three writers who went to Bolton, in Lancashire, for a couple of weeks or so to spend all their time with the local cops – in the cars during their shifts, drinking with them afterwards, getting to know them and the detail of their work.

If you don't know it, haven't lived it, then you must research it, get under the skin of it. One's imagination has to have something to feed off. If you think you can sit in front of a computer and wait for divine inspiration you will end up unconsciously rehashing all the second-hand clichés from old television series or movies, newspaper stories and your own baseless fantasies; third-hand crap, in other words.

Our writers returned with more stories and the basis for more characters than they could use. I'd thought about the merits of team writing, which is popular in America, mainly in half-hour narrative comedy. I concluded it would be unpopular in the UK, so tried to get the best out of co-operation in team meetings, then allowed each writer to go away and write a draft. What followed was the immediate, generous exchange of ideas and soon they were bypassing me and Francis Hopkinson, the script editor, giving each other characters and stories. Writers, who work so much in isolation, are such happy collaborators.

As usual we spent months auditioning. We don't do lazy casting; if you flick through an industry publication like *Spotlight*, it's easy. If you trawl, it takes time. We did few script readings, preferring simple improvisations. Can an actor unselfconsciously be in the moment? If you ask ten actors to walk across the room, nine will act walking across the room; the tenth will just . . . walk across the room. That's the one you cast.

One afternoon I was sitting inconspicuously in a corner and a middle-aged man walked in. He was built like a thick-set Lego man.

The director asked him to walk into a police station seeking answers. He'd just learned his son had died in custody. The actor, John Henshaw, nodded and after a moment, sat down in an upright chair and began quietly digging for the facts, questioning an imaginary desk sergeant. He did so with dignity but was obviously containing his grief with difficulty. Within twenty seconds I was choking up, fighting back tears. I knew we'd struck gold. It was Huw Wheldon's theory that the most moving performances came from actors with simple Anglo-Saxon names, not from exotic Latin or Celtic ones. The latter show their emotions, the former bottle them up with a stiff upper lip. The fewer tears shown by the suffering character, the more the audience will shed on his or her behalf.

Afterwards I chatted to John, asking him what he'd been doing, because he was new to me. He said he hadn't been able to get any acting jobs and was thinking about working on the bins. How could such a truthful actor be so ignored? He did brilliantly as a sergeant in *The Cops* and has worked with Ken Loach and others since. It's been good to see him acknowledged.

We shot it on the run, always following the actors, never anticipating them or constricting them with tight marks. It was an observational style with no cinematic riffs. No one was trying to enhance a showreel for Harvey Weinstein. I wanted the simple reality of people's lives, not applause for technical wizardry. It goes back to the most basic rule: no writing writing, acting acting or directing directing. Use your skills to recreate a fictional reality and then dissolve those skills; if they show, you've failed.

Again, a group of unknown actors, writers and directors found their voices and gained confidence. *The Cops* began a three-series run in the autumn of 1998 and since then I have seen so many of them growing in stature, doing good work.

The Great Con-Trick

If you can measure it, you can manage it.

The McKinsey maxim

The head of BBC TV, Huw Wheldon, told me that as far back as the seventies the BBC called in management consultants. They were given the run of the place and they questioned and observed, wielded their clipboards and looked purposeful.

After a while the senior consultant looked puzzled, so Huw asked if he could help.

'Yes, Mr Wheldon. I am confused. Could you tell me how many decision makers you employ?'

Huw said, 'What do you mean, decision makers?'

'Well, people who make actual decisions about the product, the product as it goes to the public.'

'I don't know, actually.'

'You don't know?'

Huw did a quick reckoning of all the producers and said, 'Well, at least a few hundred, I suppose.'

The consultant went white.

'In that case, Mr Wheldon, I'm afraid we can't help you.'

The cult of management, led by the high priests of expensive consultancy, continued to scar the BBC. It didn't understand creativity. Only those who had killed the child within them could prosper in this environment. The dilemma was that the BBC needed creativity but was so afraid of it that they crippled it with tight control.

A healthy BBC has a balance between budgetary order and creative disorder.

Although fluctuating in size, my company, World Productions, was bigger now. I decided to free it of management, one of the biggest con tricks of the last century. We had efficient business systems, of course. But I replaced management with leadership, self-management and creative freedom.

I had the opportunity to recruit even more kids and bring them on. I was becoming so old they all seemed kids to me: like the police, even channel controllers looked younger and younger. I had sons older than some of them. Co-founder John Heyman gave me full creative control. He never overruled me or questioned any creative decision, even when I must have caused him pain by cancelling a profitable series. In return I never questioned any of his business decisions.

Only after the work with Charles Rycroft did I realise that being busy wasn't the same as being productive.

'Booked your holiday yet? Somewhere nice?' Pom asks.

'Holiday? Him? His life's one long holiday!'

Harold had no grasp of what I did. He made things with his hands. What he did was tangible. She would crochet or knit, even when watching television. Weekends didn't disturb his routine. He would be under the Ford Prefect, his first love, or be sawing and filing in his shed.

'The devil makes work for idle hands' should have been my family's motto. All my life I've felt guilty if I wasn't working. A friend perceptively said that I chose film-making so that I could go to the cinema without guilt. It was true that I often heard myself say, 'I have to go to the Curzon tonight.' If it was work I could give myself permission.

Even after research had pointed out that being obsessively busy was inimical to creativity or any productivity, it was difficult for me to spend a day without being busy to the moment of exhaustion.

'Bone idle.' That was the accusation I dreaded.

I worked (that word again) to find out the truth. All the evidence pointed to a reverse relationship between hours worked and creative achievement. Extolling the virtues of long hours of work was an ideological matter that partly reflected the needs of capital engaged in outdated production methods. In fact, time idling, 'Doing nothing', as my family would put it, was really more productive. I also realised that the digital revolution would both abolish many jobs and change the whole nature of what we meant by work.

Typically, I accepted the evidence but didn't apply it to myself.

But at World Productions, especially as it expanded, I made it clear that I was only interested in creative results. I didn't want to 'make work'. I wasn't interested in how many hours people were at their desks or even if they ever came into the office. They could work at home or in the park or in the pub or not work at all. They wouldn't be checked or judged. The invention of the office might have made sense in the nineteenth century, but it was inimical to creative work now. I just needed to know enough so that we didn't duplicate.

Did they have good ideas? Could they find, win the confidence of, and inspire writers? Could they do the same with a production team? Could they create a persuasive pitch?

I told them to come to me if they had a problem, revealing shades of the BBC in the sixties. My job was to encourage and facilitate; to lift them when they were crippled with doubt, telling them to have the courage of my convictions; to pick them up if they failed, telling them to try again. Next time, in the old phrase, I wanted them to fail better.

I discovered I liked this pastoral role. It was satisfying, in a paternal way. I've always enjoyed being a father. I never had a problem with any crew, never doubting that when I put my foot down I would be obeyed. I rarely needed to. People don't let you down.

But I still had to find stuff to keep me busy, to satisfy the censorial voice on my shoulder. That never changed.

Have You Been Telling Stories Again?

There is more to the imagination than any moment of conscious-
ness can apprehend.

Charles Rycroft

Psychoanalysis is that kind of illness of which it purports to be the
cure.

Austrian writer Karl Kraus, an aphorism loved and
quoted with glee by Charles Rycroft

The work with Charles had been so consuming that there was an
emptiness when it came to its end. Far from being relieved to
be free of this three times a week discipline, I knew I would miss
Charles. On my last formal session he surprised me by saying he
hoped we would not lose touch, that he was always there, happy to
see me for a chat. I wouldn't have dared to suggest this, but on his
initiative our relationship changed.

I often went to see him, just to enjoy his company. His erudition
prompted me to read some poetry which I hadn't read for decades.
Our conversations ranged over his and my many interests. We also
gossiped. He became surprisingly indiscreet, perhaps because he
knew how discreet I was.

He became less of an icon and more a man, of human size. Maybe this was a subtle continuation of the analysis. He had from the start established the nature of the relationship developing between us, that it was a confrontation, an encounter between two real people. He wasn't the detached, Freudian 'Perfectly reflecting mirror'. He was there, conversing with me, a man who happened to be a therapist.

This was important. I had to relive and reinterpret not so much my relationship with Mom and Dad and others but my fantasies of them and my fantasies about myself. These lived inside me and had become part of who I was or pretended to be. Years spent turning Charles into versions of these fantasies – yet always having him there as a real, consistent man – helped me to eventually change and become who I was, to adjust my fantasies in the light of repeated examination. This led to relinquishing the exhausting process of having to act who I was anyway. This man accepted me, even after knowing I was a murderer. So maybe I was not a murderer. Maybe I was OK.

Charles's existentialist take was an echo of what I had learned in my conversations with Ronnie Laing years before, researching for the film *In Two Minds*. After Ronnie died, I read in an obituary that Charles had been Ronnie's analyst, too.

This seemed appropriate, somehow.

Charles told me the analysis hadn't ended, which surprised me. He said it would quietly go on as long as I lived. He was right.

Writing this book has been an extension of it. I have experienced distressing agony, sometimes unable to continue writing because tears were preventing me seeing the screen. I've had startling insights and made connections that seem obvious once revealed. Remembering funny incidents and family stories have warmed me, humour being as healing as tears.

I end with the question I asked as I began. Is all this true? Did it really happen? Well, yes, it all happened. But like this, as I recall it?

Most memory was traumatised out of me in the family blitzkrieg. Every item, every little artefact I called mine, was left behind in the home I was wrenched from. I entered Siberia numb, empty, starting over, needing to learn the tricks of the trade of survival in a new place, with new rules of engagement.

Who I was (becoming) was left behind.

There was a discontinuity – a new and necessary creation of a compliant false self – in order to fit in and avoid banishment. An angry self. Hiding behind it, lurking in the dark and no longer known to me, were the remnants of who I had been. It took all my concentration to discover who they required me to be. Only in my fifties was I rediscovered. Or uncovered. Or reconnected.

Maturity for me lies in allowing this little boy unconditional space within me, just to be; and in being, ignite me fully to life.

That statement also sums up decades of work with actors, creating a space and an atmosphere, devoid of fear, where they can just be, daring to tell us the truth, *their* truth. As the wise and brilliant child analyst Donald Winnicott said, the opposite of play is not work but coercion.

So my life's work on me ended up not confined to me.

All the time without that little boy was a life sentence of sincere pretence, of not being myself but acting a self: guarded behaviour masquerading as spontaneity. A double agent with no one to betray but me.

Finally, relaxation settled inside me so that I could spontaneously be the person I had impersonated and at the same time allow the person I had buried to have some room in the light. It had all been exhausting.

Being is more important than doing: it is the generator of healthy doing. Doing is no substitute for being: one is then just an active nothing, pretending to be.

That lesson is what drove me to find and love actors, writers and directors who could tell the truth.

I merely tried to create the circumstances and give them love, so they could feel safe enough to dare.

I impress on students that the storyteller in every society is central to the cohesion and the health of everyone. We live by stories. They are the way we make sense of ourselves and of the world and of ourselves in the world. They also, through the magic of the imagination of the actor, allow disparate strangers to empathise, to see their common humanity behind their cultural differences. I'm happy therefore to have spent my life in the world of 'as if', making up fictions. These are not lies. They tell deeper truths than told by those who think they only deal in hard facts. The deeper the fiction penetrates, the deeper the truths.

I respect facts but I seek the truth.

So I've revealed, in the interstices of the story in the preceding pages, truths about myself I didn't know, maybe even still don't know. Truths you will have noticed. Like in all stories, one finds connections and continuities. Being able finally to tell this story to Charles Rycroft liberated me and writing the same story here has liberated me further.

Certainly I now see connections between my early experiences and some of the films, connections masked from me before. We all go through life in a fugue state, unaware of what's driving us, ascribing conscious motives that only disguise the hidden ones.

Over the years I acquired, without seeking, a pile of old family photographs, from holiday snaps to formal wedding poses. Just the usual mix all families used to keep and hand on through the generations. I glanced at them occasionally as I moved house. None touched me. They bored me.

As I worked with Charles, I had the urge to trash them but couldn't quite bring myself to the deed. They upset and unnerved me, prodding me to tears I angrily rejected.

When I finished writing this book, I was drawn to those photos. I took them from the drawer and carefully looked at them.

The people in them are now dead. All my aunts and uncles had followed my Mom and Dad, and Grandma and Granddad, leaving my brothers and all the cousins still alive.

Here was one of Topsy, so young and happy. She died of lung cancer early in 2014. We all spent time with her towards the end, especially her older sister Merry, feeling just as helpless. I visited her a few days before she died with our son Will and we chatted affectionately about our early life together. For a few minutes her head seemed to clear and she remembered as we laughed together.

She was seventy-five. A magical, captivating, talented person, overflowing with love, cut down. A life unlived. I remain haunted by what happened to her, mysterious and irreversible. I try to move beyond that to remember her beautiful, loving personality and that talent, worn so lightly.

I wept at snaps of my parents, dressed stylishly in summer whites, as they walked together happily, arm-in-arm, along the Blackpool front; of Grandma and Granddad, old, battered and dignified, marking their Diamond Wedding; a formally posed one of them flanked by all twelve children in their Sunday best; and one of my Mom and Dad's wedding, posed behind a three-tier wedding cake, Mom in a fine white gown and Dad looking sharp in his suit, with Granddad standing behind them, still in his hat, pipe firmly in his mouth; and of Topsy as I remember her before her illness, lovely and unaffected, happy in herself.

I selected some: Topsy, my cousin Jack in his Fleet Air Arm uniform, Grandma and Granddad inspecting a fishing rod he had made and one of my Mom and Dad with Pom and Harold, together on holiday, laughing without a care in the world. I took them into Soho and had them framed.

They are now together on the wall in my hall. I see them everyday. Sometimes they upset me, but I shed healing tears.

I am comfortable with them now and I am comfortable with myself.

Most families at first glance seem unremarkably normal, conventional, even boring. But peel away the surface conventions and start to dig through the generations and you discover that they are extraordinary. High drama emerges the deeper you penetrate each individual's story. There is painful suffering, humour, courage, achievement and loss. Transcending all the petty resentments and bitterness felt here and there, what marks them all is love.

Love that sustains. Love that offers continuity. Love that gives life its meaning. Love that is renewed as each new generation takes its first unsteady steps under caring eyes.

Mine was probably no different from yours, except in detail.

All families are the same in their uniqueness.

I'm lucky. I've managed at last to reconnect, to emotionally accept my family, to come back in from the cold. They never gave up on me. I am close again to my brother Peter. I am at peace with my parents.

I have had an interesting life, full of privilege and chances, family and good friends.

Sure, it's been a painful journey. Everyone's passage through life is.

I remain a 51/49 per cent optimist.